VOLUME II

BUCKINGHAM BURIALS

A Survey of Cemeteries in Buckingham County Virginia

Compiled by
Janice J. R. Hull

HERITAGE BOOKS
2011

HERITAGE BOOKS
AN IMPRINT OF HERITAGE BOOKS, INC.

Books, CDs, and more—Worldwide

For our listing of thousands of titles see our website
at
www.HeritageBooks.com

Published 2011 by
HERITAGE BOOKS, INC.
Publishing Division
100 Railroad Ave. #104
Westminster, Maryland 21157

Copyright © 2002 Janice J. R. Hull

Other books by the author:

Buckingham Burials: A Survey of Cemeteries in Buckingham County, Virginia: Volumes 1 and 2

Index to the United States Census for Buckingham County, Virginia, Volume 1: 1810–1850

Index to the United States Census for Buckingham County, Virginia, Volume 2: 1860–1870

Cover illustration: One of the more decorative tombstones still standing in Buckingham County is this stone for Charles H. McKinney, son of Philip W. and Nannie C. McKinney. The inscription reads:

"Our little Charlie. Charles Heath, son of P. W. & Nannie C. McKinney. Born Sept. 29, 1857: Died Dec. 7, 1859"

The child's father, Philip, served as Governor of Virginia for four years (1890-1894), the only man from Buckingham to become governor of the state.

All rights reserved. No part of this book may be reproduced or transmitted in any form or by any means, electronic or mechanical, including photocopying, recording or by any information storage and retrieval system without written permission from the author, except for the inclusion of brief quotations in a review.

International Standard Book Numbers
Paperbound: 978-1-58549-746-1
Clothbound: 978-0-7884-8940-2

DEDICATION

The Compiler of this book would like to dedicate this volume to Mrs. Mildred Booker Stanton. A fine lady and friend and a descendant of many of the early families in Buckingham County, including the Morris and Booker families.

Mildred was one of the first who contacted me to offer her help in locating family cemeteries and offering her wisdom and knowledge in the genealogy of Buckingham County families.

ACKNOWLEDGMENTS

I am now finished with Volume II of Buckingham Burials. All the cemeteries that I have surveyed that were not mentioned in Volume I, are included here.

I have included four cemeteries that I was not able to identify. However, what information was available from an on-site survey has been mentioned. Historic Buckingham, Inc. will be interested in hearing from anyone who has knowledge of any of these four sites. They are listed under "Unknown."

Also, for the researcher who is interested in the oldest burying grounds in the county, I have cited three Indian mound locations that were told to me.

As with any undertaking of this kind, one of the many reasons we are doing this, is to have a central file, with a map of each site and directions on how to find each cemetery. Also the names of landowners in case a researcher needs to get permission to visit the site themselves after a close study of our records. We do not feel that this kind of information should be made a part of a general published record.

I have been assisted by many kind people in searching out the cemeteries included in this volume, and I wish to acknowledge and thank them again for their assistance and time. No one person can do a project like this by themselves, but with the help of many, it can be accomplished.

H. Spencer Adams
Billy Allen
Carrie Allen
Genieveve Agee
Mrs. Albert Baird
Ernest H. Bowling, Jr.
Percy and Gertrue Carroll
Jimmy and Patsy Davis
Irene Ellis
Bob Flippen
Fred Flood
Edith B. Harris
Nell F. Harris
Laura Hayes
Marie Hill
Myrtle C. Hill
Rita Hill
Harriet Hocker
Ola Huddleston
Nancy B. Jones
Elsie Kidd
Tana Knott
Mrs. Annie H. LeSueur
Edward LeSueur
Polly LeSueur
Ben Lewis
James D. Main
Mrs. A. W. Mann
Mrs. C. J. Morgan
John and Dorothy Morgan
John Nicholas
Stuart and Tammy Nixon
John Patterson
Bessie Ragland
Gordon Ragland Sr.
Mr. and Mrs. Gordon Rush
Frank Shumaker
Jack Shumaker
Ruby Talley Smith
Stanton Family
Mildred B. Stanton
Margaret E. Taylor
Ernest Thomas
Margaret and Katie Thomas
Francis E. Wood Sr.
Mildred J. Wood
Mary Branch Wootton
Pauline P. Word

I also wish to extend a special Thank You for all of the encouragement and support I always received from the Officers and Board of Historic Buckingham, Inc.

The survey of cemeteries in Buckingham County has been a very rewarding experience for me. It gave me an opportunity to meet many wonderful people, a chance to get a working knowledge of the land and its layout, and to learn more of the local history and family stories passed down through many generations.

Thank you one and all for the help, support, and courtesies you extended to me.

As all know who serve with Historic Buckingham, Inc., a new committee has been formed and set to work on searching out all cemeteries not yet cited. I wish them all the satisfaction and enjoyment that I experienced while working at this same endeavor.

I have moved back to my native state of Vermont, and am already working on old cemeteries here. Once the bug bites, it doesn't let go.

If anyone using this book wants to give more information or make a correction on any cemetery entry, please contact Historic Buckingham, Inc. at P. O. Box 152, Buckingham, Virginia 23921.

Sincerely,

The Compiler

Janice J. R. Hull

November 2001

Table of Contents

Abraham Family - Hwy 660 1
Agee/Moss Family - Hwy 631 1
"Allendale" Homeplace - Hwy 648 2
Anderson Family - Hwy 640 2
Austin Family - Hwy 636 (Near Int. Hwy 697) 3
Baird Family - Hwy 659 4
Bethel United Methodist Church Cemetery - Hwy 640 5
Bixler/Crews Family - Hwy 660 15
Black Cemetery at Jonestown - Hwy 15 16
Booker / Lackland / Selden Family - Hwy 15 17
Brown Family - Hwy 653 18
Brown - Willie Brown Family - Black - Hwy 655 18
Brown's Chapel United Methodist Church - Hwy 617 18
Brown/Peters Family - Hwy 653 31
Cedar Baptist Church Cemetery - Hwy 650 32
Chambers Family - Hwy 602 (Black) 64
Childress Family - Hwy 60 (Maysville C.H.) 64
Dameron - John Dameron Family - Hwy 664 64
Darneille/Darneil Family Slave Plot - Hwy 633 65
Davidson Family - Hwy 640 65
Dillwyn Town Cemetery - Hwy T1010 65
Duty Family Cemetery - Hwy 637 95
Elcan Family Slave Plot - Black - Hwy 608 95
Fones/Wright Family - Hwy 631 95
Garnett Family at "Wheatland" - Hwy 633 96
General Childress/Jamerson Family Cemetery - Hwy 630 96
Gilliam Family at "Millcote" - Hwy 612 (Cole Forest Road) 101
Gunter Family - Hwy 601 101
Hocker Family Slave Plot - Black - Hwy 708 102
Holman/Jones Family at "Oak Hill" - Hwy 642 102
Horsley family - Hwy 604 103
Jamerson/Sharpe Family - Hwy 650 104
Kyle/Davis Family Cemetery - Hwy 637 104
Laury - Dora Laury Family - Black - Hwy 660 105
Mann Family (Mann Tract Road) - Hwy 636 105
Maxey - G. W. Maxey Family - Hwy 705 106
McKinney/Jones Family Slave Cemetery - Hwy 636 (at New Store) .. 107
Miller Family/Poor House Farm - Hwy 659 108
Mt. Zion Baptist Church - Hwy 610 108
Murphey/Flood Family - Hwy 640 150
New Store Presbyterian Church Cemetery - Hwy 609 151
Newton Family - Hwy 622 (At Int. with Hwy 729) 160
O'Brien Family - Hwy 640 160
Oak Hill Baptist Church - Black - Hwy 633 161

Oliver/Nixon/Gilliam/Snoddy Family at "Grass Dale" Hwy 20
  (Near Int. with Hwy 15) 164
Pleasant Grove Baptist Church Cemetery - Hwy 24 164
Poe Family - Hwy 664 166
Rocky Mount United Methodist Church - Hwy 15/669 167
"Rolfton" Homeplace - Hwy 749 177
Rush Family Cemetery - Hwy 642 177
Salem Baptist Church - Black - Hwy 627 179
Salem United Methodist Church Cemetery - Hwy 632 180
Scruggs - John & Eliz. Scruggs Family - Hwy 636 203
Second Liberty Baptist Church (Black) - Hwy 640 203
Sharon Baptist Church Cemetery - Hwy 622 214
Shelton - F. and D. Shelton Family - Black - Hwy 663 226
Shumaker - B. F. Shumaker Family - Hwy 631 227
Slave Cemetery at "Col Alto" (Black) - Hwy 601 227
Smyrna Methodist Church Cemetery - Hwy 15 228
Stanton Family Cemetery (Black) - Hwy 677 248
Thomas Family/Thomas Farm Cemetery - Hwy 669 249
Tolbert - Sallie Tolbert Family - Hwy 640 251
Toney Family - Hwy 15 (Near Int. with Hwy 631) 252
"Town Cemetery" - Hwy 664 253
Trinity Presbyterian Church Cemetery - Hwy 670 254
Unknown - Hwy 740 266
Unknown at "Tall House" property - Hwy 631 266
Unknown on Shumaker family property - Hwy 631 266
Warminster Baptist Church Cemetery (Black) - Hwy 664 266
Welcome Wesleyan Methodist Church - Hwy 15 268
"Wheatland" Homeplace - Hwy 633 270
Wootten - Clifford Wootten Family - Hwy 640 (Slate River Forest Rd) 270
Wright 271

LAST NAME	Date of Birth	Maiden Name	Tombstone
First Name	Date of Death	Spouse	
	Age at Death		

Abraham family - Hwy 660

| ABRAHAM | | Jones | No |
| Carrie | | Abraham, Samuel E. | |

Other Info: Grave marked by fieldstones only, but known to be buried here beside her husband, Samuel, a CSA soldier. This cemetery was surveyed in Vol. I of Buckingham Burials, but at that time the name of Samuel's wife was not known.

Agee/Moss Family - Hwy 631

| AGEE | 18 Jan. 1905 | Moss | Yes |
| Ruby | 24 Nov. 1977 | | |

Inscription: "Mother."

Other Info: Grave also marked by a funeral home metal marker.

| AGEE | 1943 | Agee | Yes |
| Tommy T. | 1966 | Iris M. | |

Other Info: Grave also marked by a funeral home metal marker inscribed: "Tommy Tubbs Agee 1943 - 1966 Dunkum Funeral Home."

| AGEE | 29 Aug. 1906 | | Yes |
| Willie Anderson | 04 Apr. 1972 | | |

Inscription: "In Loving Memory."

| BANTON | 1963 | | No |
| Robert Allen | 1963 | | |

Other Info: Grave marked by a funeral home metal marker.

| BRANCH | 1955 | | Yes |
| Glen Edward | 1955 | | |

Inscription: "Son"

Other Info: Grave also marked by a funeral home metal marker.

| BRANCH | 1955 | | Yes |
| Richard Arlen | 1955 | | |

Inscription: "Son"

Other Info: Grave also marked by a funeral home metal marker.

LAST NAME First Name	Date of Birth Date of Death Age at Death	Maiden Name Spouse	Tombstone
MOSS Elizabeth T.	28 Apr. 1886 12 Dec. 1968		Yes

Inscription: "Rest In Peace."

MOSS Jeff	14 May 1879 21 Mar. 1966		Yes

Inscription: "Rest In Peace."

MOSS Marshall Lee	02 Mar. 1926 15 May 1966		Yes

Inscription: Marshall served as inscribed: "Virginia CPL HQ Co 222 Inf. Regt. World War II. ... BSM."

SHUMAKER Eddie P.	14 Feb. 1884 12 Nov. 1956		Yes
SHUMAKER Glenn David	1961 1961		No

Other Info: Grave marked by a funeral home metal marker.

TAYLOR George Cosby	05 May 1902 13 May 1967		Yes

Inscription: "Rest In Peace."

Other Info: Grave also marked by a funeral home metal marker.

WOODFIN Willie	24 July 1915 15 Aug. 1988	Taylor	Yes

Other Info: Grave also marked by a funeral home metal marker inscribed: "Willie Sue Woodfin 1915 - 1988 Dunkum Funeral Home."

"Allendale" Homeplace - Hwy 648

INDIAN MOUND			No

Other Info: Located on the North Branch of the Slate River. The local residents know where these Indian burial mounds are located, and they should always be preserved.

Anderson Family - Hwy 640

ANDERSON Earl	1897 1897		Yes

LAST NAME First Name	Date of Birth Date of Death Age at Death	Maiden Name Spouse	Tombstone
ANDERSON Elizabeth	1838	Flood Anderson, James Moses Capt.	No

Other Info: Elizabeth was the first wife of Capt. James. She is believed to be buried here alongside her husband.

ANDERSON Esta	1897 1897		Yes
ANDERSON Fleeta	1902 1903		Yes
ANDERSON Florence Virginia	1826 (circa)	Anderson, James Moses Jr.	No

Other Info: Believed to be buried here beside her husband.

ANDERSON Grover Morten	1884 1888		Yes
ANDERSON James Moses Capt.	1786 1861 - 1870	Anderson, Elizabeth Flood	No

Other Info: Capt. Flood was married twice, first to Elizabeth (Flood), secondly to Martha (Flood). He is believed to be buried here beside his first wife.

ANDERSON James Moses Jr.	1822 1879	Anderson, Florence Virginia	Yes
ANDERSON Reese Moses	1853 1906		Yes
ANDERSON Samuel Knight Polk	24 July 1846 18 Jan. 1867		No

Other Info: Son of Capt. James M. and Martha F. Anderson. He is believed to be buried here.

ANDERSON William Bennett	1857 1894		Yes
ANDERSON William Robert	15 Sep. 1849		No

Other Info: The son of Capt. James M. Anderson. He is believed to be buried here.

Austin Family - Hwy 636 (Near Int. Hwy 697)

AUSTIN A. A.	13 Feb. 1875 20 Mar. 1955		Yes

LAST NAME First Name	Date of Birth Date of Death Age at Death	Maiden Name Spouse	Tombstone
AUSTIN Mary A.	04 June 1880 24 May 1946		Yes

Baird Family - Hwy 659

BAIRD Bill Daniel	1931		No

Other Info: He was buried on Feb. 28, 1931. Son of James and Mattie Belle Baird.

BAIRD (children)			No

Other Info: Two young children, a girl about 7 yrs. of age, and a young boy of the Baird family are also buried in this cemetery.

BAIRD Clarke			No

Other Info: Known to be buried here. Her parents are James and Mattie Belle Baird.

BAIRD Hubert			No

Other Info: Son of James and Mattie Belle Baird.

BAIRD James	1860 (circa)	Baird, Mattie Belle	No

Other Info: This family cemetery has approximately 17 graves. No tombstones.

BAIRD Mattie Belle	1860s	Baird, James	No

Other Info: This family cemetery contains approximately 17 graves. No tombstones.

BAIRD Minnie	Sep. 1923		No

Other Info: She was buried in Sept. 1923. Daughter of James and Mattie Belle Baird.

Bethel United Methodist Church Cemetery - Hwy 640

ALLISON I.D. Mrs.			No

Other Info: Grave marked with a slate marker - not inscribed.

LAST NAME First Name	Date of Birth Date of Death Age at Death	Maiden Name Spouse	Tombstone
ANDERSON Cammie R.	14 Jan. 1888 23 Feb. 1974		Yes

Inscription: Footstone inscribed: "C.R.A."

ANDERSON Claude Wood	26 Apr. 1934 22 Sep. 1987		Yes

Inscription: "A Friend to Man... 1968 - 1985 Virginia House of Delegates."

ANDERSON Edward Pratt	1883 1962	Anderson, Etta Sinclair	Yes

Other Info: Shares a headstone with his wife.

ANDERSON Edward Van	28 Oct. 1841 01 Jan. 1914	Anderson, Nannie Steger	Yes

Inscription: "Our Father ... Asleep In Jesus." A second stone at the foot of the grave shows that he served as inscribed: "2 Sgt. E. V. Anderson TRK 4 VA CAV C.S.A."

ANDERSON Estelle	05 June 1905 07 Apr. 1987	Vaughn Anderson, Herman Shield	Yes

Other Info: Shares a headstone with her husband.

ANDERSON Etta Sinclair	1884 1974	Anderson, Edward Pratt	Yes

Other Info: Shares a headstone with her husband.

ANDERSON Evelyn Meade	27 Jan. 1879 06 July 1894		Yes

Inscription: "In Memory of...Daughter of E. V. and Mary B. Anderson."

ANDERSON Herman Shield	01 Sep. 1898 23 Apr. 1972	Anderson, Estelle Vaughn	Yes

Other Info: Shares a headstone with his wife.

ANDERSON James Meade	03 July 1893 11 July 1975	Anderson, Pattie Coleman	Yes

Other Info: Shares a headstone with his wife.

ANDERSON Joseph W.	26 Oct. 1878 05 Dec. 1942		Yes

Inscription: Footstone inscribed: "J.W.A."

LAST NAME First Name	Date of Birth Date of Death Age at Death	Maiden Name Spouse	Tombstone
ANDERSON Juan A.	1855 1930	 Anderson, Lillie I.	Yes

Inscription: Footstone inscribed: "J.A.A."

Other Info: Shares a headstone with his wife.

| ANDERSON
Juan R. | 05 July 1891
14 May 1978 |
Anderson, Mildred W. | |

Inscription: A second stone at the foot of the grave shows he served as inscribed: "Juan Raymond Anderson PFC US Army World War I 1891 - 1978."

Other Info: Shares a headstone with his wife.

| ANDERSON
Juan Raymond Jr. | 05 June 1931
07 Feb. 1980 |
Anderson, Anne Follkes | Yes |

Inscription: "Love Always."

| ANDERSON
Lillie I. | 1863
1957 |
Anderson, Juan A. | Yes |

Inscription: Footstone inscribed: "L.I.A."

Other Info: Shares a headstone with her husband.

| ANDERSON
Martha M. | 02 Nov. 1809
08 Dec. 1902 | Flood
Anderson, Capt. James | Yes |

Inscription: "In Memory of ... Married Capt. James Anderson ... At Rest."

| ANDERSON
Mildred W. | 27 Apr. 1898
12 Sep. 1980 |
Anderson, Juan R. | Yes |

Other Info: Shares a headstone with her husband.

| ANDERSON
Nannie | 19 Feb. 1846
20 Feb. 1922 | Steger
Anderson, Edward Van | Yes |

Inscription: "Peace Perfect Peace."

| ANDERSON
Pattie | 29 Jan. 1900
04 July 1979 | Coleman
Anderson, James Meade | Yes |

Other Info: Shares a headstone with her husband.

| ANDERSON
William B. | 25 May 1886
12 Mar. 1979 | | Yes |

Inscription: Footstone inscribed: "W.B.A."

| BRYANT
Sallie R. | 12 Mar. 1877
28 July 1950 |
Bryant, Warren A. | Yes |

LAST NAME First Name	Date of Birth Date of Death Age at Death	Maiden Name Spouse	Tombstone

Other Info: Shares a headstone with her husband.

| BRYANT Warren A. | 10 Dec. 1880 25 June 1939 | Bryant, Sallie R. | Yes |

Other Info: Shares a headstone with his wife.

| BULLARD Lula Yates | 18 Oct. 1877 10 May 1920 | Anderson Bullard, Rev. Wm. E. | Yes |

Inscription: "...Asleep In Jesus...Daughter of E. V. and M. V. Anderson...Wife of REv. W. E. Bullard."

| BULLARD Wm. E. (Rev.) | 12 Feb. 1855 27 Dec. 1906 | Bullard, Lula Yates Anderson | Yes |

Inscription: "...Joined Va. Conference Nov. 1886...Died...At West Lunenburg Parsonage." (Masonic Symbol)

| CHRISTIAN Ernest T. | 06 May 1901 17 Oct. 1977 | Christian, Martha B. | Yes |

Inscription: "Nearer My God To Thee."

| COLE Ferd W. | 15 Sep. 1883 02 Nov. 1944 | Cole, Minnie C. | Yes |

Other Info: Shares a headstone with his wife.

| COLE Juan B. | 10 Apr. 1922 29 Mar. 1923 | | Yes |

Inscription: "Son of Ferd and Minnie Cole...Gone To Be An Angel." Footstone inscribed: "Billie"

| COLE Lucy | 29 Sep. 1857 05 Feb. 1931 | Roberts Cole, Milton W. | Yes |

Other Info: Shares a headstone with her husband.

| COLE May | 1906 1927 | | Yes |

| COLE Milton W. | 07 May 1857 19 Mar. 1927 | Cole, Lucy Roberts | Yes |

Other Info: Shares a headstone with his wife.

| COLE Minnie C. | 07 Apr. 1884 13 June 1964 | Cole, Ferd W. | Yes |

Inscription: Footstone inscribed: "M.C.C."

Other Info: Shares a headstone with her husband.

LAST NAME First Name	Date of Birth Date of Death Age at Death	Maiden Name Spouse	Tombstone
COLEMAN Evelyn A.	1893 1971	Coleman, Julius A.	Yes

Other Info: Shares a headstone with her husband.

| COLEMAN
Julius A. | 1888
1961 | Coleman, Evelyn A. | Yes |

Inscription: (Masonic Symbol)

Other Info: Shares a headstone with his wife.

| COLEMAN
Minnie Morgan | 1878
1935 | | Yes |

| COWAN
Stephen Green (Rev.) | 05 Aug. 1896
07 Jan. 1980 | Cowan, Margaret Morgan | Yes |

| DAVIDSON
Annie R. | 06 Nov. 1879
26 Apr. 1912 | Davidson, Richard T. | Yes |

Inscription: "At Rest." Footstone inscribed: "A.R.D."

Other Info: Shares a headstone with her husband.

| DAVIDSON
Hallie G. | 08 Mar. 1892
12 Jan. 1959 | | Yes |

| DAVIDSON
Mary J. | | | No |

Other Info: Grave marker - not inscribed.

| DAVIDSON
Richard T. | 11 Apr. 1877
19 Dec. 1931 | Davidson, Annie R. | Yes |

Inscription: Footstone inscribed: "R.T.D."

Other Info: Shares a headstone with his wife.

| DAVIDSON
Thomas E. | | | Yes |

Inscription: He served as inscribed: "CO E 20th Va Inf C.S.A."

| DUNKUM
Isia Frances | 16 May 1881
07 Aug. 1935 | Dunkum, Robert Henry | |

Inscription: "The Light of God Surpasseth All Understanding." Footstone inscribed: "Mother."

Other Info: Shares a headstone with her husband.

| DUNKUM
Robert Henry | 16 Mar. 1870
14 Oct. 1952 | Dunkum, Isia Frances | Yes |

LAST NAME First Name	Date of Birth Date of Death Age at Death	Maiden Name Spouse	Tombstone

Inscription: "The Light of God Surpasseth All Understanding." Footstone inscribed: "Father."

Other Info: Shares a headstone with his wife.

| DUTY Eugena | 14 May 1923 | | Yes |

Other Info: Shares a stone with her infant brothers who were born and died on Dec. 31, 1927. Children of Lemuel and Ethel Duty.

| FITTZ Sally O. | Nov. 1883 May 1958 | | Yes |

| FLOOD Howell Luther | 09 Sep. 1870 03 June 1952 | | Yes |

| FLOOD William Irving | 02 Feb. 1884 30 Nov. 1930 | | Yes |

| GENTRY Mary Sue | 1837 1917 | | Yes |

| GILLIAM Annie | 15 Sep. 1864 08 Apr. 1957 | Gilliam, Spencer | Yes |

Other Info: Shares a headstone with her husband.

| GILLIAM Edward Cook | 01 Apr. 1876 02 Jan. 1953 | | Yes |

Inscription: "Asleep In Jesus."

| GILLIAM Lelia | 23 Dec. 1875 27 Dec. 1963 | Fitttz | Yes |

| GILLIAM Mary Lillian | 1874 1950 | | Yes |

| GILLIAM Robert Van | 1880 1938 | | Yes |

| GILLIAM Spencer | 29 June 1860 29 Aug. 1943 | Gilliam, Annie | Yes |

Other Info: Shares a headstone with his wife.

| GLOVER Ashland B. | 22 Sep. 1898 05 Jan. 1977 | | Yes |

| GLOVER Edward Lee | 26 Oct. 1855 28 May 1917 | | Yes |

Inscription: "Father." Footstone inscribed: "E.L.G."

LAST NAME First Name	Date of Birth Date of Death Age at Death	Maiden Name Spouse	Tombstone
GLOVER Eva	03 Oct. 1874 09 Nov. 1962	Davidson	Yes

Inscription: "Mother." Footstone inscribed: "E.D.G."

GLOVER John W.	1890 1956	Glover, Lucy A.	Yes

Other Info: Shares a headstone with his wife.

GLOVER Lewis T.	23 Aug. 1922 13 July 1974		Yes

Inscription: He served as inscribed: "S M Sgt. US Air Force."

GLOVER Lucy A.	1895 1981	Glover, John W.	Yes

Other Info: Shares a headstone with her husband.

GLOVER Marvin Agee	18 Sep. 1893 14 June 1961	Glover, Rena Roberts	Yes

Inscription: Footstone inscribed: "Father."

Other Info: Shares a headstone with his wife.

GLOVER Paul L.	02 Dec. 1900 03 Jan. 1974		Yes

GLOVER Rena	26 Aug. 1894 09 Feb. 1984	Roberts Glover, Marvin Agee	Yes

Other Info: Shares a headstone with her husband.

GLOVER Roma (Miss)	11 June 1916 23 Oct. 1986		Yes

Inscription: "In God's Care."

GLOVER Wilbur W.	19 Nov. 1905 25 July 1978		Yes

Inscription: "In Loving Memory."

HARRIS Millard Fillmore	23 Nov. 1915 30 Oct. 1977		Yes

Inscription: He served as inscribed: "U.S. Army World War II."

HEDRICK Frank	1905 1965		Yes

HORNE Margaret A.	25 Sep. 1888 09 Apr. 1922		Yes

LAST NAME First Name	Date of Birth Date of Death Age at Death	Maiden Name Spouse	Tombstone

Inscription: "Mother."

| HUBBARD
J. W. | 1858
1924 | Hubbard, Ann R. (Stinson) | Yes |

Other Info: Shares a headstone with his wife.

| JOHNSON
Yem Gill | 10 Jan. 1909
20 Feb. 1979 | Johnson, Ruth Mitchell | Yes |

| JONES
C. Robert | 21 Nov. 1901
26 Oct. 1954 | Jones, Dorothy Douglas | Yes |

| JONES
Dorothy | 25 Jan. 1906
17 July 1958 | Douglas
Jones, C. Robert | Yes |

Inscription: Footstone inscribed: "D.D.J."

| JONES
M. Tandy | 12 Sep. 1873
16 Sep. 1939 | Jones, Mary Eliza | Yes |

Inscription: Footstone inscribed: "M.T.J."

| JONES
Mary Eliza | 30 May 1874
22 Nov. 1946 | Jones, M. Tandy | Yes |

Inscription: Footstone inscribed: "M.E.J."

| LEAGUS
Mary | | | No |

Other Info: Grave marked with a slate marker - not inscribed.

| LODGE
S. D. | | | No |

Other Info: Grave marked with a slate marker - not inscribed.

| MILLS
Lamartine Paul "Buck" | 04 Dec. 1896
16 Mar. 1984 | Mills, Louise Phelps | Yes |

| MITCHELL
Doris E. | 28 Feb. 1919
23 Mar. 1919 | | Yes |

Inscription: "Doris Lives." Footstone inscribed: "D.E.M."

| MITCHELL
Joseph H. | 1863
1948 | Mitchell, Julia E. | Yes |

Inscription: "M.D." Footstone inscribed: "J.H.M."

Other Info: Shares a headstone with his wife.

| MITCHELL
Julia E. | 1886
1975 | Mitchell, Joseph H. | Yes |

LAST NAME First Name	Date of Birth Date of Death Age at Death	Maiden Name Spouse	Tombstone

Other Info: Shares a headstone with her husband.

MORGAN Billie	29 Mar. 1917 07 May 1962		Yes
MORGAN C. B. Jr.	10 Oct. 1920 15 May 1927		Yes
MORGAN Charles B.	09 Nov. 1876 10 May 1950		Yes
MORGAN Ernest Agee	02 July 1890 17 Jan. 1975		Yes

Inscription: He served as inscribed: "Wagr. U.S. Army."

MORGAN Grace A.	12 Mar. 1892 07 Oct. 1975		Yes
MORGAN Hattie R.	29 Mar. 1884 30 May 1971		Yes
MORGAN Inez A.	17 Feb. 1849 19 Oct. 1938		Yes
MORGAN John C.	04 Dec. 1894 16 Dec. 1958		Yes

Inscription: "Father."

MORGAN John P.	31 Jan. 1813 27 Oct. 1899	Morgan, Martha J.	Yes

Inscription: "Our Grandparents ... Gone But Not Forgotten."

Other Info: Shares a headstone with his wife.

MORGAN Judith Chambers	1941 1987		Yes

Other Info: Grave marked with a Funeral Home Metal Marker.

MORGAN Lollie Inez	21 Nov. 1914 24 Oct. 1918		Yes
MORGAN Martha J.	23 Jan. 1819 10 Oct. 1895	Morgan, John P.	Yes

Inscription: "Our Grandparents ... Gone But Not Forgotten." Footstone inscribed: "M.J.M."

MORGAN Mary E.	25 Oct. 1867 05 July 1942	Coleman Morgan, Robert A.	Yes

Other Info: Shares a headstone with her husband.

LAST NAME First Name	Date of Birth Date of Death Age at Death	Maiden Name Spouse	Tombstone
MORGAN Mary Louise	04 Oct. 1903		Yes
MORGAN Mary "Sid"	02 June 1932 31 Dec. 1984	Swartz Morgan, Richard M.	Yes

Other Info: Daughter of Hugh M. Swartz and Effie Swartz (Echert).

MORGAN R. Lewis	08 Sep. 1907 10 Sep. 1984	Morgan, Virgie C.	Yes

Other Info: Grave is also marked with a Funeral Home Metal Marker inscribed: "Richard Lewis Morgan, 1907 - 1984."

MORGAN Reece A.	03 Mar. 1884 23 Jan. 1935		Yes
MORGAN Richard T.	25 Apr. 1848 07 Mar. 1922		Yes
MORGAN Richie I.	29 Sep. 1874 31 Mar. 1935		Yes
MORGAN Robert A.	08 Mar. 1849 27 May 1930	Morgan, Mary E. Coleman	Yes

Other Info: Shares a headstone with his wife.

PAYNE Ossie Irene	29 Mar. 1856 03 Feb. 1938	Payne, Richard H.	Yes
PAYNE Richard H.	23 Apr. 1852 11 Jan. 1912	Payne, Ossie Irene	Yes

Inscription: "Gone But Not Forgotten."

PHELPS J. C.	1876 1937		Yes
PRICE John			No

Other Info: Grave marked - not inscribed.

PRICE Sallie			No

Other Info: Grave marked - not inscribed.

PROVINCE Margaret Slater (Mrs.)	19 June 1866 10 Feb. 1932	Province, James S.	Yes

Inscription: "At Rest." Footstone inscribed: "M.S.P."

LAST NAME First Name	Date of Birth Date of Death Age at Death	Maiden Name Spouse	Tombstone
PROVINCE Mary	04 Apr. 1880 16 Mar. 1959	Morgan Province, William P.	Yes

Other Info: Shares a headstone with her husband. Grave also marked with a Funeral Home Metal Marker.

PROVINCE William P.	28 Mar. 1883 08 Apr. 1941	Province, Mary Morgan	Yes

Other Info: Shares a headstone with his wife.

ROBERTS Eveline	1860 1941	Roberts, Troy	

Other Info: Shares a headstone with her husband.

ROBERTS Troy	1861 1946	Roberts, Eveline	Yes

Other Info: Shares a headstone with his wife.

RUSH Clem F.			No

Other Info: Known to be buried here, but no grave marker.

RUSH Ella G.	1867 1957	Rush, John S.	Yes

Other Info: Shares a headstone with her husband.

RUSH John S.	1857 1931	Rush, Ella G.	Yes

Other Info: Shares a headstone with his wife.

RUSH Vincent P.	16 Jan. 1899 08 May 1987		Yes

Inscription: "In Loving Memory."

SCRUGGS		Scruggs, John	No

Other Info: Grave marked - not inscribed. Known to be buried here beside her husband.

SCRUGGS John		Scruggs (Mrs.)	No

Other Info: Known to be buried here beside his wife, but no marker.

SIMON Evelyn Harris	12 Dec. 1921 22 May 1987		Yes

LAST NAME	Date of Birth	Maiden Name	Tombstone
First Name	Date of Death	Spouse	
	Age at Death		

Inscription: "The Most Wonderful Mother of All, Who Gave Her Time Joyfully, Her Love Generously, and Her Smile Warmly, We Love You."

| STEGER | | | No |
| Ellen | | | |

Other Info: Grave marked - not inscribed.

| STEGER | 14 Sep. 1820 | Seargent (sic) | Yes |
| Frances E. | 06 Jan. 1891 | Steger, Wm. | |

Inscription: "In Memory of ... Married Wm. Steger ... At Rest."

Other Info:

| STINSON | 1860 | | Yes |
| Ann R. Hubbard | 1937 | Stinson & Hubbard, J. W. | |

Other Info: Shares a headstone with her first husband.

| THOMPSON | 04 Aug. 1887 | | Yes |
| Oswald J. | 15 June 1974 | Thompson, Emma Barker | |

Bixler/Crews Family - Hwy 660

| BIXLER | | | No |
| Alexander | | | |

Other Info: Known to be buried here beside his parents, but grave marked by fieldstones only. He is the son of Frank and Irene C. Bixler.

| BIXLER | | | No |
| Frank | | Bixler, Irene C. | |

Other Info: Frank is known to be buried here beside his wife, but grave marked only by fieldstones.

| BIXLER | | Crews | No |
| Irene | | Bixler, Frank | |

Other Info: Irene is known to be buried here beside her husband, but grave marked by fieldstones only. Irene was the sister of James Crews.

| BRANCH | | | No |
| (Baby) | | | |

Other Info: Known to be buried here, but grave marked by fieldstones only.

| COLLINS | 25 June 1886 | | Yes |
| Harry R. | 23 Nov. 1886 | | |

Inscription: "We Miss the Bright Eyes Of Our Darling Child and the Sweet Rosy Lips That So Often On Us Smile."

LAST NAME	Date of Birth	Maiden Name	Tombstone
First Name	Date of Death	Spouse	
	Age at Death		

CREWS
Albert   No

Other Info: Known to be buried here, but grave marked only by fieldstones. Albert was the son of James Crews. He died young, just before he was to be married.

CREWS   Mar. 1874   Elder   Yes
Dora   Sep. 1922   Crews, William "Bill"

Inscription: "At Rest."

Other Info: Her husband is buried at Mulberry Grove Baptist Church Cemetery.

CREWS   Davis   No
Fannie   Crews, Jesse

Other Info: Known to be buried here, but grave marked by fieldstones only.

CREWS   No
John Whitcomb Pratt "Pratt"

Other Info: Known to be buried here, but grave marked by fieldstones only. John was the son of James Crews and Pinkie Hackett Crews.

CREWS   No
Lou   Crews, William "Billy"

Other Info: Known to be buried here beside her husband, but grave marked only by fieldstones.

CREWS   1823 (circa)   Yes
William A.   Crews, Sarah Eliza

Inscription: William A. served as inscribed: "CO K 4 VA CAV C.S.A."

Other Info: Father of James Crews.

CREWS   No
William "Billy"   Crews, Lou

Other Info: Known to be buried here beside his wife, but grave marked only by fieldstones.

Black Cemetery at Jonestown - Hwy 15

BROWN   22 Sep. 1832   Yes
Harrie   11 Nov. 1913

Inscription: "Father."

LAST NAME First Name	Date of Birth Date of Death Age at Death	Maiden Name Spouse	Tombstone
JOHNSON Mary	1888 1909		Yes

Inscription: "At Rest."

Other Info: This is a large black community cemetery with 100+ graves - only two graves have headstones. Two graves are marked with funeral home metal markers but they were unreadable. Could this be a Pollard family slave burying ground that then became a burying ground for black families after the Civil War? Does anyone know?

Booker / Lackland / Selden Family - Hwy 15

BLAND Emily L.	1819 1913		Yes
LOUDON Elvira			Yes

Other Info: No dates inscribed for this burial.

SELDEN Anna W.	1888 1888		Yes
SELDEN Caroline E.	1880 1888		Yes

Other Info: "Carrie" died from the measles.

SELDEN Emma B.	1855 1916	Selden, Samuel M.	Yes
SELDEN Esther W.	1898 1916		Yes
SELDEN John R.	1883 1914		Yes
SELDEN Samuel M.	1850 1912	Selden, Emma B.	Yes

Other Info: Samuel M., his wife, and their five children are all listed on one headstone, along with Elvira Loudon and Emily L. Bland, who might have been servants, or they might have been other family members. One son, John Randolph Selden, who had a separate Woodmen of the World headstone, was listed in the original cemetery listing in Vol. I. This additional information on this family cemetery is an important part of this cemetery record.

SELDEN Samuel M. Jr.	1874		Yes

Other Info: Samuel Jr.'s death date was not inscribed on the headstone.

LAST NAME	Date of Birth	Maiden Name	Tombstone
First Name	Date of Death	Spouse	
	Age at Death		

Brown Family - Hwy 653

BROWN   No
                                    Brown, Gabriel Willis

   Other Info: The single grave at this cemetery is burial place of "Willis" Brown's second wife. Grave marked only by fieldstones, and probably impossible to find today. The road that this home was on ran from Hwy 627 over past "Montrose" and came back out onto Hwy 653, a fairly well-travelled road at one time.

Brown - Willie Brown Family - Black - Hwy 655

ANDERSON   No
Mattie   24 July 1944
                  70 yr.

   Other Info: Grave is marked by a funeral home metal marker. Mattie Anderson is the mother of John Nicholas, buried elsewhere in the county. There is also a fieldstone marker in this same cemetery that has the initials "C.H." carved on it. Also approximately 40 other graves marked by fieldstones only.

BROWN   No
Willie

   Other Info: There are approximately 40 graves marked by fieldstones only in this cemetery. Not known which grave belongs to Willie Brown.

Brown's Chapel United Methodist Church - Hwy 617

ABSHER   09 July 1909   Yes
Albert Lee   02 June 1989   Absher, Elizabeth

Inscription: "Married Aug. 3, 1930."

Other Info: Grave also marked by a funeral home metal marker.

ABSHER   04 Aug. 1902   Wood   Yes
Belle   31 Dec. 1983   Absher, Oscar Watson

Other Info: Shares a headstone with her husband.

ABSHER   06 July 1868   Compton   Yes
Betty   14 Jan. 1944   Absher, Lee B.

Other Info: Shares a headstone with her husband.

ABSHER   24 Aug. 1873   Yes
Charles C.   02 Nov. 1948   Absher, Minnie E.

LAST NAME First Name	Date of Birth Date of Death Age at Death	Maiden Name Spouse	Tombstone

Inscription: Footstone inscribed: "Father."

Other Info: Shares a headstone with his wife.

| ABSHER Daniel Lee | 1922 1996 | | No |

Other Info: Grave marked by a funeral home metal marker.

| ABSHER Edith G. | 18 Jan. 1930 23 July 1983 | | Yes |

Inscription: "At Rest."

| ABSHER Ellen Carbaugh | 25 Jan. 1903 11 Aug. 1969 | Absher, William Bee | Yes |

Other Info: Shares a headstone with her husband.

| ABSHER Fanny A. | 1897 1960 | Absher, William E. | Yes |

Other Info: Shares a headstone with her husband.

| ABSHER Harriette Agnes | 15 Dec. 1929 26 Dec. 1931 | | Yes |

Inscription: "Darling We Miss Thee."

| ABSHER Lane Edward | 25 July 1911 10 Apr. 1935 | | Yes |

Inscription: "Our Loved One." Footstone inscribed: "L.E.A."

| ABSHER Lee B. | 21 Jan. 1871 27 Feb. 1945 | Absher, Betty Compton | Yes |

Other Info: Shares a headstone with his wife.

| ABSHER Millie | May 1893 Apr. 1965 | Herndon Absher, Walter Paris | Yes |

Other Info: Shares a headstone with her husband.

| ABSHER Minnie E. | 07 Nov. 1878 09 Mar. 1957 | Absher, Charles C. | Yes |

Inscription: Footstone inscribed: "Mother."

Other Info: Shares a headstone with her husband.

| ABSHER Oscar Watson | 25 Oct. 1891 21 July 1956 | Absher, Belle Wood | Yes |

Inscription: "My Beloved Husband."

LAST NAME	Date of Birth	Maiden Name	Tombstone
First Name	Date of Death	Spouse	
	Age at Death		

Other Info: Shares a headstone with his wife.

| ABSHER | 11 Jan. 1881 | | Yes |
| Walter Paris | 24 Nov. 1971 | Absher, Millie Herndon | |

Inscription: He served as inscribed: "Virginia Mech MG Co 33 Infantry World War I."

Other Info: Shares a headstone with his wife.

| ABSHER | 03 Oct. 1893 | | Yes |
| William Bee | 05 Dec. 1978 | Absher, Ellen Carbaugh | |

Inscription: Footstone shows he served as inscribed: "PFC US Army World War I."

Other Info: Shares a headstone with his wife.

| ABSHER | 1904 | | Yes |
| William E. | 1964 | Absher, Fanny A. | |

Other Info: Shares a headstone with his wife.

| AGEE | 1872 | | Yes |
| Cornelius Hamilton | 1967 | Agee, Rosa K. C. | |

| AGEE | 29 June 1871 | | Yes |
| Frank Garland | 22 Dec. 1897 | | |

Inscription: "Brother."

Other Info: Shares a headstone with his sister, M. C. Agee.

| AGEE | 17 Mar. 1904 | | Yes |
| Frank Garland | 17 Dec. 1991 | | |

| AGEE | 09 Aug. 1834 | | Yes |
| Garland Price Lt. | 01 June 1899 | Agee, Mary Nuckols | |

Inscription: "He served as shown by the designation of "Lt."

| AGEE | 12 Feb. 1806 | | Yes |
| Jacob Jr. Capt. | 1842 | Agee, Mary Price | |

Other Info: Shares a headstone with his wife.

| AGEE | 1809 | Price | Yes |
| Mary | 1850 | Agee, Capt. Jacob Jr. | |

Other Info: Shares a headstone with her husband.

| AGEE | 11 May 1845 | Nuckols | Yes |
| Mary | 28 Nov. 1919 | Agee, Lt. Garland Price | |

LAST NAME First Name	Date of Birth Date of Death Age at Death	Maiden Name Spouse	Tombstone
AGEE Mary Catherine	18 July 1866 14 June 1892		Yes

Inscription: "Sister."

Other Info: Shares a headstone with her brother, F. G. Agee.

| AGEE
Rosa Kate | 1883
1948 | Claiborne
Agee, Cornelius Hamilton | Yes |

Inscription: "Wife of Cornelius Hamilton Agee."

| AGEE
Virginia Hooper | 11 July 1903
01 Nov. 1981 | | Yes |

| AGEE
Wm. C. | | | Yes |

Inscription: "Uncle. He Hath Entered the Pearly Gates."

Other Info: No dates inscribed on this headstone.

| BARKER
Edna W. | 17 May 1891
01 Oct. 1981 | Barker, Wm. Lee | Yes |

Inscription: "Gone But Not Forgotten."

Other Info: Shares a headstone with her husband.

| BARKER
Robert J. | 03 Sep. 1916
28 Nov. 1944 | | Yes |

Inscription: He served as inscribed: "PFC 120 INF 30 DIV World War II."

| BARKER
Wm. Lee | 1886
1954 | Barker, Edna W. | Yes |

Inscription: "Gone But Not Forgotten."

Other Info: Shares a headstone with his wife.

| BESENDORFER
Erich Whitman | 01 Oct. 1969
27 Sep. 1990 | | Yes |

Inscription: "Always In Our Hearts."

| BRANSFORD
Glenna | 30 Sep. 1904
31 Oct. 1992 | Bransford, Walter P. | Yes |

Inscription: "Precious Lord Take My Hand."

Other Info: Shares a headstone with her husband.

| BRANSFORD
Walter P. | 05 Nov. 1901
29 June 1982 | Bransford, Glenna | Yes |

LAST NAME First Name	Date of Birth Date of Death Age at Death	Maiden Name Spouse	Tombstone

Inscription: "Precious Lord Take My Hand."

Other Info: Shares a headstone with his wife.

| CARTER
Lee Roy | 01 Jan. 1899
15 July 1990 | Carter, Nannie Oliver | Yes |

Inscription: "In God's Care. Wed June 6, 1948."

Other Info: Shares a headstone with his wife.

| CARTER
Nannie | 03 June 1909
20 Mar. 1990 | Oliver
Carter, Lee Roy | Yes |

Inscription: "In God's Care. Wed June 6, 1948."

Other Info: Shares a headstone with her husband.

| CHILDRESS
Helen | 06 Mar. 1900
26 Oct. 1971 | | Yes |

| CHILDRESS
Robert L. | 06 Apr. 1892
14 Sep. 1974 | | Yes |

| CHILDRESS
Sarah B. | 05 Feb. 1958 | | Yes |

Inscription: "Mother."

| CLAIBORNE
Laura | 08 Aug. 1821
29 July 1901 | Garnett
Claiborne, Thomas O. | Yes |

Other Info: Shares a headstone with her husband.

| CLAIBORNE
Martha Elizabeth | 20 June 1844
14 Nov. 1902 | Claiborne, Sgt. Temple Irving | Yes |

Other Info: Shares a headstone with her husband.

| CLAIBORNE
Temple Irving Sgt. | 18 Jan. 1844
20 Sep. 1916 | Claiborne, Martha E. | Yes |

Other Info: Shares a headstone with his wife.

| CLAIBORNE
Thomas O. | 16 Mar. 1809
26 Feb. 1892 | Claiborne, Laura Garnett | Yes |

Other Info: Shares a headstone with his wife.

| DAVIS
Florence T. | 10 Oct. 1894
17 Dec. 1987 | Davis, John W. | Yes |

Inscription: Footstone inscribed: "Mother."

Other Info: Shares a headstone with her husband.

LAST NAME First Name	Date of Birth Date of Death Age at Death	Maiden Name Spouse	Tombstone
DAVIS John W.	21 Sep. 1883 27 June 1975	Davis, Florence T.	Yes

Inscription: Footstone inscribed: "Father."

Other Info: Shares a headstone with his wife.

DAVIS Kenneth E.	13 Feb. 1920 13 June 1976		Yes

Inscription: He served as inscribed: "PFC Army Air Forces World War II."

DAVIS Willie Oscar	18 Mar. 1905 07 June 1986		Yes
DENNIS Edmund Smith	11 Jan. 1887 13 Jan. 1948	Dennis, Edna England	Yes

Other Info: Shares a headstone with his wife.

DENNIS Edna	13 Feb. 1884 03 July 1971	England Dennis, Edmund Smith	Yes

Other Info: Shares a headstone with her husband.

DOLAN Rachel A.	22 Oct. 1886 10 Aug. 1965		Yes

Inscription: "At Rest." Footstone inscribed: "Grandmother."

DUNKUM Rosa L.	20 Feb. 1883 26 Feb. 1969	Dunkum, W. Elijah	Yes

Inscription: "Married Dec. 27, 1904."

Other Info: Shares a headstone with her husband.

DUNKUM W. Elijah	17 June 1884 16 June 1971	Dunkum, Rosa L.	Yes

Inscription: "Married Dec. 27, 1904."

Other Info: Shares a headstone with his wife.

ENGLAND Anna Palmore	05 Aug. 1855 01 Apr. 1944		Yes
ENGLAND W. I.	03 Aug. 1851 06 Apr. 1923		Yes

Inscription: "Another Link Is Broken In Our House Hold Band But A Chain Is Forming In A Better Land." Footstone inscribed: "W.I.E."

LAST NAME First Name	Date of Birth Date of Death Age at Death	Maiden Name Spouse	Tombstone
GORMUS Alfred T.	29 July 1883 09 May 1971	Gormus, Lillian E.	Yes

Inscription: "Resting Beneath the Sunlight Trail."

Other Info: Shares a headstone with his wife.

GORMUS Bert H.	05 May 1915 21 May 1961		Yes

Inscription: "The Gift Of God Is Eternal LIfe."

GORMUS Lawrence B.	22 June 1910 29 Sep. 1969		Yes
GORMUS Lillian E.	18 Sep. 1891 19 May 1977	Gormus, Alfred T.	Yes

Inscription: "Resting Beneath the Sunlight Trail."

Other Info: Shares a headstone with her husband.

HALL Gerald Ray	05 May 1929 09 Dec. 1984		Yes

Inscription: He served as inscribed: "CPL US Army World War II."

HUDGINS Mattie	18 July 1878 24 Apr. 1958	Gormus	Yes

Inscription: "Mother."

LESUEUR Frank Evans	16 Aug. 1917 03 Feb. 1995	LeSueur, Pauline Dunkum	Yes
LIGHTFOOT DeLores A.	15 July 1908 22 Feb. 1985	Lightfoot, James C.	Yes

Other Info: Shares a headstone with her husband.

LIGHTFOOT James C.	31 Mar. 1905 04 Jan. 1970	Lightfoot, DeLores A.	Yes

Other Info: Shares a headstone with his wife.

LYLE Claude O.	1910 1977		Yes

Inscription: He served as inscribed: "PFC US Army World War II."

MARKS Margaret A.	1946 1990		Yes

Other Info: Grave also marked by a funeral home metal marker.

LAST NAME First Name	Date of Birth Date of Death Age at Death	Maiden Name Spouse	Tombstone
MEADOR Alice G.	1888 1952		Yes
MEADOR Elizabeth Walker	05 Apr. 1871 22 Oct. 1875		Yes

Inscription: "Dau. of T. B. & Mary W. Meador. Though Lost To Sight To Memory Dear."

MEADOR Frank W.	1883 1952		Yes
MEADOR James L.	1872 1941		Yes
MEADOR Mary W.	1849 1919		Yes
MEADOR Thomas B.			Yes

Inscription: He served as inscribed: "CO A 57 VA Inf. C.S.A."

Other Info: No dates inscribed on this headstone.

MEADOR William B.	1877 1935		Yes
MILLER Villa Allison	06 Apr. 1914 07 May 1993	Miller, Anna Marie D.	Yes

Inscription: Footstone shows he served as inscribed: "S1 US Navy World War II."

OLD Beulah D.	1916 1995		No

Other Info: Grave marked by a funeral home metal marker.

OLIVER Alice J.	22 Sep. 1880 30 July 1972		Yes

Inscription: "Mother. Rest In Peace."

OLIVER Carrie	03 Feb. 1907 10 Apr. 1984	Whitlow Oliver, Spencer Lewis	Yes

Inscription: "Forever In Our Hearts." Footstone inscribed: "Mother."

Other Info: Shares a headstone with her husband.

OLIVER Edgar	12 Oct. 1902 22 May 1934		Yes

Inscription: "Gone But Not Forgotten." Footstone inscribed: "E.O."

LAST NAME First Name	Date of Birth Date of Death Age at Death	Maiden Name Spouse	Tombstone
OLIVER Henry Carol	02 Jan. 1907 21 Sep. 1977		Yes

Inscription: "How Great Thou Art."

| OLIVER
James L. | 09 June 1917
16 July 1944 | | Yes |

Inscription: "Father. We Miss You." Footstone inscribed: "J.L.O."

| OLIVER
James Lewis | 1944
1996 | | No |

Other Info: Grave marked by a funeral home metal marker.

| OLIVER
Lucille T. | 22 June 1919
16 Apr. 1992 | Oliver, Murray L. | Yes |

Inscription: "Mother. We Will Meet Again."

Other Info: Shares a headstone with her husband.

| OLIVER
Murray L. | 14 June 1912
07 Mar. 1967 | Oliver, Lucille T. | Yes |

Inscription: "Father. We Will Meet Again."

Other Info: Shares a headstone with his wife.

| OLIVER
Spencer Lewis | 03 Nov. 1904
03 Sep. 1982 | Oliver, Carrie Whitlow | Yes |

Inscription: "Forever In Our Hearts." Footstone inscribed: "Father."

Other Info: Shares a headstone with his wife.

| OLIVER
William W. | 21 Aug. 1880
22 Sep. 1945 | | Yes |

Inscription: "Gone But Not Forgotten." Footstone inscribed: "W.W.O."

| POE
Aubrey Jack | 23 Apr. 1931
06 Dec. 1990 | | Yes |

| POE
Florence | 26 Oct. 1904
25 Oct. 1969 | Childress | Yes |

| POE
James P. | 1851
1936 | | Yes |

| POE
John W. | 08 Nov. 1874
03 Jan. 1966 | | Yes |

Inscription: Footstone inscribed: "J.W.P."

LAST NAME First Name	Date of Birth Date of Death Age at Death	Maiden Name Spouse	Tombstone
POE Liza V.	1848 1933		Yes
POE Maomi	02 May 1901 29 Mar. 1990	Maxey Poe, William Ernest	Yes

Other Info: Shares a headstone with her husband.

POE Martha Frances	29 Dec. 1872 22 July 1930		Yes

Inscription: "She Has Been A Faithful Wife, and Good Mother. She Believed and Sleeps In Jesus."

POE Mary	15 July 1902 10 Apr. 1934	Absher Poe, William E.	Yes

Inscription: "Wife of William E. Poe."

Other Info: Shares a headstone with her two infants.

POE Ruth			Yes

Inscription: "Baby."

Other Info: Shares a headstone with her mother, Mary A. Poe; also an infant brother.

POE William			Yes

Inscription: "Baby"

Other Info: Shares a headstone with his mother, Mary A. Poe; also an infant sister.

POE William Ernest	12 Nov. 1896 17 Sep. 1960	Poe, Maomi Maxey	Yes

Other Info: Shares a headstone with his wife.

SHUMAKER John J.	1871 1953		Yes

Inscription: "Buck."

SLOUGH Carlton M.	13 May 1921 08 Aug. 1990	Slough, Annette A.	Yes

Other Info: Grave also marked by a funeral home metal marker.

SNODDY Ashby W.	27 May 1907 13 Oct. 1980	Snoddy, Okie S.	Yes

LAST NAME First Name	Date of Birth Date of Death Age at Death	Maiden Name Spouse	Tombstone

Other Info: Shares a headstone with his wife.

| SNODDY
Okie S. | 31 Mar. 1907
29 Aug. 1981 | Snoddy, Ashby W. | Yes |

Other Info: Shares a headstone with her husband.

| SNYDER
Mattie O. | 08 Sep. 1914
15 Apr. 1993 | | Yes |

Inscription: "Rest In Peace Mom."

| THOMAS
Annie B. | 19 May 1911
21 Nov. 1988 | Thomas, Robert J. | Yes |

Inscription: "Forever In Our Hearts."

Other Info: Shares a headstone with her husband.

| THOMAS
Brian Keith Sr. | 11 Oct. 1967
16 May 1993 | Thomas, Terry Marie | Yes |

Inscription: "Married June 20, 1986."

| THOMAS
G. Gordon | 24 May 1914
26 Mar. 1987 | Thomas, Sarah D. | Yes |

Inscription: "Married July 20, 1940."

| THOMAS
J. F. | 09 Mar. 1856
30 Dec. 1924 | | Yes |

Inscription: "He Died As He Lived A Christian."

| THOMAS
Karen Elizabeth | 15 Nov. 1986 | | Yes |

Inscription: "Daughter of Brian & Terry Thomas."

| THOMAS
Minerva C. | 27 June 1860
23 Mar. 1937 | | Yes |

Inscription: "Not Dead, But Sleeping In Christ." Footstone inscribed: "M.C.T."

| THOMAS
Robert J. | 28 June 1909
13 Feb. 1988 | Thomas, Annie B. | Yes |

Inscription: "Forever In Our Hearts."

Other Info: Shares a headstone with his wife.

| VAN KEUREN
Marcella | 02 Feb. 1899
14 June 1960 | Childress | Yes |

LAST NAME First Name	Date of Birth Date of Death Age at Death	Maiden Name Spouse	Tombstone
WEST Alice			Yes

Inscription: "Dau. of John S. West. She Was An Affectionate Daughter and A Faithful Friend."

Other Info: No dates inscribed on this headstone.

WEST Dudley Rogers	11 Sep. 1901 25 July 1970		Yes
WEST Eugene Francis	14 Oct. 1865 1891		Yes

Inscription: "Brother. He Was Faithful To Every Duty."

WEST Jacob A.	16 Jan. 1845 13 Dec. 1910		Yes

Inscription: "Brother. Though Lost To Sight. To Memory Dear." Footstone shows that he served as inscribed: "1 Lieut. Jacob A. West CO C 3 VA RES. C.S.A."

WEST John Edmund	07 July 1853 30 Dec. 1935		Yes
WEST John Francis	15 Jan. 1899 01 Apr. 1988	West, Sue Roberson	Yes
WEST John S.	02 Oct. 1815 06 Mar. 1878	West, Sarah Elizabeth	Yes

Inscription: "Father. He Died As He Lived. A Christian."

WEST Margaret Staehlin	16 June 1870 20 June 1947		Yes
WEST Martha J.	18 Feb. 1851 07 Nov. 1901		Yes

Inscription: "In Memory of ... Daughter of John S. and Sarah E. West."

WEST Sarah Elizabeth	11 Feb. 1827 25 June 1894	West, John S.	Yes

Inscription: "Mother. Wife of John S. West. She Shall Wake On the Resurrection Morn."

WEST Sue	05 Aug. 1909 12 Oct. 1992	Roberson West, John Francis	Yes
WEST Tyree			Yes

LAST NAME	Date of Birth	Maiden Name	Tombstone
First Name	Date of Death	Spouse	
	Age at Death		

Inscription: "Son of John S. West...Earth Has No Sorrows That Heaven Cannot Heal."

Other Info: No dates inscribed on this headstone.

| WILLIAMS | 25 Jan. 1899 | | Yes |
| Fred O. | 05 Nov. 1965 | Williams, R. Garnett Agee | |

| WOOD | 26 Aug. 1908 | Hudgins | Yes |
| Anna | 25 Feb. 1993 | Wood, James Milton | |

Inscription: "Married Dec. 31, 1928. In God We Trust."

Other Info: Shares a headstone with her husband.

| WOOD | 05 Apr. 1974 | | Yes |
| Christopher Shawn | 17 May 1990 | | |

Inscription: "An Inspiration To All Who Knew Him."

| WOOD | 03 Jan. 1909 | | Yes |
| James Milton | 05 Oct. 1987 | Wood, Anna Hudgins | |

Inscription: "Married Dec. 31, 1928. In God We Trust."

Other Info: Shares a headstone with his wife.

| WOODS | | | Yes |
| (Infant) | 13 Oct. 1939 | | |

Inscription: "Our Darling. Infant Son of Mr. & Mrs. I. E. Woods."

| WOODS | 21 Feb. 1895 | | Yes |
| Ira E. | 16 May 1956 | Woods, Pearl A. | |

Inscription: Footstone shows he served as inscribed: "Ira Everett Woods Virginia SC2 USNRF."

Other Info: Shares a headstone with his wife.

| WOODS | 10 Nov. 1898 | | Yes |
| Pearl A. | 11 July 1991 | Woods, Ira E. | |

Other Info: Shares a headstone with her husband. Her grave is also marked by a funeral home metal marker.

| WOOTTON | 11 Mar. 1900 | Poe | Yes |
| Inez | 10 Dec. 1945 | Wootton, Osten D. | |

Other Info: Shares a headstone with her husband.

| WOOTTON | 07 Nov. 1903 | | Yes |
| Osten D. | 29 Mar. 1970 | Wootton, Inez Poe | |

Other Info: Shares a headstone with his wife.

LAST NAME	Date of Birth	Maiden Name	Tombstone
First Name	Date of Death	Spouse	
	Age at Death		

Brown/Peters Family - Hwy 653

BANTON   17 May 1928   Yes
Alex Sizer Wilson   14 Dec. 1929

     Other Info: Originally buried in this family cemetery, but moved to Scottsville Community Cemetery. The son of Charles M. and "Dottie" Banton.

BANTON   1874   Yes
Charles Mitchell   1929   Banton, "Dottie" N. L. P.

     Other Info: Originally buried in this family cemetery, but removed to Scottsville Community Cemetery.

BANTON   09 July 1906   Yes
Francis Mitchell   22 Nov. 1920

     Other Info: Originally buried in this family cemetery, but moved to the Scottsville Community Cemetery. The son of Charles M. and "Dottie" Banton.

BANTON   1881   Peters   Yes
Narcissus Lee "Dottie"   1975   Banton, Charles M.

     Other Info: Originally buried in this family cemtery, but moved to the Scottsville Community Cemetery.

BROWN   1810 (circa)   No
Gabriel   Brown, Martha A. B.

     Other Info: Known to be buried here beside his wife.

BROWN   1816 (circa)   Baird   No
Martha A.   Brown, Gabriel

     Other Info: Known to be buried here beside her husband.

CURRIER   21 Oct. 1877   Peters   Yes
Ardella   02 Aug. 1965   Currier, Richard Ernest

     Inscription: "A Precious One From Us Has Gone, A Voice I Loved Is Still. A Place Is Vacant In My Home, Which Never Can Be Filled."

     Other Info: Shares a headstone with her husband.

CURRIER   22 Apr. 1884   Yes
Richard Ernest   25 Sep. 1961   Currier, Ardella Peters

     Inscription: "A Precious One From Us Has Gone, A Voice I Loved Is Still. A Place Is Vacant In My Home, Which Never Can Be Filled."

     Other Info: Shares a headstone with his wife.

LAST NAME First Name	Date of Birth Date of Death Age at Death	Maiden Name Spouse	Tombstone
HURT (infant)	02 Sep. 1937		Yes

Inscription: "Our Darling Infant Son of Stuart and Elizabeth Hurt. Budded On Earth To Bloom In Heaven."

HURT (infant son)	15 June 1949 16 June 1949		Yes

Inscription: "Our Darling Infant Son of Stuart and Elizabeth Hurt. Budded On Earth To Bloom In Heaven."

PETERS Emily			No

Other Info: Known to be buried here, but grave marked by fieldstones only. She was the daughter of Curtis Bannister Peters and Mamie Dudley Peters.

PETERS (infant)			No

Other Info: Markers at head and foot of grave, but no inscriptions. Known to be the infant son of Joseph and Addie Bruce Peters.

PETERS Jefferson A.	1850 1931	Peters, Parkie E. B.	Yes
PETERS Parkie E.	30 Mar. 1852 26 Feb. 1917	Brown Peters, Jefferson A.	Yes

Inscription: "Asleep In Jesus."

Other Info: Daughter of Gabriel and Martha A. Baird Brown.

RICE Thomas Edward	08 Apr. 1964 25 Apr. 1967		Yes

Inscription: "He Is Just Sleeping."

TILLMAN John			No

Other Info: Grave marked by a funeral home metal marker, mostly unreadable.

TILLMAN Martha E.	25 Sep. 1874 16 Mar. 1929		Yes

Cedar Baptist Church Cemetery - Hwy 650

ADAMS Lelia A.	1914 1966	Adams, T. Chambers	Yes

LAST NAME	Date of Birth	Maiden Name	Tombstone
First Name	Date of Death	Spouse	
	Age at Death		

Other Info: Shares a headstone with her husband.

| ADAMS | 1906 | | Yes |
| T. Chambers | 1974 | Adams, Lelia A. | |

Other Info: Shares a headstone with his wife.

| ADCOCK | 26 Apr. 1921 | Hardiman | Yes |
| Bessie Charlotte | 08 July 1945 | Adcock, David Walker | |

Inscription: "Wife of ... At Rest." Footstone inscribed: "B.H.A."

| ADCOCK | 16 May 1895 | | Yes |
| Carrie P. | 31 Dec. 1982 | Adcock, Wesley T. | |

Other Info: Shares a headstone with her husband.

| ADCOCK | 22 Aug. 1920 | | Yes |
| David Walker | 20 Dec. 1982 | Adcock, Bessie C.H. | |

Inscription: "At Rest."

| ADCOCK | 25 Apr. 1877 | | Yes |
| Wesley T. | 15 Nov. 1957 | Adcock, Carrie P. | |

Other Info: Shares a headstone with his wife.

| ALLEN | 21 Oct. 1921 | | Yes |
| Charlie B. | 26 Feb. 1970 | Allen, Carrie S. | |

Inscription: "At Rest." Footstone inscribed: "Father."

| ALLEN | 01 Mar. 1919 | | Yes |
| Frank Acie | 31 May 1962 | Allen, Mary Lesueur | |

Inscription: "We Will Meet Again." Footstone inscribed: "F.A.A. Sr."

| ALLEN | 03 Jan. 1915 | | Yes |
| Gladys D. | 01 Nov. 1991 | Allen, J. Lenard | |

Inscription: "Wed May 4, 1940." Footstone inscribed: "Mother."

Other Info: Shares a headstone with her husband.

| ALLEN | 09 Apr. 1914 | | Yes |
| J. Lenard | 07 Dec. 1992 | Allen, Gladys D. | |

Inscription: "Wed May 4, 1940." Footstone inscribed: "Father."

Other Info: Shares a headstone with his wife.

| ALLEN | 27 May 1920 | Harris | Yes |
| Mary | 04 Nov. 1995 | Allen, "Billy" W.S. | |

Inscription: "Married July 10, 1942."

LAST NAME First Name	Date of Birth Date of Death Age at Death	Maiden Name Spouse	Tombstone

Other Info: Shares a headstone with her husband.

| ALLEN
Ronald Lee | 11 Oct. 1948
17 Oct. 1948 | | Yes |

Inscription: "In Memory Of Our Darling." Footstone inscribed: "R.L.A."

| ALLEN
Willie Samuel | 11 May 1920
12 July 1995 | Allen, Mary Harris | Yes |

Inscription: "Billy." "Married July 10, 1942."

Other Info: Shares a headstone with his wife.

| ATKINSON
John W. | 1874
1939 | Atkinson, Willie W. | Yes |

Inscription: "Dear Parents Though We Miss You Much We Know You Rest With God." "Father."

Other Info: Shares a headstone with his wife.

| ATKINSON
Willie W. | 1877
1940 | Atkinson, John W. | Yes |

Inscription: "Dear Parents Though We Miss You Much We Know You Rest With God." "Mother."

Other Info: Shares a headstone with her husband.

| AYERS
Nannie Sue | 1860
1938 | | Yes |

Other Info: The name should be spelled "Ayres."

| AYRES
Dora | | | Yes |

Other Info: No dates inscribed on the headstone, but known to be buried here.

| AYRES
John R. | | | Yes |

Inscription: He served as inscribed: "Co. C 25 VA Inf. C.S.A."

Other Info: No dates inscribed on the headstone.

| AYRES
Kate | | | Yes |

Other Info: No dates inscribed on the headstone, but known to be buried here.

| AYRES
Sarah | | | Yes |

LAST NAME First Name	Date of Birth Date of Death Age at Death	Maiden Name Spouse	Tombstone

Other Info: No dates inscribed on the headstone, but known to be buried here.

AYRES
  Willie   Yes

Other Info: No dates inscribed on the headstone, but known to be buried here.

BANTON   17 Jan. 1937   Yes
  Albert Glover   29 May 1970

Inscription: "Wheater." Footstone inscribed: "Husband."

BANTON   26 Sep. 1921   Yes
  Alex   27 Apr. 1987

Inscription: He served as inscribed: "PFC US Army World War II."

BANTON   25 Mar. 1890   Yes
  Alexander   10 Mar. 1970   Banton, Lillian C.

Inscription: Footstone inscribed: "Father."

Other Info: Shares a headstone with his wife.

BANTON   13 Mar. 1911   Yes
  Charles H.   18 Nov. 1990 Banton, Carrie Lee Huddleston

Inscription: "Devoted Father."

BANTON   24 Feb. 1884   Yes
  Ella B.   17 July 1964   Banton, Henry G.

Inscription: Footstone inscribed: "E.B.B."

Other Info: Shares a headstone with her husband.

BANTON   02 Apr. 1906   Yes
  Emmett Mitchell   08 June 1964

BANTON   04 Nov. 1930   Yes
  Eugene K. Jr.   02 Nov. 1977

Inscription: "There Is Rest In Heaven." Footstone inscribed: "Eugene Kary Banton Jr."

BANTON   08 Feb. 1895   Yes
  Eugene K. Sr.   30 Aug. 1950

Inscription: "Gone But Not Forgotten." Footstone inscribed: "E.K.B. Sr."

BANTON   01 Sep. 1919   Yes
  Eugene Kenneth   13 Aug. 1929

Inscription: "Till We Meet Again."

LAST NAME First Name	Date of Birth Date of Death Age at Death	Maiden Name Spouse	Tombstone
BANTON Henry G.	03 Feb. 1879 03 July 1952	Banton, Ella B.	Yes

Inscription: Footstone inscribed: "H.G.B."

Other Info: Shares a headstone with his wife.

| BANTON
L. E. | | | Yes |

Other Info: No dates inscribed on this headstone, but known to be buried here.

| BANTON
Lillian C. | 03 Mar. 1889
14 Oct. 1965 | Banton, Alexander | Yes |

Inscription: Footstone inscribed: "Mother."

Other Info: Shares a headstone with her husband.

BANTON Lucy	22 May 1906 03 Mar. 1939	Walker	Yes
BANTON Mary L.	12 Apr. 1909 23 Oct. 1951		Yes
BANTON Robert Lee	1920 1920		Yes

Other Info: Shares a headstone with his brother, W. Banton.

| BANTON
Walter | 1911
1911 | | Yes |

Other Info: Shares a headstone with his brother, R.L. Banton.

| BARKER
(Baby) | | | Yes |

Inscription: "Son of Sidney Allen Barker and .. Born and Died 19__."

Other Info: Very difficult to read.

| BARKER
Evie | | | Yes |

Other Info: No dates inscribed on her flat tombstone.

| BARKER
Frank | 19 Oct. 1852
28 Nov. 1926 | | Yes |

Inscription: "His Toils Are Past His Work Is Done He Fought the Fight The Victory Won."

LAST NAME First Name	Date of Birth Date of Death Age at Death	Maiden Name Spouse	Tombstone

BARKER
Frank (Mrs.) — Tombstone: Yes

Other Info: No dates inscribed, or Christian name given, but known to be buried here.

BARKER
Frank R.   09 Sep. 1920 — Tombstone: Yes

Inscription: He served as inscribed: "Virginia PVT. US Army."

BARKER
John A. — Tombstone: Yes

Other Info: No dates inscribed on his flat tombstone.

BARKER
Lucy — Tombstone: Yes

Other Info: No dates inscribed, but known to be buried here.

BARKER
Sidney Allen   23 Mar. 1927 / 23 Apr. 1989 — Tombstone: Yes

Inscription: He served as inscribed: "PFC US Army World War II."

BARKER
Wiley — Tombstone: Yes

Other Info: No dates inscribed, but known to be buried here.

BARKSDALE
Mollie — Tombstone: Yes

Other Info: No dates inscribed on this stone, but known to be buried here.

BLACKWELL
Douglas Wayne   26 Oct. 1917 / 21 Jan. 1990 — Tombstone: Yes

Inscription: He served as inscribed: "S. Sgt. U.S. Army World War II."

BLACKWELL
Joseph W. Jr.   16 Jan. 1910 / 18 Sep. 1949 — Tombstone: Yes

Inscription: He served as inscribed: "Virginia PFC 35 Infantry 18 Div."

BLACKWELL
Mattie   01 Oct. 1880 / 26 Aug. 1972   Rogers — Tombstone: Yes

Inscription: "Mother."

BLACKWELL
Robert L.   26 Feb. 1948 / 08 May 1949 — Tombstone: Yes

Inscription: Footstone inscribed: "R.L.B."

LAST NAME First Name	Date of Birth Date of Death Age at Death	Maiden Name Spouse	Tombstone
BLACKWELL Roy Franklin	15 Feb. 1905 16 Jan. 1934		Yes

Inscription: Footstone inscribed: "R.F.B."

BRANSFORD John			Yes

Other Info: No dates inscribed, but known to be buried here.

BROCK Deems B.	11 Jan. 1861 20 Feb. 1930	Brock, Flora E.	Yes

Inscription: "Father."

Other Info: Shares a headstone with his wife.

BROCK Flora E.	08 May 1862 26 Jan. 1938	Brock, Deems B.	Yes

Inscription: "Mother."

Other Info: Shares a headstone with her husband.

BRYANT Bell(e)			Yes

Other Info: No dates inscribed on headstone, but known to be buried here.

CATLETT Phillip B.	25 Aug. 1917 29 Aug. 1992	Catlett, Rosa Swann	Yes

Inscription: "Father."

CHRISTIAN Annie			Yes

Other Info: No dates inscribed on this headstone, but known to be buried here.

CHRISTIAN Annie			Yes

Other Info: No dates inscribed on this headstone, but known to be buried here.

CHRISTIAN Charles L.			Yes

Inscription: He served as inscribed: "Co. C 22 VA Inf. C.S.A."

Other Info: No dates inscribed on this headstone.

CHRISTIAN Fitz (Lee)			Yes

LAST NAME First Name	Date of Birth Date of Death Age at Death	Maiden Name Spouse	Tombstone

Other Info: No dates inscribed on this headstone, but known to be buried here. (1885-1964)

CHRISTIAN Yes
John (Henry)

Other Info: No dates inscribed on this headstone, but known to be buried here.

CHRISTIAN Yes
Lucy (Jane)

Other Info: No dates inscribed on this headstone, but known to be buried here.

CHRISTIAN Yes
Robert

Other Info: No dates inscribed on this headstone, but known to be buried here.

COLLINS Yes
John

Other Info: No dates inscribed, but known to be buried here.

DAVIDSON No
Deliah White

Other Info: Known to be buried here, but no markers.

DAVIS 29 Oct. 1911 Yes
Roy M. 03 Sep. 1988 Davis, Louise Hardiman

Inscription: "Devoted Father."

DEAN 01 Nov. 1918 Yes
Carrie Alma 19 Aug. 1920

Inscription: "In God's Care." Footstone inscribed: "Daughter."

DEAN 22 Aug. 1909 Barker Yes
Etta 16 Jan. 1976 Dean, L. Ernest

Inscription: "Mother. We Shall Meet Again."

Other Info: Shares a headstone with her husband.

DEAN 21 Dec. 1866 Yes
John William 25 July 1943 Dean, Martha Harris

Inscription: "In My Father's House Are Many Mansions." Footstone inscribed: "Father."

Other Info: Shares a headstone with his wife.

LAST NAME First Name	Date of Birth Date of Death Age at Death	Maiden Name Spouse	Tombstone
DEAN L. Ernest	08 June 1909 26 Sep. 1979	 Dean, Etta Barker	Yes

Inscription: "Father. We Shall Meet Again."

Other Info: Shares a headstone with his wife.

| DEAN
Louis R. | 18 June 1870
04 Dec. 1959 |
Dean, Mary Sharpe | Yes |

Inscription: "At Rest."

Other Info: Shares a headstone with his wife.

| DEAN
Martha | 30 Sep. 1883
26 Aug. 1965 | Harris
Dean, John William | Yes |

Inscription: "In My Father's House Are Many Mansions." Footstone inscribed: "Mother."

Other Info: Shares a headstone with her husband.

| DEAN
Mary | 12 July 1880
22 Nov. 1956 | Sharpe
Dean, Louis R. | Yes |

Inscription: "At Rest."

Other Info: Shares a headstone with her husband.

| DEAN
(Robert) Lee | | | Yes |

Other Info: No dates inscribed but known to have been born July 2, 1861, and he died on June 23, 1947.

| DUNCAN
George W. | | | Yes |

Inscription: "Footstone inscribed: "Son."

Other Info: Shares a headstone with his father and mother. No dates inscribed for George W.

| DUNCAN
Pearl D. | 03 Mar. 1903
30 May 1995 |
Duncan, W. Church | Yes |

Inscription: "Mother."

Other Info: Shares a headstone with her husband.

| DUNCAN
Robert | | | No |

Other Info: An infant. Known to be buried here, but no markers.

LAST NAME First Name	Date of Birth Date of Death Age at Death	Maiden Name Spouse	Tombstone
DUNCAN Robert James	15 Dec. 1851 03 Nov. 1923		Yes

Inscription: "Gone But Not Forgotten."

DUNCAN Robert L.	03 May 1882 08 Aug. 1946	Duncan, Willie J.	Yes

Inscription: "Father." Footstone inscribed: "Father."

Other Info: Shares a headstone with his wife and his son, George.

DUNCAN (W.) Church	01 May 1892 20 Sep. 1976	Duncan, Pearl D.	Yes

Inscription: "Father."

Other Info: Shares a headstone with his wife.

DUNCAN Willie C.			No

Other Info: Known to be buried here, but no markers.

DUNCAN Willie J.	29 May 1883 24 Nov. 1927	Duncan, Robert L.	Yes

Inscription: "Mother." Footstone inscribed: "Mother."

Other Info: Shares a headstone with her husband and her son, George.

DUNKUM (Baby)			Yes

Other Info: No dates inscribed on the headstone, but known to be buried here.

DUNKUM Charles Acy	09 Feb. 1874 04 Aug. 1925	Dunkum, Emma T.	Yes

Inscription: "Father." Footstone inscribed: "Father."

Other Info: Shares a headstone with his wife and his son, Stephen.

DUNKUM Emma T.	02 Feb. 1875 29 Dec. 1947	Dunkum, Charles Acy	Yes

Inscription: "Mother." Footstone inscribed: "Mother."

Other Info: Shares a headstone with her husband, and her son, Stephen.

DUNKUM Eugene E.	09 June 1933		Yes

Inscription: He served as inscribed: "Virginia PVT 1C1 Coast Art. Corps."

LAST NAME First Name	Date of Birth Date of Death Age at Death	Maiden Name Spouse	Tombstone
DUNKUM Lenwood			Yes

Other Info: No dates on the headstone, but known to be buried here. Infant Son of Myrtle Dunkum.

DUNKUM Paul Beattie	12 Oct. 1916 24 June 1972		Yes

Inscription: "He Worked A Lifetime For Others." He served as inscribed on his footstone: Virginia Cpl Army Air Forces."

DUNKUM Stephen W.	20 Oct. 1912 01 Dec. 1925		Yes

Inscription: "Son." Footstone inscribed: " Son."

Other Info: Shares a headstone with his father and mother, Charles A. & Emma T. Dunkum."

DUNSFORD Amaranda			Yes

Other Info: No dates inscribed, but known to be buried here.

DUNSFORD Willie			No

Other Info: (Female.) Known to be buried here, but no markers.

ELGIN John D.	13 Nov. 1922 25 Sep. 1981	Elgin, Frances H.	Yes

Inscription: "Precious Lord Take My Hand."

FARRAR Eva Louise	03 June 1921 25 Apr. 1943		Yes

Inscription: "At Rest."

FARRAR John Spencer	09 Mar. 1908 07 Dec. 1975		Yes

Inscription: He served as inscribed: "Sgt. U.S. Army World War II."

FARRAR Kenneth Wayne	27 Dec. 1935 14 July 1937		Yes

Inscription: "Son of Earl & Effie Farrar Jr. Safe In the Arms Of Jesus." Footstone inscribed: "Son."

FARRAR Lewis Edgar	12 May 1904 04 Sep. 1969		Yes

Inscription: "God Will Take Care." Footstone inscribed: "L.E.F."

LAST NAME First Name	Date of Birth Date of Death Age at Death	Maiden Name Spouse	Tombstone
FARRAR Lewis Edgar	09 Mar. 1873 16 June 1958	Farrar, Pocahontas J.	Yes

Inscription: "God Be With You Till We Meet Again." Footstone inscribed: "Father."

Other Info: Shares a headstone with his wife.

| FARRAR Pocahontas J. | 09 Mar. 1876 16 July 1958 | Farrar, Lewis Edgar | Yes |

Inscription: "God Be With You Till We Meet Again." Footstone inscribed: "Mother."

Other Info: Shares a headstone with her husband.

| FARRIS | | | Yes |

Other Info: (Not known if Male or Female.) Known to be buried here, but no markers.

| FARRIS Mary | | | Yes |

Other Info: No dates inscribed on this headstone, but known to be buried here. (B. Feb. 27, 1857 - D. Apr. 25, 1936.)

| HARDIMAN Charles D. | 16 July 1884 26 July 1972 | Hardiman, Emma Sharpe | Yes |

Other Info: Shares a headstone with his wife.

| HARDIMAN Elizabeth L. | 11 Feb. 1911 03 May 1992 | Hardiman, Howard Sherman Sr. | Yes |

Inscription: "Loving Mother."

| HARDIMAN Emma | 23 June 1884 11 May 1940 | Sharpe Hardiman, Charles D. | Yes |

Other Info: Shares a headstone with her husband.

| HARDIMAN Leonard Reeves | 12 Sep. 1881 16 Nov. 1946 | Hardiman, Mary Lillian | Yes |

Inscription: "At Rest."

| HARDIMAN Luther Wilfred | 24 Aug. 1882 19 July 1945 | Hardiman, Susie W. | Yes |

Inscription: "Rest Father Rest."

| HARDIMAN Mary Lillian | 13 June 1884 24 July 1972 | Hardiman, Leonard Reeves | Yes |

LAST NAME First Name	Date of Birth Date of Death Age at Death	Maiden Name Spouse	Tombstone

Inscription: "At Rest."

| HARDIMAN
Susie W. | 06 Nov. 1887
24 May 1975 | Hardiman, Luther Wilfred | Yes |

Inscription: "Rest Mother Rest." Footstone inscribed: "S.W.H."

| HARDIMAN
Wesley Earl | 02 Sep. 1918
17 June 1944 | | Yes |

Inscription: He served as inscribed: "In Memory Of Our Son S. Sgt. ... Born In Dillwyn, Virginia ... Died In Action In France ..."

| HARDIMAN
Wilfred Curtis | 09 Jan. 1908
01 Aug. 1942 | | Yes |

Inscription: "Gone To God." Footstone inscribed: "W.C.H."

| HARRIS
Alma M. | 22 July 1899
21 Dec. 1958 | Harris, John E. | Yes |

Inscription: "Married Nov. 7, 1919.'

Other Info: Shares a headstone with her husband.

| HARRIS
Bernard Elijah | 11 Oct. 1907
07 May 1965 | | Yes |

| HARRIS
Beulah | 13 Mar. 1920
10 Oct. 1980 | Stephens
Harris, James Dabney | Yes |

Other Info: Shares a headstone with her husband.

| HARRIS
Charlie T. | 1907
1974 | Harris, Edna B(ell) | Yes |

Other Info: Shares a headstone with his wife.

| HARRIS
Edna | 1896
1974 | Bell
Harris, Charlie T. | Yes |

Other Info: Shares a headstone with her husband.

| HARRIS
Eunice Pittiet | 13 Jan. 1916
21 Oct. 1923 | | Yes |

| HARRIS
(Infant) |
10 July 1934 | | Yes |

Inscription: "Our Darling ... Infant Son of John E. & Alma M. Harris."

| HARRIS
James D. | 1846
1911 | Harris, Judith A. | Yes |

Inscription: "Father." Footstone inscribed: "J.D.H."

LAST NAME	Date of Birth	Maiden Name	Tombstone
First Name	Date of Death	Spouse	
	Age at Death		

Other Info: Shares a headstone with his wife.

| HARRIS | 12 Feb. 1922 | | Yes |
| James Dabney | 15 Nov. 1991 | Harris, Beulah Stephens | |

Other Info: Shares a headstone with his wife.

| HARRIS | 13 July 1881 | | Yes |
| James Walter | 29 Nov. 1957 | | |

Inscription: Footstone inscribed: "Brother."

| HARRIS | | | Yes |
| John | | | |

Other Info: No dates inscribed on this stone, but known to be buried here.

| HARRIS | 10 Feb. 1896 | | Yes |
| John E. | 12 Dec. 1961 | Harris, Alma M. | |

Inscription: "Married Nov. 7, 1919."

Other Info: Shares a headstone with his wife.

| HARRIS | 30 Oct. 1887 | | Yes |
| Joseph D. | 27 May 1968 | Harris, Nannie E. | |

Inscription: "Our Loved Ones."

Other Info: Shares a headstone with his wife.

| HARRIS | 1860 | | Yes |
| Judith A. | 1929 | Harris, James D. | |

Inscription: "Mother." Footstone inscribed: "J.A.H."

Other Info: Shares a headstone with her husband.

| HARRIS | 1876 | | Yes |
| Mary E. | 1941 | Harris, Willie E. | |

Inscription: Footstone inscribed: "M.E.H."

Other Info: Shares a headstone with her husband.

| HARRIS | 22 Mar. 1891 | | Yes |
| Mary Frances | 07 Oct. 1955 | | |

Inscription: Footstone inscribed: "Sister."

| HARRIS | 06 Mar. 1894 | | Yes |
| Nannie E. | 06 July 1936 | Harris, Joseph D. | |

Inscription: "Our Loved Ones."

LAST NAME First Name	Date of Birth Date of Death Age at Death	Maiden Name Spouse	Tombstone

Other Info: Shares a headstone with her husband.

| HARRIS
Paula Elizabeth | 09 June 1971
07 Oct. 1989 | | Yes |

Inscription: "Daughter. She Passed Through Heaven's Gates and Walked In Paradise."

| HARRIS
Robert H. | 26 June 1901
27 May 1974 | Harris, Therie N. | Yes |

Inscription: "Thy Kingdom Come."

Other Info: Shares a headstone with his wife.

| HARRIS
Robert H. Jr. | 14 Aug. 1925
22 Nov. 1925 | | Yes |

Inscription: Footstone inscribed: "R.H.H."

Other Info: Shares a headstone with his twin brother, William.

| HARRIS
Ruth Virginia | 24 Apr. 1913
21 Jan. 1978 | | Yes |

| HARRIS
Therie N. | 23 Aug. 1904
05 Dec. 1988 | Harris, Robert H. | Yes |

Inscription: "Thy Kingdom Come."

Other Info: Shares a headstone with her husband.

| HARRIS
Thomas Alfred | 08 Oct. 1899
09 June 1964 | Harris, Mattie LeSueur | Yes |

Inscription: "A Loving Husband and A Devoted Father."

| HARRIS
William E. | 14 Aug. 1925
22 Dec. 1925 | | Yes |

Inscription: Footstone inscribed: "W.E.H."

Other Info: Shares a headstone with his twin brother, Robert, Jr.

| HARRIS
Willie E. | 1856
1922 | Harris, Mary E. | Yes |

Inscription: Footstone inscribed: "W.E.H."

Other Info: Shares a headstone with his wife.

| HILL
Mary C. | 22 Nov. 1872
02 Feb. 1937 | | Yes |

LAST NAME First Name	Date of Birth Date of Death Age at Death	Maiden Name Spouse	Tombstone
HILL Samuel J.	24 Dec. 1856 28 May 1934		Yes
HUDDLESTON Albert G.	1879 1952	Huddleston, Mary C.	Yes

Inscription: Footstone inscribed: "Father."

HUDDLESTON (Infant)	10 Apr. 1916 15 Apr. 1916		Yes

Inscription: "Infant Son of Albert & Mary Huddleston."

HUDDLESTON James A.	1869 1957	Huddleston, Josephine G.	Yes

Inscription: Footstone inscribed: "Father."

Other Info: Shares a headstone with his wife.

HUDDLESTON Josephine G.	1867 1936	Huddleston, James A.	Yes

Inscription: Footstone inscribed: "Mother."

Other Info: Shares a headstone with her husband.

HUDDLESTON Mary C.	1882 1968	Huddleston, Albert G.	Yes

Inscription: Footstone inscribed: "Mother."

HUDNALL Harry Lee	21 Jan. 1924 21 Dec. 1975	Hudnall, Gracie B.	Yes

Inscription: He served as inscribed: "P.F.C. W.W.II."

HUSKEY Loyd Hudson	01 Oct. 1916 10 July 1984	Huskey, Mary Etta Dunn	Yes
HUSKEY Raymond Frank	25 May 1946 08 Aug. 1965		Yes

Inscription: Footstone inscribed: "Son."

JAMERSON Bertha Banton	31 Oct. 1898 15 Mar. 1968		Yes

Inscription: "Rest In Peace." Footstone inscribed: "B.B.J."

JAMERSON Billy Lee	12 Mar. 1923 19 Jan. 1939		Yes

Other Info: Shares a headstone with his twin brother, Joseph W. Jamerson.

LAST NAME First Name	Date of Birth Date of Death Age at Death	Maiden Name Spouse	Tombstone
JAMERSON Bossieux J.	30 June 1889 17 July 1969	Jamerson, Margaret V.	Yes

Inscription: He served as inscribed on the footstone: "Virginia PVT Co A 10 BN IRTC World War I."

Other Info: Shares a headstone with his wife.

JAMERSON Carrington Morel	17 June 1933 16 May 1981	Jamerson, Dorothy S.	Yes
JAMERSON Dora		Banton	Yes

Other Info: No dates inscribed on this headstone, but known to be buried here.

JAMERSON Dorothy Beatrice	31 Mar. 1925 23 Apr. 1984		Yes

Inscription: "Every Blade In the Field - Every Leaf In the Forest - Lays Down Its Life In Its Season As Beautifully As It Was Taken Up."

JAMERSON Earl Leroy	20 Feb. 1928 18 July 1936		Yes
JAMERSON Earl W.	1894 1956	Jamerson, Millie L.	Yes

Other Info: Shares a headstone with his wife.

JAMERSON Flora	27 June 1898 28 May 1981	Brock Jameson, Thomas E. "Pete"	Yes

Inscription: "Thy Kingdom Come."

Other Info: Shares a headstone with her husband.

JAMERSON (Infant)	21 Oct. 1921		Yes

Inscription: "Infant Son of Flora B. & Thomas E. Jamerson."

JAMERSON Jessie M.	31 July 1925 25 Sep. 1993	Jamerson, Mary	Yes

Inscription: "Loving Husband Of Mary."

JAMERSON Joseph W.	12 Mar. 1923 12 Aug. 1923		Yes

Other Info: Shares a headstone with his twin brother, Billy Lee Jamerson.

| JAMERSON
Kimbow | | | No |

LAST NAME First Name	Date of Birth Date of Death Age at Death	Maiden Name Spouse	Tombstone

Other Info: Known to be buried here, but no markers.

| JAMERSON
Margaret V. | 29 Aug. 1905
25 Aug. 1993 | Herndon
Jamerson, Bossieux J. | Yes |

Other Info: Shares a headstone with her husband. Grave is also marked by a funeral home metal marker.

| JAMERSON
Mary A. | 08 Sep. 1904
07 Dec. 1986 | Jamerson, Russell M. | Yes |

Inscription: "Precious Lord Take My Hand."

Other Info: Shares a headstone with her husband.

| JAMERSON
Mattie E. | 19 Sep. 1891
21 Apr. 1992 | Jamerson, Robert D. | Yes |

Other Info: Shares a headstone with her husband.

| JAMERSON
Michael Elton | 24 May 1951
22 May 1980 | | Yes |

| JAMERSON
Millie L. (Kozuhowski) | 1898
1972 | Jamerson, Earl W. | Yes |

Other Info: Shares a headstone with her first husband.

| JAMERSON
Phyllis | 25 Oct. 1934
16 Nov. 1990 | Adams
Jamerson, Andrew David | Yes |

| JAMERSON
Robert Carroll | 23 May 1915
27 Sep. 1978 | | Yes |

Inscription: He served as inscribed: "Sgt. US Army World War II."

| JAMERSON
Robert D. | 29 June 1875
14 Feb. 1959 | Jamerson, Mattie E. | Yes |

Other Info: Shares a headstone with his wife.

| JAMERSON
Russell M. | 02 Apr. 1898
07 Apr. 1979 | Jamerson, Mary A. | Yes |

Inscription: "Precious Lord Take My Hand."

Other Info: Shares a headstone with his wife.

| JAMERSON
Silvey W. | 17 Dec. 1904
30 May 1972 | | Yes |

| JAMERSON
Thomas E. | 20 Feb. 1896
10 Feb. 1978 | Jamerson, Flora Brock | Yes |

Inscription: "Pete." "Thy Kingdom Come."

LAST NAME	Date of Birth	Maiden Name	Tombstone
First Name	Date of Death	Spouse	
	Age at Death		

Other Info: Shares a headstone with his wife.

| JAMESON | 08 Oct. 1881 | | Yes |
| Joshua O. | 20 Dec. 1952 | Jameson, Werta E. | |

Inscription: Footstone inscribed: "Father."

Other Info: Shares a headstone with his wife.

| JAMESON | 20 Sep. 1885 | | Yes |
| Werta E. | 09 Aug. 1968 | Jameson, Joshua O. | |

Inscription: Footstone inscribed: "Mother."

Other Info: Shares a headstone with her husband.

| KOZUHOWSKI | 24 May 1899 | | Yes |
| Chester P. | 01 Sep. 1973 | Kozuhowski, Millie L. J. | |

Inscription: He served as inscribed: "New Jersey SC1 US Navy World War II."

| LeSUEUR | 31 Jan. 1925 | | Yes |
| Andrew Moses | 25 Mar. 1988 | | |

Inscription: Footstone inscribed: "A.M.L."

| LeSUEUR | 19 Aug. 1917 | | Yes |
| Anna Guy | 19 Oct. 1943 | LeSueur, Billie D. | |

Inscription: "At Rest."

| LeSUEUR | 03 Mar. 1908 | | Yes |
| (Baby) | 04 Mar. 1908 | | |

Inscription: "Infant Son Of Willie D. and Mattie G. LeSueur."

| LeSUEUR | 28 Apr. 1914 | | Yes |
| Beulah T. | 02 Mar. 1991 | LeSueur, John D. | |

Inscription: "We Will Meet Again." Footstone inscribed: "Mother."

Other Info: Shares a headstone with her husband.

| LeSUEUR | 1916 | | No |
| Billie D. | 1995 | LeSueur, Anna Guy | |

Other Info: Grave marked by a funeral home metal marker.

| LeSUEUR | 1884 | Dunsford | Yes |
| Blanch | 1959 | LeSueur, Joshua Lee | |

Inscription: Footstone inscribed: "B.D.L."

Other Info: Shares a headstone with her husband.

LAST NAME First Name	Date of Birth Date of Death Age at Death	Maiden Name Spouse	Tombstone
LeSUEUR Carrie Frances	26 Nov. 1921 06 July 1946		Yes
LeSUEUR Clarence W.	08 Nov. 1920 14 Apr. 1992		Yes
LeSUEUR Edgar O.	26 June 1892 24 July 1984	LeSueur, Martha B.	Yes

Other Info: Shares a headstone with his wife.

LeSUEUR Floyd Bernard	27 Sep. 1904 25 Dec. 1991	LeSueur, Kathleen Vestal	Yes
LeSUEUR Frank H.	16 Sep. 1906 23 Apr. 1908		Yes
LeSUEUR J. J.	20 Nov. 1848 09 Mar. 1928		Yes

Inscription: "Weep Not, He Is At Rest."

LeSUEUR J. Leonard	20 Nov. 1909 15 Jan. 1982	LeSueur, Annie H.	Yes

Inscription: "Rest In Peace."

LeSUEUR John Cleveland	20 Nov. 1884 09 Apr. 1966	LeSueur, Sallie J.	Yes

Inscription: Footstone inscribed: "Father."

Other Info: Shares a headstone with his wife.

LeSUEUR John D.	28 June 1905 05 Oct. 1959	LeSueur, Beulah T.	Yes

Inscription: "We Will Meet Again." Footstone inscribed: "Father."

Other Info: Shares a headstone with his wife.

LeSUEUR John Randolph	02 Sep. 1954 30 Mar. 1958		Yes

Inscription: "Son."

LeSUEUR Joseph W.	16 Apr. 1874 22 May 1936	LeSueur, Mattie S. O.	Yes

Other Info: Shares a headstone with his wife.

LeSUEUR Joshua James	17 Jan. 1920 30 Dec. 1969	LeSueur, Viola Taylor	Yes

Inscription: Footstone inscribed: "Husband."

LAST NAME First Name	Date of Birth Date of Death Age at Death	Maiden Name Spouse	Tombstone
LeSUEUR Joshua Lee	1887 1989	LeSueur, Blanch D.	Yes

Other Info: Shares a headstone with his wife.

| LeSUEUR
Martha B. | 27 Oct. 1890
07 Mar. 1956 | LeSueur, Edgar O. | Yes |

Other Info: Shares a headstone with her husband.

| LeSUEUR
Martha B. | | | No |

Other Info: Known to be buried here, but no markers.

| LeSUEUR
Mary Lee | 09 Nov. 1917
20 Dec. 1981 | | Yes |

Inscription: "Now Cometh Eternal Rest."

| LeSUEUR
Mary Stone | 1915
1957 | | Yes |

Inscription: Footstone inscribed: "M.S.L."

| LeSUEUR
Mattie G. | 05 Nov. 1875
15 Aug. 1918 | LeSueur, Willie D. | Yes |

Inscription: Footstone inscribed: "M.G.L."

Other Info: Shares a headstone with her husband.

| LeSUEUR
Mattie S. | 20 Sep. 1876
06 Apr. 1941 | Oliver
LeSueur, Joseph W. | Yes |

Other Info: Shares a headstone with her husband.

| LeSUEUR
Mattie Sue | 10 July 1891
04 July 1969 | Thomas
LeSueur, Travis Conrad | Yes |

Other Info: Shares a headstone with her husband.

| LeSUEUR
Robert M. | | | Yes |

Other Info: No dates inscribed, but known to be buried here.

| LeSUEUR
Robert Moses | 19 Apr. 1891
22 Aug. 1960 | | Yes |

Inscription: Footstone inscribed: "Father."

| LeSUEUR
Sallie | 27 Aug. 1884
20 Mar. 1960 | Jamerson
LeSueur, John C. | Yes |

LAST NAME First Name	Date of Birth Date of Death Age at Death	Maiden Name Spouse	Tombstone

Inscription: Footstone inscribed: "Mother."

Other Info: Shares a headstone with her husband.

| LeSUEUR
Sarah J. | 17 Aug. 1857
31 Jan. 1927 | | Yes |

Inscription: "Asleep In Jesus."

| LeSUEUR
Travis Conrad | 07 Apr. 1896
12 July 1985 | LeSueur, Mattie S. T. | Yes |

Other Info: Shares a headstone with his wife.

| LeSUEUR
Travis Lee | 15 Sep. 1920
24 Sep. 1987 | | Yes |

| LeSUEUR
Viola | 08 June 1928
28 June 1992 | Taylor
LeSueur, Joshua James | Yes |

Inscription: "Moowa." Footstone inscribed: "Wife."

| LeSUEUR
W. J. | | | Yes |

Other Info: No dates inscribed, but known to be buried here.

| LeSUEUR
Wilbur Randolph | 23 Aug. 1928
28 Dec. 1964 | | Yes |

Inscription: Footstone inscribed: "W.R.L."

| LeSUEUR
Willie | 24 Nov. 1886
06 July 1932 | Dun(s)ford | Yes |

Inscription: Footstone inscribed: "Mother."

| LeSUEUR
Willie A. | 22 May 1904
03 Mar. 1976 | | Yes |

Inscription: "Buck."

| LeSUEUR
Willie Archer | 04 Sep. 1910
02 Feb. 1992 | | Yes |

| LeSUEUR
Willie D. | 03 Mar. 1864
27 Apr. 1947 | LeSueur, Mattie G. | Yes |

Inscription: Footstone inscribed: "W.D.L."

Other Info: Shares a headstone with his wife.

| LOWE
Charles A. | 1898
1974 | Lowe, Lottie C. | Yes |

LAST NAME	Date of Birth	Maiden Name	Tombstone
First Name	Date of Death	Spouse	
	Age at Death		

Inscription: "Thy Kingdom Come."

Other Info: Shares a headstone with his wife.

| LOWE | 1903 | | Yes |
| Lottie C. | 1982 | Lowe, Charles A. | |

Inscription: "Thy Kingdom Come."

Other Info: Shares a headstone with her husband.

| MARTIN | 1899 | | Yes |
| Carson Jeff | 1965 | Martin, Florine D. | |

Inscription: He served as inscribed on his footstone: "Carson Jeff Martin Virginia Cpl Co B 325 Infantry World War I April 25, 1899 July 7, 1965."

Other Info: Shares a headstone with his wife.

| MARTIN | 1905 | | Yes |
| Florine D. | 1970 | Martin, Carson Jeff | |

Other Info: Shares a headstone with her husband.

| MARTIN | 02 Sep. 1937 | | Yes |
| Shirley Jean | 15 Nov. 1937 | | |

Inscription: "Fom Mother's Arms To the Arms Of Jesus."

| MARTIN | 31 Mar. 1924 | | Yes |
| Wilber C. | 07 Sep. 1924 | | |

Inscription: "Son of Florine & C. J. Martin. From Mother's Arms To the Arms Of Jesus."

| MCCRAW | 1853 | | Yes |
| Anna C. | 1916 | McCraw, Thomas E. | |

Other Info: Shares a headstone with her husband.

| MCCRAW | 23 Feb. 1895 | | Yes |
| Guy | 24 Jan. 1961 | McCraw, Pearl H. | |

Other Info: Shares a headstone with his wife.

| MCCRAW | 21 Apr. 1897 | | Yes |
| Pearl H. | 21 May 1978 | McCraw, Guy | |

Other Info: Shares a headstone with her husband.

| MCCRAW | 1847 | | Yes |
| Thomas E. | 1923 | McCraw, Anna C. | |

Other Info: Shares a headstone with his wife.

LAST NAME First Name	Date of Birth Date of Death Age at Death	Maiden Name Spouse	Tombstone
MEADOR Hubert L.	21 Nov. 1908 12 May 1971	Meador, Mary E. S.	Yes

Inscription: "Father." Footstone inscribed: "Father."

Other Info: Shares a headstone with his wife.

MEADOR Mary E.	30 Dec. 1916 12 May 1971	Sharpe Meador, Hubert L.	Yes

Inscription: "Mother." Footstone inscribed: "Mother."

Other Info: Shares a headstone with her husband.

MOSS Daisy		(Newton)	Yes

Other Info: No dates inscribed on this headstone, but known to be buried here.

NICHOLAS Dainy L.	04 Nov. 1940 26 Apr. 1972		Yes

Inscription: "Gone But Not Forgotten."

OLIVER Annie J.	12 June 1870 03 Jan. 1939	Oliver, Walter S.	Yes

Other Info: Shares a headstone with her husband.

OLIVER Florence	05 June 1896 06 Sep. 1945	Thomas Oliver, Percy L.	Yes

Inscription: "At Rest." Footstone inscribed: "F.T.O."

OLIVER (Infant)	31 Aug. 1921		Yes

Inscription: "Infant Son of Mary B. & Robert A. Oliver."

OLIVER Joseph Roy	15 June 1909 02 June 1985		Yes

Inscription: "Hyghtie."

OLIVER Mamie Toney	16 Apr. 1915 21 June 1984		Yes

Inscription: "Asleep In Jesus."

OLIVER Mary	25 July 1891 04 Jan. 1972	Brock Oliver, Robert Aubrey	Yes

Inscription: "Ma Mary."

LAST NAME	Date of Birth	Maiden Name	Tombstone
First Name	Date of Death	Spouse	
	Age at Death		

Other Info: Shares a headstone with her husband.

| OLIVER | 19 June 1895 | | Yes |
| Percy L. | 07 May 1951 | Oliver, Florence T. | |

Inscription: "A Hard Worker and A Devoted Father." Footstone inscribed: "P.L.O."

| OLIVER | 11 Apr. 1897 | | Yes |
| Robert Aubrey | 05 Aug. 1943 | Oliver, Mary Brock | |

Inscription: He served as inscribed: "Virginia PVT 468 Engrs. World War I."

Other Info: Shares a headstone with his wife.

| OLIVER | 14 Feb. 1923 | | Yes |
| Rufus Aubrey | 23 Nov. 1969 | | |

Inscription: He served as inscribed: "Virginia BM1 US Navy WW II Korea Vietnam."

| OLIVER | 22 Apr. 1872 | | Yes |
| Walter S. | 10 Mar. 1928 | Oliver, Annie J. | |

Other Info: Shares a headstone with his wife.

| OLIVER | 09 Aug. 1905 | | Yes |
| William Spencer | 10 June 1976 | | |

Inscription: "Willie Boy."

| OWNBY | 02 Apr. 1991 | | Yes |
| Newel | 10 July 1920 | Ownby, Grace McCraw | |

Inscription: He served as inscribed: "Adj. US Navy World War II Korea." "Married Jan. 9, 1948."

| PERKINS | 05 Apr. 1904 | | Yes |
| Esther C. | 26 Jan. 1949 | | |

Inscription: "At Rest."

| PERRY | 13 Jan. 1967 | | Yes |
| Jimmy (Frank) Jr. | 20 Aug. 1989 | | |

Inscription: Two lines of inscription are unreadable; the third line is inscribed: "On the Outer Banks."

| POE | 08 Feb. 1906 | | Yes |
| Etta H. | 19 May 1989 | Poe, J. Elmo | |

Inscription: "Precious Lord Take My Hand."

Other Info: Shares a headstone with her husband.

LAST NAME First Name	Date of Birth Date of Death Age at Death	Maiden Name Spouse	Tombstone
POE Irvin N.	22 June 1927 19 June 1991	Poe, Virginia Worley	Yes
POE J. Elmo	30 Oct. 1905 21 July 1992	Poe, Etta H.	Yes

Inscription: "Precious Lord Take My Hand."

Other Info: Shares a headstone with his wife.

POE John Robert	01 July 1898 26 Jan. 1988	Poe, Willie Sue Dean	Yes

Inscription: "Precious Lord Take My Hand."

Other Info: Shares a headstone with his wife.

POE John W.	26 May 1933 28 Oct. 1956		Yes

Inscription: "Gone, But Not Forgotten." Footstone inscribed: "Son."

POE Willie Sue	09 Jan. 1907 10 Dec. 1979	Dean Poe, John Robert	Yes

Inscription: "Precious Lord Take My Hand."

Other Info: Shares a headstone with her husband.

POWERS C. Burns	1915 1974	Powers, Nell (Lowe)	Yes

Inscription: "Thy Kingdom Come."

RAINEY Anne Trent	1918 1975		Yes

SEAY Richard			Yes

Other Info: No dates inscribed on the headstone, but known to be buried here.

SHARP Jannie P.			Yes

Other Info: No dates inscribed on headstone, but known to be buried here. (Died in 1969.)

SHARP Warren D.	02 Oct. 1909 30 Sep. 1973	Sharp, Agnes P.	Yes

Inscription: "Father. In Precious Memory." Footstone shows he served as inscribed: "Warren Daniel Sharp Virginia S1 USNR World War II."

LAST NAME First Name	Date of Birth Date of Death Age at Death	Maiden Name Spouse	Tombstone
SHARP William T.	09 Apr. 1920		Yes

Inscription: He served as inscribed: "Virginia Pvt. U.S. Army."

| SHARP(E)
Mary Ann | 20 May 1851
22 June 1936 | Sharpe, Alex | Yes |

Inscription: "She Was A Kind and Affectionate Wife. A Fond Mother and A Friend To All."

| SHARPE
Alex | | Sharp(e), Mary Ann | Yes |

Inscription: He served as inscribed: "Co C 3 VA Res C.S.A."

Other Info: No dates inscribed on this headstone.

| SHARPE
Anne Jannie | 07 May 1883
27 May 1955 | Sharpe, James Daniel | Yes |

Other Info: Shares a headstone with her husband.

| SHARPE
James Daniel | 19 Sep. 1882
22 May 1968 | Sharpe, Anne Jannie | Yes |

Other Info: Shares a headstone with his wife.

| SHARPE
William H(oward) | | | Yes |

Other Info: No dates inscribed on headstone, but known to be buried here. (Died May 13, 1985.)

| STEELE
(Baby) | | | Yes |

Inscription: "Infant Son of John H. & Ollie M. Steele."

Other Info: No dates inscribed, but known to have died in 1922.

| STEPPE
Virginia | 21 Sep. 1907
28 Mar. 1990 | Blackwell | Yes |
| THOMAS
Albert B. | 22 Feb. 1913
20 Dec. 1991 | Thomas, Anna W. | Yes |

Inscription: "My Loving Husband. Rest In Peace."

| THOMAS
Albert B. Jr. | 14 Nov. 1940
15 Jan. 1977 | | Yes |

Inscription: "At Rest. Our Loving Son. Gone But Not Forgotten."

LAST NAME First Name	Date of Birth Date of Death Age at Death	Maiden Name Spouse	Tombstone
THOMAS Ann J.	1879 1944	Thomas, John D.	Yes

Inscription: Footstone inscribed: "A.J.T."

Other Info: Shares a headstone with her husband.

THOMAS Annie S.	22 July 1877 31 Jan. 1968	Thomas, Willie W.	Yes

Inscription: "Earth Has No Sorrow That Heaven Cannot Heal." Footstone inscribed: "Mother."

Other Info: Shares a headstone with her husband.

THOMAS E. J. (Mrs.)	06 Aug. 1847 28 Jan. 1927	Thomas, James E.	Yes
THOMAS George R.	18 Apr. 1870 08 Jan. 1941		Yes

Inscription: "Gone But Not Forgotten."

THOMAS George Wesley	23 Sep. 1878 01 Sep. 1938	Thomas, Sarah Josephine	Yes

Inscription: "Our Loved Ones."

Other Info: Shares a headstone with his wife.

THOMAS Gracie L.	24 Sep. 1920 22 July 1988	Thomas, Morris Lemuel	Yes

Other Info: Shares a headstone with her husband.

THOMAS Irene	02 Sep. 1876 12 Feb. 1961	Dawson Thomas, William P.	Yes

Inscription: "Beyond the Sunset."

Other Info: Shares a headstone with her husband.

THOMAS J. L.	26 Nov. 1876 15 Jan. 1954	Thomas, Martha C.	Yes

Inscription: "Our Father. At Rest." Footstone inscribed: "J.L.T."

THOMAS James A.	13 Oct. 1901 16 Feb. 1967	Thomas, Ida Poe	Yes

Inscription: "Father."

Other Info: Shares a headstone with his wife and infant son.

LAST NAME First Name	Date of Birth Date of Death Age at Death	Maiden Name Spouse	Tombstone
THOMAS James A. Jr.	24 Sep. 1923 18 Dec. 1924		Yes

Inscription: "Son."

Other Info: Shares a headstone with his father and mother.

| THOMAS
James E. | | Thomas, E. J. (Mrs.) | Yes |

Inscription: He served as inscribed: "Co C 25 VA Inf C.S.A."

Other Info: No dates inscribed on the headstone.

| THOMAS
Janie H. | 24 Aug. 1885
16 June 1974 | | Yes |

Inscription: "My Presence Shall Go With Thee. Ex 33:14." Footstone inscribed: "Mother."

| THOMAS
John D. | 1873
1943 | Thomas, Ann J. | Yes |

Inscription: Footstone inscribed: "J.D.T."

Other Info: Shares a headstone with his wife.

| THOMAS
Martha C. | 12 June 1878
05 Mar. 1964 | Thomas, J. L. | Yes |

Inscription: "Our Mother."

| THOMAS
Mary Emma | | | Yes |

Other Info: No dates inscribed on the headstone, but known to be buried here.

| THOMAS
Morris L. | 30 July 1913
03 Jan. 1978 | Thomas, Gracie L. | Yes |

Inscription: He served as inscribed on the footstone: "Morris Lemuel Thomas S2 US Navy World War II."

Other Info: Shares a headstone with his wife.

| THOMAS
Nannie (Dunsford) | | Archer | Yes |

Other Info: No dates inscribed, but known to be buried here. Born in 1883, and died in 1964.

| THOMAS
Nannie S. | 31 May 1886
02 Mar. 1971 | Thomas, Walter E. | Yes |

Inscription: "Gone But Not Forgotten." Footstone inscribed: "N.S.T."

LAST NAME First Name	Date of Birth Date of Death Age at Death	Maiden Name Spouse	Tombstone

Other Info: Shares a headstone with her husband.

THOMAS Randolph King	1914 1980		No

Other Info: Grave marked by a funeral home metal marker.

THOMAS Sarah Josephine	27 Oct. 1880 19 Dec. 1954	Thomas, George Wesley	Yes

Inscription: "Our Loved Ones."

Other Info: Shares a headstone with her husband.

THOMAS Thomas Edwin	06 Dec. 1922 28 June 1932		Yes

Inscription: "In Heaven There Is One Angel More."

THOMAS Thomas R.	19 May 1877 28 June 1960		Yes

Inscription: "Uncle."

THOMAS Walter E.	09 Mar. 1879 27 Apr. 1949	Thomas, Nannie S.	Yes

Inscription: "Gone But Not Forgotten." Footstone inscribed: "W.E.T."

Other Info: Shares a headstone with his wife.

THOMAS William P.	15 Sep. 1886 06 Sep. 1953	Thomas, Irene Dawson	Yes

Inscription: "Beyond the Sunset."

Other Info: Shares a headstone with his wife.

THOMAS William Russell	03 Dec. 1911 14 Feb. 1989	Thomas, Frances Worley	Yes

Inscription: "Father ... Together Forever."

THOMAS Willie E.	06 Jan. 1902 05 Apr. 1919		Yes

Inscription: "Our Brother."

THOMAS Willie Elmore	1931 1932		Yes

Inscription: "Junior." Footstone inscribed: "Elmo Thomas Jr." (sic)

Other Info: Shares a headstone with his father.

LAST NAME First Name	Date of Birth Date of Death Age at Death	Maiden Name Spouse	Tombstone
THOMAS Willie Elmore	1910 1978		Yes

Other Info: Shares a headstone with his infant son.

| THOMAS
Willie W. | 03 Dec. 1867
14 Oct. 1941 | Thomas, Annie S. | Yes |

Inscription: "Earth Has No Sorrow That Heaven Cannot Heal." Footstone inscribed: "Father."

Other Info: Shares a headstone with his wife.

| TONEY
Harry James | 1900
1970 | | Yes |
| TONEY
Lillian A. | | | Yes |

Other Info: No dates inscribed on this headstone, but known to be buried here.

| TRENT
Anna T. | 1883
1964 | Trent, Stephen W. | Yes |

Other Info: Shares a headstone with her husband.

| TRENT
Catherine G. | 1830
1915 | Trent, Thomas W. | Yes |

Other Info: Shares a headstone with her husband.

| TRENT
John G. | 1924
1994 | | No |

Other Info: Grave marked by a funeral home metal marker.

| TRENT
Stephen W. | 1871
1949 | Trent, Anna T. | Yes |

Other Info: Shares a headstone with his wife.

| TRENT
Thomas T. | 03 Oct. 1927
17 July 1992 | | Yes |
| TRENT
Thomas W. | 1821
1903 | Trent, Catherine G. | Yes |

Other Info: Shares a headstone with his wife.

| TRENTHAM
David H. | 23 Aug. 1944
08 Apr. 1990 | Trentham, Frances H. | Yes |

Inscription: "Devoted Husband."

LAST NAME First Name	Date of Birth Date of Death Age at Death	Maiden Name Spouse	Tombstone
WALLACE Joseph Denton	10 May 1918 02 Dec. 1975		Yes

Inscription: He served as inscribed: "PVT US Army World War II."

WALLACE Sarah E. (Bessie)	02 June 1896 15 Dec. 1989	Dunkum	Yes
WRIGHT (Baby)			Yes

Other Info: No dates inscribed on this headstone, but known to be buried here. Infant of Elmo Wright.

WRIGHT Elmo W.	04 Nov. 1907 31 Dec. 1985	Wright, Frances S.	Yes

Other Info: Grave also marked with a funeral home metal marker inscribed: "Elmo Walker Wright 1907 - 1986(sic)." Shares a headstone with his wife.

WRIGHT Eva Mosbie Toney	1878 1958	Wright, Thomas Jackson	Yes

Inscription: "Mother." Footstone inscribed: "Eva M. Wright."

Other Info: Shares a headstone with her husband.

WRIGHT Frances S.	04 Apr. 1916 09 July 1988	Wright, Elmo Walker	Yes

Other Info: Shares a headstone with her husband.

WRIGHT Joseph L.			Yes

Other Info: No dates inscribed on this headstone, but known to be buried here. (B. 1910 - D. 1963.)

WRIGHT Phillip Archer	12 Aug. 1897 18 Feb. 1992		Yes
WRIGHT Thomas Jackson	1864 1925	Wright, Eva Mosbie Toney	Yes

Inscription: "Father." Footstone inscribed: "T. J. Wright."

Other Info: Shares a headstone with his wife.

WRIGHT William T.			Yes

Other Info: No dates inscribed on this headstone, but known to be buried here. (1902-1915)

LAST NAME	Date of Birth	Maiden Name	Tombstone
First Name	Date of Death	Spouse	
	Age at Death		

Chambers Family - Hwy 602 (Black)

CHAMBERS 　　　　　　　　　　　　　　　　　　　　　　　　　　　　No
John Russell　　20 May 1934
　　　　　　　　56 yr 01 mo 11 dy

　　Other Info: Grave marked with a Funeral Home Metal Marker.

CHAMBERS　　　　　　　　　　　　　　　　　　　　　　　　　　　　No
Peter　　　　　10 Dec. 1943
　　　　　　　　71 yr

　　Other Info: Grave marked with a Funeral Home Metal Marker.

Childress Family - Hwy 60 (Maysville C.H.)

CHILDRESS　　　　　　　　　　　　　　　　　　　　　　　　　　　　No
(children)

　　Other Info: The graves were visible in 1920, but all visible signs have since
　　　　　　　　disappeared.

Dameron - John Dameron Family - Hwy 664

DAMERON　　　　1808 (circa)　　　　　　　　　　　　　　　　　　　No
John　　　　　　　　　　　　　　Dameron, (Lucy) Eliza Harris

　　Other Info: The general location of this cemetery is known. No grave markers.
　　　　　　　　At least eleven children in this family, three of whom are known to
　　　　　　　　be buried here.

DAMERON　　　　1822 (circa)　　　　　　Harris　　　　　　　　　　　No
(Lucy) Eliza　　　　　　　　　　　　　　Dameron, John

　　Other Info: Known to be buried here alongside her husband, and three
　　　　　　　　unmarried daughters.

DAMERON　　　　1844 (circa)　　　　　　　　　　　　　　　　　　　No
Margaret

　　Other Info: Unmarried daughter of John and (Lucy) Eliza Harris Dameron.

DAMERON　　　　1851 (circa)　　　　　　　　　　　　　　　　　　　No
Mary

　　Other Info: Unmarried daughter of John and (Lucy) Eliza Harris Dameron.

DAMERON　　　　1846 (circa)　　　　　　　　　　　　　　　　　　　No
Nancy

　　Other Info: Unmarried daughter of John and (Lucy) Eliza Harris Dameron.

LAST NAME	Date of Birth	Maiden Name	Tombstone
First Name	Date of Death	Spouse	
	Age at Death		

Darneille/Darneil Family Slave Plot - Hwy 633

Other Info: This cemetery contains 150 - 200 graves. It was believed to be a slave cemetery before the Civil War, and a cemetery for the freed blacks after the War. Graves marked by fieldstones only.

Davidson Family - Hwy 640

| DAVIDSON | | | No |

Other Info: There are at least three graves here marked by fieldstones only. At least one is a child as the grave is very short. No names known except that they were members of a Davidson family.

Dillwyn Town Cemetery - Hwy T1010

| ADCOCK | | | No |
| Mary (Miss) | | | |

Other Info: No grave marker, but known to be buried near the corner of the headstone of A. J. and A.F. Thomas headstone. Mary is the daughter of Wesley Adcock.

| ADCOCK | | | No |
| Wesley | | | |

Other Info: No grave marker, but his grave is either under the fence by the middle gate or near the boundry of the Pearson family plot.

| ALMOND | 30 Apr. 1925 | | Yes |
| Janie M. | 15 Sep. 1983 | Almond, Davis | |

| AMISS | 01 Oct. 1882 | Moss | Yes |
| Eva | 27 Sep. 1969 | Amiss, Phillip W. | |

| AMISS | 09 July 1910 | | Yes |
| John Calvin | 15 May 1972 | | |

Inscription: He served as inscribed: "Virginia PVT Army Air Forces World War II."

| AMISS | 22 Feb. 1878 | | Yes |
| Phillip W. | 24 Apr. 1977 | Amiss, Eva Moss | |

| ANDERSON | 03 Sep. 1911 | | Yes |
| Alexander Marshall | 06 Oct. 1955 | | |

| APPERSON | 29 Dec. 1912 | | Yes |
| John P. | 04 Apr. 1968 | | |

LAST NAME First Name	Date of Birth Date of Death Age at Death	Maiden Name Spouse	Tombstone
APPERSON Mary G.	15 Nov. 1882 18 Nov. 1974		Yes
BABER Mary	04 July 1895 13 Sep. 1977	Hardiman Baber, Granville R.	Yes

Inscription: "Wife of Granville R. Baber."

BANTON "Hick"			No

Other Info: Headstone not inscribed, but known to be Hick Banton - other data not available.

BANTON Jessie Pendleton	07 Oct. 1894 08 Aug. 1971		Yes

Other Info: Shares a headstone with John Jacob Pendleton.

BANTON John A.	12 Sep. 1903 08 Aug. 1944		Yes

INSCRIPTION: He served as inscribed: "Virginia PFC Infantry World War II."

BANTON Samuel	29 June 1915 11 Sep. 1944		Yes

Inscription: He served as inscribed: "Virginia TEC 5 175 Inf 29 Div World War II"

BANTON Sidney A.	21 Apr. 1881 10 May 1963		Yes
BEATTY Clarence C.	01 Feb. 1896 20 Mar. 1964	Beatty, Lucille B.	Yes

Inscription: He served as inscribed: "Virginia PFC 2 CO 20 Engineers World War I." Footstone inscribed: "C.C.B."

BEATTY Lucille B.	14 Feb. 1907 28 Sep. 1985	Beatty, Clarence C.	Yes

Inscription: Footstone inscribed: "L.B.B."

BENNINGHOVE Irvin Jr.	17 Dec. 1928 14 Aug. 1969		Yes

Inscription: He served as inscribed: "Virginia PVT Co D 10 INF Regt."

BERRY J. Ivanhoe	04 Dec. 1874 03 Apr. 1936	Berry, Josephine	Yes

Other Info: In front of this grave are two unmarked graves; they are known to be Josephine Berry, the wife of J. Ivanhoe Berry, and their daughter, whose name is not known at this time.

LAST NAME First Name	Date of Birth Date of Death Age at Death	Maiden Name Spouse	Tombstone
BERRY W.S.	31 Aug. 1901 24 May 1925		Yes

Inscription: "Son of Josephine & J. I. Berry...Dearest Brother Thou Has Left Us, Here Thy Loss We Deeply Feel. But Tis God That Hath Bereft Us, He Can All Our Sorrows Heal."

BLANKS Terrell	23 Aug. 1911 18 Sep. 1977		Yes
BRICKEY Ronald C.	05 June 1944 08 June 1984		Yes

Inscription: "Ring The Bells Of Heaven."

BRYANT Nannie S.	12 Apr. 1912 27 Aug. 1966	Bryant,	Yes

Other Info: Her husband is known to be buried in the unmarked grave beside her.

CALL			No

Other Info: No grave marker, but known to be either Dick Call or Ernest Call.

CALL			No

Other Info: No grave marker, but known to be either Dick Call or Ernest Call.

CALL Addie M.	1905 1964		Yes
CALL Alfred	1879 1976	Call, Josephine	No

Other Info: Grave marked with a Funeral Home Metal Marker.

CALL Charles E.	1917 1980		Yes

Inscription: He served as inscribed: "Sgt. US Army World War II."

CALL Cosby	1907 1964		No

Other Info: Grave marked with a Funeral Home Metal Marker.

CALL Edna G.	04 July 1893 25 Dec. 1978		Yes
CALL George W.	1917 1986		No

Other Info: Grave marked with a Funeral Home Metal Marker.

LAST NAME First Name	Date of Birth Date of Death Age at Death	Maiden Name Spouse	Tombstone
CALL George Washington	30 Nov. 1921 28 June 1972	Call, Mable Call	Yes
CALL Josephine		Call, Alfred	No

Other Info: No grave marker, but known to be buried here beside her husband.

CALL Mattie F.	02 May 1885 06 July 1950	Call, Robert J.	Yes

Other Info: Shares a headstone with her husband.

CALL Patti Jane	1890 1960		Yes

Inscription: "Mother."

CALL Robert J.	15 July 1875 21 Mar. 1943	Call, Mattie F.	Yes

Other Info: Shares a headstone with his wife.

CALL Rosa Lee	1894 1971		No

Other Info: Grave marked with a Funeral Home Metal Marker.

CATLETT Alfred N.	07 Oct. 1885 11 Apr. 1937		Yes
CATLETT Florence M.	03 June 1918 19 Oct. 1962		Yes
CATLETT Garnett E.	18 Nov. 1920 13 Feb. 1972		Yes

Inscription: He served as inscribed: Virginia TEC 5 BTRY A 967 FA BN World War II."

CATLETT John Edward	13 Sep. 1922 11 Jan. 1980		Yes

Inscription: He served as inscribed: "PFC US Army World War II."

CATLETT Margaret M.	26 Apr. 1926 29 Nov. 1957		Yes
CATLETT William E.	18 Jan. 1947 22 Jan. 1954		Yes
CHARLTON Edgar Anderson	26 Feb. 1887 09 May 1970	Charlton, Theresa Johnson	Yes

LAST NAME First Name	Date of Birth Date of Death Age at Death	Maiden Name Spouse	Tombstone
CHARLTON J. Spottswood	09 Jan. 1923		Yes
CHARLTON John J.	1853 1922	Charlton, S. L.	Yes

Other Info: "Father. Husband of S. L. Charlton."

CHARLTON John R.	1883 1945		Yes
CHARLTON S. L.	1857 1944	Charlton, John J.	Yes

Inscription: "Mother."

CHARLTON Theresa	01 Mar. 1895 08 Feb. 1981	Johnson Charlton, Edgar Anderson	Yes
CHILDRESS Dennis Elvin Jr.	26 Feb. 1964 28 Feb. 1964		Yes
CHRISTIAN Andrew M.	08 Jan. 1930 13 Oct. 1978		Yes

Inscription: He served as inscribed: "CPL US Marine Corps Korea."

CHRISTIAN Bernard Lee Jr. "Bernie"	24 Aug. 1943 10 Sep. 1967		Yes

Inscription: "Son."

CHRISTIAN James Donald	01 June 1941		Yes

Inscription: "Son of Mary L. Huddleston Christian Toney. Given In Memory by Stepfather Sidney Toney."

CLAIBORNE Aubra	21 Apr. 1890 14 May 1966	Price Claiborne, Marshall P. Sr.	Yes

Other Info: Shares a headstone with her husband.

CLAIBORNE Marshall P. Sr.	12 Mar. 1873 19 Aug. 1939	Claiborne, Aubra Price	Yes

Other Info: Shares a headstone with his wife.

COLEMAN Mack	1907 1971	Coleman, Ollie	Yes
CONNER Beulah	1873 1961		Yes

LAST NAME First Name	Date of Birth Date of Death Age at Death	Maiden Name Spouse	Tombstone
CONNER Janie	1875 1955	Cobb Conner, William Rolfe	Yes

Other Info: Shares a headstone with her husband.

CONNER William Rolfe	1874 1952	Conner, Janie Cobb	Yes

Other Info: Shares a headstone with his wife.

COOK Arminta M.	1853 1931	Cook, Silas M.	Yes

Other Info: Shares a headstone with her husband.

COOK Silas M.	1848 1924	Cook, Arminta M.	Yes

Other Info: Shares a headstone with his wife.

COOPER Edward Mercer	12 Nov. 1902 28 Mar. 1976	Cooper, Virginia Phaup	Yes
CRAFT David Arnold	28 Mar. 1950 11 Nov. 1984		Yes

Inscription: "Memories - Love's Greatest Gift."

CREASEY Robert L.	04 Feb. 1887 26 Nov. 1951	Creasey, Betty S.	Yes

Inscription: He served as inscribed: "World War I." "Father. At Rest."

CULBRETH Dolly		Hooper Culbreth, Harry Clay	Yes

Other Info: This grave has an unengraved marker on it. It is assumed that Mrs. Culbreth is buried here beside her husband.

CULBRETH Harry Clay	1865 1948		Yes
CULBRETH Mary Truitt	1840 1916		Yes
DAVIS Charles Eugene	16 July 1930 11 Feb. 1952		Yes

Inscription: He served as inscribed: "Virginia CPL 2035 Area SVC Unit."

DAVIS Lucy Clarke	15 Oct. 1920 12 Nov. 1923		Yes

Inscription: "Daughter of Pearl A. & P. G. Davis." "A Little Bud of Love To Bloom With God Above."

LAST NAME First Name	Date of Birth Date of Death Age at Death	Maiden Name Spouse	Tombstone
DAVIS Martha K.	25 Feb. 1923 23 Feb. 1978		Yes

Inscription: "Asleep In Jesus." Footstone inscribed: "M.K.D."

| DAVIS
Pearl H. | 14 Nov. 1898
20 May 1975 | Davis, Percy G. Sr. | Yes |

Inscription: "Thy Will Be Done."

Other Info: Shares a headstone with her husband.

| DAVIS
Percy G. Sr. | 15 Nov. 1881
12 Feb. 1962 | Davis, Pearl H. | Yes |

Inscription: "Thy Will Be Done."

Other Info: Shares a headstone with his wife.

| DAVIS
Rosa S. | 26 Mar. 1882
29 Feb. 1968 | | Yes |

Inscription: "Mother."

| DAWSON
Virgil Wayne Sr. | 13 Oct. 1910
08 June 1974 | | Yes |

| DEAN
George W. | 21 Feb. 1915
17 Dec. 1976 | Dean, Margaret C. | Yes |

Inscription: A military headstone set at the foot of his grave is inscribed as follows: "George William Dean "PFC US Army World War II Feb. 21, 1915 Dec. 17, 1976."

| DUNKUM
Janie | 09 Jan. 1897
20 Dec. 1976 | Wood
Dunkum, Julian Clyde | Yes |

Other Info: Shares a headstone with her husband.

| DUNKUM
Julian Clyde | 18 Aug. 1895
10 May 1975 | Dunkum, Janie Wood | Yes |

Other Info: Shares a headstone with his wife.

| DUNKUM
Leslie Bersch | 26 Mar. 1956
22 July 1974 | | Yes |

| DUNN
Joyce Ann | 12 Nov. 1943
17 Apr. 1978 | | Yes |

| DYCHES
Garland Dr. | 28 June 1910
03 Oct. 1984 | Dyches, Mary N. | Yes |

| EDMONDS
Thyra | | | No |

LAST NAME	Date of Birth	Maiden Name	Tombstone
First Name	Date of Death	Spouse	
	Age at Death		

Other Info: This child, who died sometime after 1926, is known to be one of the first persons buried in this cemetery. It is not known where her grave is located.

| EDWARDS | 24 July 1912 | | Yes |
| Ruth Gleaner | 29 Sep. 1915 | | |

Inscription: "Daughter of J.M. and M.F. Edwards."

| EMERT | 1891 | Sutton | Yes |
| Myra | 1971 | Emert, Samuel Rufus | |

| EMERT | 1893 | | Yes |
| Samuel Rufus | 1953 | Emert, Myra Sutton | |

| EVANS | 1865 | | Yes |
| John | 1948 | Evans, Louisa W. | |

| EVANS | 1869 | | Yes |
| Louisa W. | 1945 | Evans, John | |

| FARISS | 18 Aug. 1904 | | Yes |
| Oakley Taylor | 13 May 1950 | | |

| FARRAR | 10 Feb. 1902 | | Yes |
| Richard Mayo | 18 Oct. 1973 | Farrar, Minnie Jamerson | |

Inscription: "Rest In Peace."

| FIELDING | | | Yes |
| Dianna Pearson | 15 Aug. 1946 | | |

| FITZGERALD | 22 July 1856 | | Yes |
| Elizabeth A. | 30 Mar. 1923 | Fitzgerald, Emmett W. | |

Inscription: "Mother."

| FITZGERALD | 28 Mar. 1854 | | Yes |
| Emmett W. | 03 Feb. 1923 | Fitzgerald, Elizabeth A. | |

Inscription: "Father."

| FOSTER | 18 Apr. 1825 | Hobson | Yes |
| Catherine | 18 May 1901 | | |

Inscription: Back: "Foster"

Other Info: Shares a headstone with her daughter, Emma Foster Price.

| GARRETT | 08 Mar. 1909 | | Yes |
| John E. | 05 Jan. 1962 | | |

Inscription: "Father."

LAST NAME First Name	Date of Birth Date of Death Age at Death	Maiden Name Spouse	Tombstone
GARTON Lily	28 Apr. 1908 13 Sep. 1973	Garton, John	Yes

Inscription: "Rest In Peace."

GILLIAM Luther P.	14 Mar. 1885 26 Oct. 1952	Gilliam, Susie Shepherd	Yes
GILLIAM Susie	23 Jan. 1909 03 Apr. 1984	Shepherd Gilliam, Luther P.	Yes

Other Info: Daughter of Benjamin F. and Willie Sue Shepherd.

GODSEY Ernest L. Jr.	24 Dec. 1947 21 Dec. 1969		Yes
GODSEY Johnny M. "Snake"	05 Jan. 1944 21 Sep. 1976		Yes

Inscription: "In Loving Memory."

GOIN Bobby			No

Other Info: No grave marker, but known to be buried here.

GOIN Emily Frances	08 Dec. 1881 02 Mar. 1966		Yes
GOIN Leslie Thomas	10 Aug. 1914 01 June 1973		Yes
GOIN Robert L.	09 Nov. 1910 04 June 1956		Yes
GOIN Sarah S.	05 May 1882 16 Feb. 1947		Yes
GOINS Floyd Lacy	27 Feb. 1887 29 Apr. 1946		Yes
GORDON			No

Other Info: Husband and wife known to be buried here, but no grave markers, and no other data available at this time.

GORMUS John Junior	1968 1970		No

Other Info: Grave marked with a Funeral Home Metal Marker.

GORMUS John Willie	14 Oct. 1916 04 Feb. 1962		Yes

LAST NAME	Date of Birth	Maiden Name	Tombstone
First Name	Date of Death	Spouse	
	Age at Death		

Inscription: He served as inscribed: "Virginia PFC Engineers World War II PH."

| GRIFFIN | | | Yes |
| Gerald L. | 04 July 1935 | | |

Inscription: He served as inscribed: "Maryland Wagoner 110 Field ARTY 29 Div."

| HACKETT | | | Yes |
| L. | 23 Sep. 1941 | | |

| HAMBY | 1919 | | No |
| | 1963 | | |

Other Info: Grave marked with a Funeral Home Metal Marker - mostly unreadable.

| HAMBY | | | No |

Other Info: Grave marked with a Funeral Home Metal Marker - mostly unreadable.

| HAMBY | 10 July 1928 | | Yes |
| Graham G. | 21 June 1976 | | |

| HAMBY | 1954 | | No |
| Graham Graniel Jr. | 1972 | | |

Other Info: Grave marked with a Funeral Home Metal Marker.

| HAMBY | 04 Dec. 1923 | | Yes |
| Jasper D. | 25 Mar. 1951 | | |

Inscription: He served as inscribed: "PVT US Army World War II."

Other Info: There are two known unmarked graves to the West of this one. They are both known to be Hamby's, but no other data available at this time.

| HAMBY | 21 Aug. 1913 | | Yes |
| Retha Rebecca A. | 12 Dec. 1984 | | |

| HANES | 1871 | | Yes |
| Ada C. | 1948 | Hanes, J. B. | |

| HANES | 02 Sep. 1901 | | Yes |
| Garland Brown | 01 Sep. 1906 | | |

Inscription: "Son of J. B. and Ada Hanes." "Safe In the Arms of Jesus."

Other Info: This body was moved to this cemetery in the 1940s from the family graveyard at Humanity Hall on Hwy 617 in Buckingham County.

LAST NAME First Name	Date of Birth Date of Death Age at Death	Maiden Name Spouse	Tombstone
HANES J. B.	28 Nov. 1865 12 Dec. 1915	Hanes, Ada C.	Yes

Inscription: (Masonic Symbol) "I Have Fought A Good Fight. I Have Finished The Course. I Have Kept The Faith. 2 Tim IV 7."

Other Info: This body was moved to this cemetery in the 1940s from the family graveyard at Humanity Hall on Hwy 617 in Buckingham County.

| HANES
Meade Carter | 19 July 1898
05 May 1913 | | Yes |

Inscription: "Son of J.B. and Ada G. Hanes." "When We See Our Precious Darling That We Tended With Such Care, Rudely Taken From Our Bosom, How Our Aching Hearts Despair."

Other Info: This body was moved to this cemetery in the 1940s from the family graveyard at Humanity Hall on Hwy 617 in Buckingham County.

| HANES
Nancy Lee | 13 July 1914
20 Mar. 1975 | Trible
Hanes, J. Blackwell Jr. | Yes |

Inscription: "Wife of J. Blackwell Hanes Jr."

| HANES
Samuel H. | 25 May 1910
27 June 1973 | | Yes |

Inscription: He served as inscribed: "Virginia TEC 5 US Army World War II."

| HARDIMAN
Mollie S. | 27 Sep. 1877
10 Mar. 1938 | Hardiman, William E. | Yes |

Inscription: (U.D.C. Symbol)

| HARDIMAN
William E. | 14 Sep. 1877
04 Jan. 1958 | Hardiman, Mollie S. | Yes |

Inscription: (Masonic Symbol)

| HARDIMAN
William Jr. | 20 May 1908
16 Dec. 1965 | | Yes |

Inscription: (Masonic Symbol)

HARRIS Clyde	23 May 1904 04 Feb. 1971	Harris, Jessie Murray	Yes
HARVEY Carrie	27 Feb. 1896 20 Feb. 1985	Cheatham Harvey, Jesse L.	Yes
HARVEY Catherine	29 Apr. 1924 04 June 1974	Beatty Harvey, Jesse Buford	Yes
HARVEY Jesse Buford	14 Mar. 1921 13 Oct. 1984	Harvey, Catherine Beatty	Yes

LAST NAME First Name	Date of Birth Date of Death Age at Death	Maiden Name Spouse	Tombstone
	Inscription: He served as inscribed: "TEC 3 US Army World War II."		
HARVEY Jesse L.	1886 1949	Harvey, Carrie Cheatham	Yes
HEATH Sam	15 Oct. 1903 10 May 1977		Yes
HUDDLESTON Churchill Jackson	15 Apr. 1889 01 July 1983		Yes
	Inscription: He served as inscribed: "F2 US Navy World War I."		
HUDDLESTON Thomas J.	27 Jan. 1880 26 Oct. 1948	Huddleston, Willie Addie	Yes
	Inscription: "Gone But Not Forgotten."		
HUDDLESTON Willie Addie	21 May 1884 14 Feb. 1925	Huddleston, Thomas J.	Yes
	Inscription: "Our Mother. Wife of T. J. Huddleston. She Believeth and Sleeps In Jesus."		
HUSTON Conway			No
	Other Info: The Odd Fellows started this cemetery. A Mr. Davis gave the land to the Odd Fellows for this purpose. There are no records of the earlier burials. This man was known to be the first person buried here. His grave is located either under the willow oak tree by the Alex. M. Anderson grave, or under the fence in this same area.		
JAMERSON Alfred Coghill	01 Aug. 1896 26 Aug. 1957		Yes
	Inscription: Footstone inscribed: "A.C.J."		
JAMERSON Clarence Keith	17 Feb. 1926 17 May 1952		Yes
JAMERSON Earnest F.	14 May 1920 20 May 1974		Yes
	Inscription: He served as inscribed: "PFC US Army."		
JAMERSON James E.	16 July 1889 01 Nov. 1957		Yes
	Inscription: He served as inscribed: "Virginia PVT Sup Co 314 F1D Arty World War I." Footstone inscribed: "J.E.J."		
JAMERSON James Myrtle	03 Jan. 1893 07 May 1961		Yes

LAST NAME	Date of Birth	Maiden Name	Tombstone
First Name	Date of Death	Spouse	
	Age at Death		

Inscription: He served as inscribed: "Virginia PFC CO A 331 Inf. 83 Division World War I."

| JAMERSON | 13 Aug. 1890 | | Yes |
| John Henry | 31 Jan. 1967 | | |

| JAMERSON | 28 Apr. 1890 | | Yes |
| Joseph C. | 02 Mar. 1957 | | |

Inscription: He served as inscribed: "Virginia PVT Sup Co 320 Inf 80 Div World War I." Footstone inscribed: "Father."

| JAMERSON | 22 Oct. 1924 | Farrar | Yes |
| Lillie | 16 Oct. 1978 | Jamerson, Whitcomb | |

| JAMERSON | 23 Nov. 1898 | | Yes |
| Lois Amiss | 01 July 1978 | | |

| JAMERSON | 04 June 1939 | | Yes |
| Samuel N. "Sammy" | 22 Nov. 1977 | | |

| JAMERSON | 12 June 1924 | Butler | Yes |
| Wanda | 29 Dec. 1983 | | |

| JAMERSON | 1886 | | No |
| William Henry | 1969 | | |

Other Info: Grave marked by a Funeral Home Metal Marker.

| JONES | 02 July 1905 | | Yes |
| Rives Jefferson | 13 Mar. 1976 | Jones, Virginia Maxey | |

Inscription: "Married Oct. 9, 1929."

| KNOTT | 30 Mar. 1921 | | Yes |
| Franklin F. | 19 July 1948 | | |

Inscription: He served as inscribed: "Virginia PFC Co L 120 Infantry World War II. BSM & OLC - PH & OLC."

| KYLE | 1886 | | Yes |
| Annie P. | 1943 | Kyle, George L. | |

| KYLE | 1878 | | Yes |
| George L. | 1956 | Kyle, Annie P. | |

| LeSUEUR | 30 Nov. 1912 | | Yes |
| Jack | 16 Nov. 1976 | | |

| MARKS | 1871 | | Yes |
| Charles L. | 1945 | Marks, Sallie Wood | |

Inscription: (Masonic Symbol)

Other Info: Shares a headstone with his wife.

LAST NAME First Name	Date of Birth Date of Death Age at Death	Maiden Name Spouse	Tombstone
MARKS Sallie	1888 1973	Wood Marks, Charles L.	Yes

Other Info: Shares a headstone with her husband.

| MAXEY Alfred G. | 19 Dec. 1895 21 Oct. 1968 (sic) | | Yes |

Inscription: A second stone at the foot of the grave shows that he served as inscribed: "Virginia PFC 331 Infantry 83 Div. World War I Dec. 19, 1895 Oct. 23, [sic] 1968."

| MAXEY Elizabeth M. | 30 Oct. 1881 01 Dec. 1952 | | Yes |

Inscription: Footstone inscribed: "Mother."

| MAXEY Ella | 30 Apr. 1940 | Thomas Maxey, Horasha Elijah | Yes |

Inscription: Shares a headstone with her husband.

| MAXEY Horasha Elijah | 14 Apr. 1912 | Maxey, Ella Thomas | Yes |

Inscription: Footstone inscribed: "Father."

Other Info: Shares a headstone with his wife.

| MAXEY Mary | 10 Mar. 1893 25 Nov. 1981 | Bryant Maxey, Thomas E. | Yes |

Inscription: "In God's Care." Footstone inscribed: "Mother."

Other Info: Shares a headstone with her husband.

| MAXEY Mary E. | 10 Mar. 1890 24 Aug. 1959 | Maxey, Waldo A. | Yes |

Other Info: Shares a headstone with her husband.

| MAXEY Thomas E. | 11 Feb. 1893 01 Nov. 1960 | Maxey, Mary Bryant | Yes |

Inscription: "In God's Care." Footstone inscribed: "Father."

Other Info: Shares a headstone with his wife.

| MAXEY W. Lawrence | 1914 1933 | | Yes |

Inscription: "In God's Care."

| MAXEY Waldo A. | 07 Dec. 1876 13 Mar. 1935 | Maxey, Mary E. | Yes |

LAST NAME First Name	Date of Birth Date of Death Age at Death	Maiden Name Spouse	Tombstone

Other Info: Shares a headstone with his wife.

| MEADOWS Florence | 16 Oct. 1914 29 Mar. 1975 | Kyle | Yes |

Inscription: "Mother."

| MEDLIN Harry Milton | 13 Jan. 1890 20 Nov. 1949 | Medlin, Lee Harden | Yes |

Inscription: (Masonic Symbol)

Other Info: Shares a headstone with his wife.

| MEDLIN Lee | 11 Oct. 1892 26 Feb. 1987 | Harden Medlin, Harry Milton | Yes |

Other Info: Shares a headstone with her husband.

| MILES | | Miles, Bessie S. | No |

Other Info: Known to be buried here, but no grave marker, and given name not available.

| MILES Alma Clayton | 22 July 1939 21 Jan. 1956 | | Yes |

| MILES Bernard N. | 29 June 1927 09 May 1986 | | Yes |

Inscription: He served as inscribed: "Pvt. US Army World War II."

| MILES Bessie S. | 20 Oct. 1887 13 June 1951 | | Yes |

| MILES Eddie | 1901 1964 | | No |

Other Info: Grave marked with a Funeral Home Metal Marker.

| MILES John Cosby | 29 Mar. 1890 17 Feb. 1957 | | Yes |

| MILES John M. "Jack" | 1902 1970 | | Yes |

Inscription: "Father."

| MILES Kate Shumaker | 27 Aug. 1875 10 Jan. 1935 | | Yes |

LAST NAME First Name	Date of Birth Date of Death Age at Death	Maiden Name Spouse	Tombstone
MILES Mary V.	02 Sep. 1871 26 Feb. 1958	 Miles, William H.	Yes

Other Info: Shares a headstone with her husband.

MILES Thomas Henry	10 Jan. 1923 04 Apr. 1970		Yes

Inscription: He served as inscribed: "Virginia Pvt. Co. D. 14 Medical Tng Bn World War II."

MILES William H.	09 June 1870 08 July 1953	 Miles, Mary V.	Yes

Other Info: Shares a headstone with his wife.

MOORE Annie	12 Oct. 1884 22 Feb. 1975	Harden Moore, William Wirt	Yes

Inscription: "Mother."

Other Info: Shares a headstone with her husband.

MOORE William Wirt	17 Dec. 1884 21 July 1968	 Moore, Annie Harden	Yes

Inscription: "Father."

Other Info: Shares a headstone with his wife.

MORRISON Grace	25 Apr. 1942 26 Apr. 1986	Godsey	Yes

Inscription: "Wife." "Till Jesus Comes."

Other Info: Grave also marked with a Funeral Home Metal Marker.

MOSS Charlie D.	10 Aug. 1900 29 Mar. 1959	 Moss, Evie Sharp	Yes

Other Info: Shares a headstone with his wife.

MOSS Clannie L.	27 Sept. 1907 15 July 1976	 Moss, John E.	Yes

Inscription: "Precious Lord Take My Hand."

MOSS Eva			No

Other Info: Mrs. Moss, and her husband, are both known to be buried here, side-by-side, but there are no marked headstones.

MOSS Evie	17 July 1893 17 Feb. 1982	Sharp Moss, Charlie D.	Yes

LAST NAME First Name	Date of Birth Date of Death Age at Death	Maiden Name Spouse	Tombstone

Other Info: Shares a headstone with her husband.

| MOSS
Frank L. | 30 June 1915
10 Apr. 1980 | Moss, Jissie C. | Yes |

Inscription: "Precious Lord Take My Hand."

Other Info: Shares a headstone with his wife.

| MOSS
Jissie C. | 19 June 1914
12 Oct. 1981 | Moss, Frank L. | Yes |

Inscription: "Precious Lord Take My Hand."

Other Info: Shares a headstone with her husband.

| MOSS
John Robert | 12 Sep. 1902
06 July 1977 | Moss, Laura Toney | Yes |

Inscription: "Father. Married Apr. 24, 1924."

| MOSS
Joseph H. | 05 July 1902
21 Oct. 1918 | | Yes |

Inscription: "Asleep In Jesus."

| MOSS
Marshall J. | 12 Oct. 1924
26 Jan. 1965 | | Yes |

Inscription: "Our Father Which Art In Heaven." Footstone inscribed: "Father."

| MOSS
Phillip S. | 17 July 1874
07 July 1916 | | Yes |

Inscription: "We Shall Meet Again."

| MOSS
Robert Andrew | 24 Apr. 1897
27 Dec. 1967 | | Yes |

Inscription: He served as inscribed: "Virginia Pvt US Army World War I." Footstone inscribed: "Father."

| MOSS
Russell Sr. | 08 May 1910
19 Dec. 1981 | Moss, Virginia W. | Yes |

Inscription: "Father. Our Father Who Art In Heaven."

Other Info: Shares a headstone with his wife.

| MOSS
Virginia W. | 07 June 1910
21 Feb. 1966 | Moss, Russell Sr. | Yes |

Inscription: "Mother. Our Father Who Art In Heaven."

Other Info: Shares a headstone with her husband.

LAST NAME First Name	Date of Birth Date of Death Age at Death	Maiden Name Spouse	Tombstone
MOSS W. E.	19 Mar. 1902 02 May 1925		Yes

Inscription: "At Rest."

| MURPHY
Alfred N. | 1914
1967 | | No |

Other Info: Grave marked with a Funeral Home Metal Marker. Brother of John Rolf Murphy.

| MURPHY
Charlie L. | 15 Feb. 1951
20 Oct. 1982 | | Yes |

Inscription: "Gone, But Not Forgotten."

| MURPHY
Charlie W. | 26 Aug. 1880
03 Dec. 1942 | Murphy, Clara C. | Yes |

OTHER Info: Shares a headstone with his wife.

| MURPHY
Clara C. | 31 Dec. 1885
18 Mar. 1965 | Murphy, Charlie W. | Yes |

Other Info: Shares a headstone with her husband.

| MURPHY
Emmett N. | 02 Mar. 1880
13 Sep. 1964 | | Yes |

Inscription: "Gone, But Not Forgotten."

MURPHY Garland Terry	28 Sep. 1957 27 May 1958		Yes
MURPHY George W.	14 Sep. 1911 24 Aug. 1944		Yes
MURPHY Harry Lynn	29 Jan. 1955 25 Nov. 1973		Yes

Inscription: "Son."

| MURPHY
Hillie L. | 06 Mar. 1884
21 Mar. 1955 | | Yes |

Inscription: "Mother."

| MURPHY
John Rolf | 1905
1975 | | No |

Inscription: Grave marked with a Funeral Home Metal Marker. Brother of Alfred N. Murphy.

| MURPHY
Leo | 18 Apr. 1907
30 Mar. 1977 | | Yes |

LAST NAME First Name	Date of Birth Date of Death Age at Death	Maiden Name Spouse	Tombstone

Inscription: "Son."

| MURPHY
Richard Donald | 20 Mar. 1959
20 Dec. 1969 | | Yes |
| MURPHY
Sarah L. | 10 Jan. 1903
20 Nov. 1983 | Goins | Yes |

Inscription: "Mother...In Loving Memory."

| MURPHY
W. Hubert | 04 Nov. 1920
28 Apr. 1972 | | Yes |
| MURPHY
Wilbur | 29 Dec. 1927
21 July 1980 | | Yes |

Inscription: He served as inscribed: "CS3 US Navy Korea."

| MURPHY
William G. | 08 Apr. 1920
16 Oct. 1943 | | Yes |

Inscription: He served as inscribed: "Virginia PVT Co C7 INF 3 INF Div. World War II."

| NORVELL
Charlie S. | 22 Sep. 1875
15 Aug. 1955 | Novell, Mary J. | Yes |

Other Info: Shares a headstone with his wife.

| NORVELL
Mary J. | 13 Apr. 1880
20 Oct. 1956 | Norvell, Charlie S. | Yes |

Other Info: Shares a headstone with her husband.

| PAGE
Maggie | 29 July 1881
18 May 1943 | Moss | Yes |

Inscription: "At Rest."

PAGE Teresa Lynn	23 Nov. 1979 24 Nov. 1979		Yes
PATTESON Leonard F.	29 May 1906 18 Apr. 1982		Yes
PEARSON	15 Mar. 1925 17 Mar. 1925		Yes

Inscription: "Infant Son of C. E. & Edna H. Pearson."

| PEARSON | 11 Oct. 1927 | | Yes |

Inscription: "Infant daughter of C.E. and Edna H. Pearson."

LAST NAME First Name	Date of Birth Date of Death Age at Death	Maiden Name Spouse	Tombstone
PEARSON Annie	23 Aug. 1881 05 Apr. 1965	Charlton Pearson, S.B.	Yes
PEARSON Mary Edna	04 Apr. 1904 30 Apr. 1968	Hardiman Pearson, C. E.	Yes
PEARSON S. B.	02 Aug. 1871 20 Oct. 1932	Pearson, Annie Charlton	Yes
PENDLETON Benjamin H.	13 Dec. 1888 18 July 1962		Yes

Inscription: He served as inscribed: "Virginia 1st Sgt. Cen Off Tng Sch World War I. " Footstone inscribed: "B.H.P."

PENDLETON Charles	30 June 1847 02 Aug. 1930		Yes
PENDLETON Cora	14 May 1874 13 Mar. 1971	Ranson	Yes

Inscription: Footstone inscribed: "C.R.P."

PENDLETON Daniel R.	18 June 1888 27 Oct. 1930		Yes

Inscription: (Crossed Rifles and "USA" inscribed across the top of the tombstone.) "No Pains, No Griefs, No Anxious Fear, Can Reach Our Loved One Sleeping Here."

PENDLETON John Jacob	03 Feb. 1885 02 May 1945		Yes

Other Info: Shares a headstone with Jessie Pendleton Banton.

PENDLETON Mac P.	18 July 1885 25 July 1914		Yes
PENDLETON Mack	05 Sep. 1857 23 Jan. 1931		Yes
PRICE Emma	1857 1937	Foster Price, Robert Henry	Yes

Inscription: "Mother." Back: "Foster"

Other Info: Shares a headstone with her mother.

PRICE James Herman	15 Jan. 1886 08 Mar. 1960	Price, Annie Butler	Yes

Inscription: Footstone inscribed: "Father."

PRICE Robert Henry	1846 1912	Price, Emma Foster	Yes

LAST NAME First Name	Date of Birth Date of Death Age at Death	Maiden Name Spouse	Tombstone
	Inscription: ""Father." Back: "Price"		
PRICE Robert I.	1884 1964		Yes
RAINEY Nancy J.	15 July 1946 20 Feb. 1971		Yes
RAINEY Rufus P.	26 Jan. 1896 19 Feb. 1960		Yes
	Inscription: "Father."		
RAKES Forrest Daniel	05 Jan. 1918 14 July 1984	Rakes, Mabel Ayres	Yes
	Inscription: "Father. In Loving Memory."		
RANSON Buford N.	16 Nov. 1911 23 Dec. 1975		Yes
	Inscription: "Son."		
RANSON Estelle F.	13 Oct. 1878 07 June 1957	Ranson, Radford B. Sr.	Yes
	Inscription: "Mother."		
RANSON Griffith T.	30 Oct. 1911 03 Sep. 1984		Yes
RANSON Patty	26 June 1944 26 June 1944		Yes
	Inscription: Infant Daughter of R.K. and Irene J. Ranson		
RANSON R. Bennett Jr.	19 Jan. 1907 19 June 1958		Yes
	Inscription: "Son."		
RANSON Radford B. Sr.	19 Sep. 1879 20 Aug. 1962	Ranson, Estelle F.	Yes
	Inscription: "Father."		
RANSON Tommy	21 Feb. 1946 23 Feb. 1946		Yes
	Inscription: Infant Son of R.K. and Irene J. Ranson		
RIDDLEBURGER Mark S.	16 Aug. 1978 10 Dec. 1978		Yes
ROBERTSON Liza Jane	14 May 1932 Oct. 1932		Yes

LAST NAME First Name	Date of Birth Date of Death Age at Death	Maiden Name Spouse	Tombstone
ROBERTSON Matt A.	02 Sep. 1894 27 June 1958		Yes
RUSH Lou	09 Aug. 1920 23 May 1962	Taylor Rush, Rolfe L. Jr.	Yes

Other Info: Shares a headstone with her husband.

| RUSH
Rolfe L. Jr. | 18 Oct. 1922
17 Dec. 1976 |
Rush, Lou Taylor | Yes |

Other Info: Shares a headstone with his wife.

| SALMON
Elsie | 25 Apr. 1924
07 Nov. 1983 | Catlett | Yes |
| SCHUMAKER [sic]
Charlie E. | 29 Dec. 1915
11 Feb. 1945 | | Yes |

Inscription: He served as inscribed: "Virginia PFC 152 INF World War II."

| SCOTT
Aubrey Coinard | 03 Sep. 1903
05 Feb. 1964 | | Yes |

Inscription: He served as inscribed: "Virginia TSGT 530 Ordnance Co. World War II." Footstone inscribed: "A.C.S."

| SCOTT
James L. | 23 Feb. 1931
31 July 1982 | | Yes |

Inscription: He served as inscribed: "A2C US Air Force Korea"." Footstone inscribed: "J.L.S."

| SCOTT
Sarah E. | 1918
1962 | | Yes |
| SCOTT
William Aubrey | 09 Nov. 1929
07 Sep. 1953 | | Yes |

Inscription: He served as inscribed: "Virginia A3C 7111 Mtr. Vehicle SQ AF." Footstone inscribed: "W.A.S."

| SCRUGGS
Charles M. | 12 Sep. 1895
03 Feb. 1966 | | Yes |

Inscription: He served as inscribed: "Virginia PVT 15 Co 155 Depot Brig World War I."

| SCRUGGS
Mary Elizabeth | 02 Mar. 1899
25 May 1935 | | Yes |
| SCRUGGS
Mary L. | 11 May 1890
26 Oct. 1920 | | Yes |

LAST NAME	Date of Birth	Maiden Name	Tombstone
First Name	Date of Death	Spouse	
	Age at Death		

Inscription: "Safe In The Arms Of Jesus."

Other Info: There are two unmarked graves beside this one who are known to be Scruggs family members, but at this time the names are not available.

| SEAY | 10 Sep. 1886 | | Yes |
| Branch Abner | 26 Oct. 1965 | Seay, Myrtle Steele | |

Inscription: (Masonic Symbol)

| SEAY | 06 June 1888 | Steele | Yes |
| Myrtle | 09 Jan. 1973 | Seay, Branch Abner | |

| SEAY | 19 Mar. 1917 | | Yes |
| Thelma Elizabeth | 24 Aug. 1985 | | |

| SELF | 11 Aug. 1895 | Lightfoot | Yes |
| Annie | 23 Oct. 1975 | Self, Frank Hill | |

Other Info: Shares a headstone with her husband and son.

| SELF | 09 Nov. 1891 | | Yes |
| Frank Hill | 22 Oct. 1972 | Self, Annie Lightfoot | |

Other Info: Shares a headstone with his wife and son.

| SELF | 07 June 1917 | | Yes |
| George Luther | 06 June 1942 | | |

Inscription: "Lost At Sea."

Other Info: Shares a headstone with his father and mother.

| SHARP | 10 Oct. 1885 | | Yes |
| J. Wiley | 04 Aug. 1935 | Sharp, Nannie T. | |

Inscription: "Gone But Not Forgotten."

| SHARP | 1912 | | Yes |
| John Littleton | 1979 | Sharp, Mattie V. | |

Inscription: He served as inscribed: "PVT US Army World War II."

| SHARP | 09 July 1909 | | Yes |
| Mattie V. | 11 Dec. 1977 | Sharp, John Littleton | |

| SHARP | 04 Nov. 1887 | | Yes |
| Nannie T. | 23 Dec. 1974 | Sharp, J. Wiley | |

| SHUMAKER | 1944 | | Yes |
| Acie C. | 1981 | Shumaker, Margaret W. | |

Inscription: "Father." "Married April 7, 1973."

| LAST NAME | Date of Birth | Maiden Name | Tombstone |
| First Name | Date of Death | Spouse | |
	Age at Death		
SHUMAKER Annie	04 June 1893 01 Dec. 1937	Taylor Shumaker, George Pratt	Yes

Other Info: Shares a headstone with her husband.

SHUMAKER B. Frank	05 Aug. 1880 20 June 1957	Shumaker, Carrie G.	Yes

Other Info: Shares a headstone with his wife.

SHUMAKER Carrie G.	10 Jan. 1882 30 Jan. 1958	Shumaker, B. Frank	Yes

Other Info: Shares a headstone with her husband.

SHUMAKER Charlie E.	29 Dec. 1915 11 Feb. 1945		Yes

Inscription: He served as inscribed: "Virginia PFC 152 INF World War II."

SHUMAKER Charlie H.	04 July 1890 07 Nov. 1971	Shumaker, Emma D.	Yes

Inscription: "Father."

Other Info: Shares a headstone with his wife.

SHUMAKER Emma D.	15 June 1886 05 Oct. 1944	Shumaker, Charlie H.	Yes

Inscription: "Mother."

Other Info: Shares a headstone with her husband.

SHUMAKER Fannie S.	18 May 1908 05 Nov. 1977	Shumaker, Sidney H.	Yes

Inscription: "Mother."

Other Info: Shares a headstone with her husband and son.

SHUMAKER Garnet Gray	10 Aug. 1911 14 May 1962		Yes

SHUMAKER George Pratt	15 Mar. 1882 15 Apr. 1945	Shumaker, Annie Taylor	Yes

Other Info: Shares a headstone with his wife.

SHUMAKER Hattie	05 Jan. 1875 24 May 1959	Taylor Shumaker, John Hill	Yes

Inscription: Footstone inscribed: "Mother."

LAST NAME First Name	Date of Birth Date of Death Age at Death	Maiden Name Spouse	Tombstone
	Other Info: Shares a headstone with her husband.		
SHUMAKER Henry T.	02 Oct. 1906 31 May 1971		Yes
SHUMAKER Jacie	28 Feb. 1898 20 Jan. 1984	Moss	Yes
	Inscription: "Mother...Precious Lord Take My Hand."		
SHUMAKER Joe F.	31 May 1934		Yes
	Inscription: "Son."		
	Other Info: Shares a headstone with his father and mother.		
SHUMAKER John Hill	12 June 1873 02 Dec. 1961	Shumaker, Hattie Taylor	Yes
	Inscription: Footstone inscribed: "Father."		
	Other Info: Shares a headstone with his wife.		
SHUMAKER John W.	17 Aug. 1913 06 Oct. 1982	Shumaker, Louise S.	Yes
	Inscription: "Precious Lord Take My Hand."		
SHUMAKER Marshall R.	14 May 1917 03 Dec. 1985		Yes
	Other Info: Grave is also marked with a Funeral Home Metal Marker inscribed: "Marshall Roy Shumaker, 1917-1985."		
SHUMAKER Mazie G.	29 Mar. 1899 20 Oct. 1973		Yes
SHUMAKER Minnie E.	05 Mar. 1918 20 Oct. 1982	Shumaker, Percy Mack	Yes
	Other Info: Shares a headstone with her husband.		
SHUMAKER Myrtis L.	1884 1943	Shumaker, Norvell E.	Yes
	Other Info: Shares a headstone with her husband.		
SHUMAKER Nellie T. Inscription: "Mother."	19 Feb. 1937 26 Apr. 1982		Yes
SHUMAKER Norvell E.	1871 1938	Shumaker, Myrtis L.	Yes

LAST NAME	Date of Birth	Maiden Name	Tombstone
First Name	Date of Death	Spouse	
	Age at Death		

Other Info: Shares a headstone with his wife.

| SHUMAKER | 02 Mar. 1905 | | Yes |
| Percy Mack | 27 June 1980 | Shumaker, Minnie E. | |

Other Info: Shares a headstone with his wife.

| SHUMAKER | 16 June 1904 | | Yes |
| Russell A. | 11 Oct. 1970 | | |

Inscription: He served as inscribed: "Virginia PVT Anti-Tank Co 395 INF World War II." Footstone inscribed: "R.A.S."

| SHUMAKER | 09 Nov. 1889 | | Yes |
| Sidney H. | 16 Nov. 1945 | Shumaker, Fannie S. | |

Inscription: "Father."

Other Info: Shares a headstone with his wife and son.

| SHUMAKER | 04 Sep. 1897 | | Yes |
| William Hill | 09 Apr. 1970 | | |

Inscription: "Brother."

| SMITH | 11 Oct. 1844 | Reese | Yes |
| Ann | 12 Apr. 1920 | Smith, William Arnold | |

Other Info: Shares a headstone with her husband.

| SMITH | 23 July 1884 | Shepard | Yes |
| Carrie | 21 Apr. 1976 | Smith, Robert Garnett | |

Inscription: "Mother" Footstone inscribed: "C.S.S."

| SMITH | 15 Oct. 1890 | Denton | Yes |
| Mabel | 16 June 1974 | Smith, William Moses Sr. | |

| SMITH | 06 July 1884 | | Yes |
| Robert Garnett | 09 Apr. 1943 | Smith, Carrie Shepard | |

Inscription: "Father." Footstone inscribed: "R.G.S."

| SMITH | 10 Feb. 1845 | | Yes |
| William Arnold | 20 Dec. 1923 | Smith, Ann Reese | |

Inscription: He served as inscribed: "C.S.A. CO. K. 4 Reg. VA CAV."

Other Info: Sharles a headstone with his wife.

| SMITH | 23 Sep. 1921 | | Yes |
| William Moses Jr. | 27 Nov. 1976 | | |

Inscription: (Masonic Symbol)

LAST NAME First Name	Date of Birth Date of Death Age at Death	Maiden Name Spouse	Tombstone
SMITH William Moses Sr.	02 May 1886 20 Feb. 1951	Smith, Mabel Denton	Yes

Inscription: (Masonic Symbol)

SNODDY John Robert	22 Apr. 1899 17 Mar. 1941	Snoddy, Reubie Nicholas	Yes
SNODDY Reubie	06 Feb. 1898 26 Sep. 1978	Nicholas Snoddy, John Robert	Yes
SNODDY William W. "Oolie"	20 Apr. 1922 13 Jan. 1965		Yes
SORRENTINO Ella C.	09 Nov. 1894 29 Dec. 1970	Sorrentino, Joseph	Yes

Other Info: Shares a headstone with her husband.

SORRENTINO Joseph	02 July 1889 20 Sep. 1976	Sorrentino, Ella C.	Yes

Other Info: Shares a headstone with his wife.

SPENCER Carolyn Ann	15 Sep. 1956 05 Feb. 1960		Yes

Inscription: "Daughter of Ann & R.B. Spencer, Jr."

SPENCER Fannie	07 Dec. 1888 27 Apr. 1967	Charlton Spencer, Robert Bruce	Yes
SPENCER Robert Bruce	21 Jan. 1886 23 Nov. 1960	Spencer, Fannie Charlton	Yes
SPENCER William Shepherd	22 June 1962 26 May 1964		Yes

Inscription: "Son of Ann & R. B. Spencer, Jr."

SPRINGER Charles G.	10 Apr. 1882 19 Apr. 1946	Springer, Kate Price	Yes

Other Info: Shares a headstone with his wife.

SPRINGER Kate	05 Aug. 1888 24 May 1927	Price Springer, Charles G.	Yes

Other Info: Shares a headstone with her husband.

| STEELE
"Old Man" | | | No |

LAST NAME	Date of Birth	Maiden Name	Tombstone
First Name	Date of Death	Spouse	
	Age at Death		

Other Info: No grave marker, but grave known to be just off the boundry of the Pearson family plot. This is Myrtle Steele Seay's father.

| TALBOTT | 1937 | | No |
| Barbara Jean | 1937 | | |

Other Info: Grave Marked with a Funeral Home Metal Marker.

| TALBOTT | 19 Mar. 1928 | | Yes |
| Edwin Ellis "Pete" | 10 Mar. 1968 | | |

Inscription: Military stone at foot of grave is inscribed as follows: "Edwin Ellis Talbott, Virginia PFC US Army Korea March 19, 1928 March 10, 1968."

| TALBOTT | | | No |
| Gloria Faye | 1954 | | |

Other Info: Grave Marked with A Funeral Home Metal Marker.

| TALBOTT | 21 June 1890 | | Yes |
| Raleigh A. | 27 Feb. 1968 | | |

| TAYLOR | 13 July 1915 | | Yes |
| Beatrice C. | 07 Dec. 1980 | Taylor, Arnie | |

Inscription: "Married Jan. 30, 1932."

| TAYLOR | 02 Aug. 1870 | | Yes |
| Ellen T. | 07 June 1951 | | |

| TAYLOR | 07 May 1934 | | Yes |
| John E. | 06 Nov. 1973 | | |

| TAYLOR | 21 June 1896 (sic) | | Yes |
| Robert | 26 Oct. 1970 | Taylor, Annie T. | |

Inscription: A second stone at the foot of the grave shows that he served as inscribed: "PVT Sup Co 61 Infantry World War I Oct. 16, 1892 (sic) Oct. 26, 1970."

| TAYLOR | 18 Aug. 1926 | | Yes |
| Robert W. | 22 May 1971 | Taylor, Mary L. | |

| TAYLOR | 07 June 1949 | | Yes |
| Tiny Estelle | 14 Oct. 1949 | | |

Inscription: "In God's Care."

| TAYLOR | 15 Jan. 1915 | | Yes |
| Willie Walker | 25 Sep. 1977 | | |

Inscription: "He Built A Monument Of Love In the Hearts Of All Who Knew Him."

LAST NAME First Name	Date of Birth Date of Death Age at Death	Maiden Name Spouse	Tombstone
THOMAS Andrew Jennings	08 May 1898 17 June 1980	Thomas, Alice Farrar	Yes

Inscription: "God Be With You Till We Meet Again."

THOMPSON Gracie Geneva	12 Mar. 1935 20 Feb. 1984	Thompson, George Paul	Yes
TONEY Bessie	18 Jan. 1901 08 June 1968	Worsham	Yes

Inscription: "Mother."

Other Info: Shares a headstone with her husband.

TONEY John Lee	08 Aug. 1893 20 Dec. 1951	Toney, Bessie Worsham	Yes

Inscription: "Father." A second stone at the foot of the grave shows he served as inscribed: "John Lee Toney Virginia PVT 155 Depot Brigade World War I Aug. 8, 1893 Dec. 20, 1951."

Other Info: Shares a headstone with his wife.

TONEY John Lee	06 Oct. 1928 01 Dec. 1975		Yes

Inscription: "Father."

TONEY Mary Lou	21 Oct. 1912 29 June 1977	Toney, Sidney A.	Yes

Inscription: "Asleep In Jesus."

Other Info: Shares a headstone with her husband.

TONEY Sidney A.	29 Oct. 1913 24 Nov. 1986	Toney, Mary Lou	Yes

Inscription: "Asleep In Jesus."

Other Info: Shares a headstone with his wife.

TONEY Walter M.	05 Dec. 1931 25 June 1972		Yes

Inscription: "Son." A second stone at the foot of the grave says he served as inscribed: "Walter Melvin Toney Virginia A3C US Air Force Korea Dec. 5, 1931 June 25, 1972."

TRENTHAM Lena W.	22 Aug. 1918 21 Nov. 1980	Trentham, N. Harman	Yes

Inscription: "Precious Lord Take My Hand."

LAST NAME First Name	Date of Birth Date of Death Age at Death	Maiden Name Spouse	Tombstone
VIAR Nannie	09 Mar. 1907 11 Apr. 1977	Call	Yes
WAKEFIELD George E.	22 Sep. 1922 23 Aug. 1974	Wakefield, Julia Call	Yes

Other Info: Shares a headstone with his wife.

| WAKEFIELD
Julia | 09 May 1923
06 Dec. 1980 | Call
Wakefield, George E. | Yes |

Other Info: Shares a headstone with her husband.

| WEEKS
John Overton | 11 June 1937
21 Dec. 1953 | | Yes |

Inscription: "At Rest."

| WEEKS
Marvin O. | 05 Apr. 1909
14 Oct. 1974 | | Yes |
| WEEKS
William Clifton | 21 Nov. 1875
17 Sep. 1935 | | Yes |

Inscription: "At Rest."

| WHITE
H. Murray | 13 Nov. 1861
15 Oct. 1925 | White, Kate E. | Yes |

Other Info: Shares a headstone with his wife.

| WHITE
Kate E. | 11 Mar. 1851
14 Dec. 1942 | White, H. Murray | Yes |

Other Info: Shares a headstone with her husband.

WHITLOW Rosa S.	21 July 1911 28 Aug. 1984		Yes
WOOD Fred Glover Jr.	20 July 1934 22 July 1934		Yes
WOODFIN Geela	29 Aug. 1958 04 Dec. 1982	Hanley Woodfin, William Ray	Yes

Inscription: "Married July 24, 1976. In Loving Memory."

Other Info: Shares a headstone with her husband.

| WOODFIN
William Ray | 04 Aug. 1951
04 Dec. 1982 | Woodfin, Geela Hanley | Yes |

Inscription: "Married July 24, 1976. In Loving Memory."
Other Info: Shares a headstone with his wife.

LAST NAME First Name	Date of Birth Date of Death Age at Death	Maiden Name Spouse	Tombstone
WOOTEN Wiley L.	12 May 1914 29 Apr. 1984		Yes

Inscription: He served as inscribed: "PFC US Army World War II."

WORSHAM Cora S.	1869 1926	Worsham, John D.	Yes

Other Info: Shares a headstone with her husband.

WORSHAM John D.	1872 1945	Worsham, Cora S.	Yes

Other Info: Shares a headstone with his wife.

WORSHAM Mary Florence "Jo"	10 Sep. 1889 10 May 1970		Yes

Duty Family Cemetery - Hwy 637

DUTY David Lemuel	13 Sep. 1887 09 Nov. 1929		Yes

Inscription: Footstone inscribed: "D.L.D."

Other Info: There are many other graves here marked with fieldstones.

Elcan Family Slave Plot - Black - Hwy 608

Other Info: This cemetery which contains approx. 15 graves marked by fieldstones only, is on land which was a part of the original Elcan farm, and is believed to be the slave burying ground.

Fones/Wright Family - Hwy 631

AGEE Agnes Wright S.	27 Aug. 1909 26 Jan. 1981	Wright	Yes
AGEE Joe Gilbert	01 Apr. 1948 01 Apr. 1948		Yes
FONES Mary Virginia	22 July 1862 01 Oct. 1947		Yes

Inscription: "Loved By All."

FONES Solon Boston	02 Aug. 1908 12 Apr. 1932		Yes

Inscription: "At Rest."

LAST NAME First Name	Date of Birth Date of Death Age at Death	Maiden Name Spouse	Tombstone
FONES William A.	31 Aug. 1851 25 Jan. 1916		Yes

Inscription: (Masonic Symbol) "We Will Meet Again." Footstone inscribed: "W.A.F."

OWNBY Terry Teresa	13 Feb. 1962 24 Feb. 1962		Yes
QUESSENBERRY Nancy	04 Apr. 1916 24 Jan. 1957	Wright	Yes
WRIGHT Emanuel F.	17 Feb. 1861 16 June 1949		Yes
WRIGHT Evelyn Joyce	03 Oct. 1943 06 Mar. 1944		Yes
WRIGHT Flora Estelle	09 Oct. 1902 05 Oct. 1959		Yes
WRIGHT Mary Elizabeth	08 July 1877 06 Nov. 1944		Yes

Garnett Family at "Wheatland" - Hwy 633

ELLIOTT Nannie	1850s 1870s	Garnett Elliott, Horace	

Other Info: The general location of this cemetery is known, but no grave markers. This mother and her newborn infant died at the birth, and both were buried here. Mr. Horace Elliott is buried at Smyrna Church.

General Childress/Jamerson Family Cemetery - Hwy 630

BANTON Lena C.	1876 1965	Banton, Tandy H.	Yes

Other Info: Shares a headstone with her husband.

BANTON Tandy H.	1886 1967	Banton, Lena C.	Yes

Other Info: Shares a headstone with his wife.

BRAY Charles C.	02 Apr. 1946 31 Aug. 1951		Yes

Inscription: Footstone inscribed: "C.C.B."

LAST NAME First Name	Date of Birth Date of Death Age at Death	Maiden Name Spouse	Tombstone
BRAY Crawford	17 July 1925 16 July 1986		Yes

Inscription: He served as inscribed: "S1 US Navy World War II."

Other Info: Grave also marked by a funeral home metal marker.

BRAY Joan E.	27 Oct. 1949 13 Nov. 1949		Yes

Inscription: Footstone inscribed: "J.E.B."

CHIDESTER Clyde L.	12 Feb. 1923 16 Mar. 1990	Chidester, Mary J.	Yes

Other Info: Shares a headstone with his wife.

CHIDESTER Mary J.	16 Mar. 1926 07 Sep. 1976	Chidester, Clyde L.	Yes

Other Info: Shares a headstone with her husband.

CHILDRESS Elizabeth V.	20 Aug. 1832 19 May 1919	Childress, James	Yes

Inscription: "In Memory Of Our Mother. At Rest." Footstone inscribed: "E.V.C."

CHILDRESS Frank A.	24 Sep. 1868 26 June 1934		Yes

Inscription: "Let Our Father's Will Be Done." Footstone inscribed: "F.A.C."

HEMBREE Henry C.	27 June 1911 18 Oct. 1991	Hembree, Maggie J.	Yes

Other Info: Grave also marked by a funeral home metal marker inscribed: "Henry Clay Hembree ... "

JAMERSON Alice I.	30 Nov. 1924 27 Oct. 1925		Yes

JAMERSON Annie L.	03 Apr. 1914 24 Jan. 1989	Jamerson, R. Claude	Yes

Inscription: "Married Mar. 30, 1935."

Other Info: Shares a headstone with her husband.

JAMERSON (Baby)	Nov. 1945		Yes

JAMERSON (Baby Girls)	1972		No

Other Info: Grave marked by a funeral home metal marker.

LAST NAME First Name	Date of Birth Date of Death Age at Death	Maiden Name Spouse	Tombstone
JAMERSON Berta	12 May 1899 04 July 1942	Amos Jamerson, Robert Mitchell	Yes

Inscription: "Mother." Footstone inscribed: "B.A.J."

| JAMERSON
Bettie V. | 24 Jan. 1895
08 Dec. 1950 | | Yes |

Inscription: "God Be With You Till We Meet Again." Footstone inscribed: "B.V.J."

| JAMERSON
Carrie | 22 Dec. 1898
07 Nov. 1969 | Sharp
Jamerson, John Walter | Yes |

Other Info: Shares a headstone with her husband. Her grave is also marked with a funeral home metal marker.

| JAMERSON
Charlie M. | 06 Sep. 1891
23 Nov. 1971 | | Yes |

Other Info: Grave also marked by a funeral home metal marker inscribed: "Charlie Marshall Jamerson 1891-1971."

| JAMERSON
Clayton Allen | 16 July 1930
21 July 1930 | | Yes |

Inscription: "At Rest."

| JAMERSON
David Ray Jr. | 05 Oct. 1970
07 Oct. 1970 | | Yes |

Inscription: "Love You Son, Mother."

| JAMERSON
Dolly A. | 1872
1972 | Jamerson, Josiah T. | Yes |

Inscription: Footstone inscribed: "Mother."

Other Info: Shares a headstone with her husband.

JAMERSON Elven O.	09 Aug. 1937 03 Mar. 1940		Yes
JAMERSON Estelle Virginia	27 Nov. 1935 03 Nov. 1941		Yes
JAMERSON Floyd M.	11 Apr. 1923 23 Dec. 1957		Yes
JAMERSON Frank	20 Mar. 1888 03 June 1971	Jamerson, Mattie R.	Yes

Other Info: Shares a headstone with his wife.

| JAMERSON
Herman Gordon | 20 Apr. 1912
13 Jan. 1972 | | Yes |

LAST NAME First Name	Date of Birth Date of Death Age at Death	Maiden Name Spouse	Tombstone
JAMERSON (Infant Son)	09 Jan. 1954		Yes

Inscription: "Infant Son of Mr. & Mrs. Emmett W. Jamerson. Gone But Not Forgotten."

JAMERSON John D.	08 Mar. 1865 10 Feb. 1941		Yes

Inscription: "Gone But Not Forgotten."

JAMERSON John Walter	29 Oct. 1889 29 June 1970	Jamerson, Carrie Sharp	Yes

Other Info: Shares a headstone with his wife.

JAMERSON Josiah T.	1870 1960	Jamerson, Dolly A.	Yes

Inscription: Footstone inscribed: "Father."

Other Info: Shares a headstone with his wife.

JAMERSON Judson H.	05 Dec. 1910 19 Apr. 1976	Jamerson, Juanita H.	Yes

JAMERSON Julius Harding	28 Apr. 1922 27 Mar. 1924		Yes

Inscription: " ... Son of B.C. & N.F. Jamerson. Budded On Earth To Bloom In Heaven." Footstone inscribed: "J.H.J."

JAMERSON Leonard Lee	1920 1943		Yes

Inscription: He served as inscribed: "PVT. U.S. Army World War II."

JAMERSON Lewis Daniel	03 Nov. 1920 07 June 1986		Yes

Other Info: Grave also marked by a funeral home metal marker.

JAMERSON Mable	02 May 1906 25 June 1907		Yes

Inscription: "In Memory Of ... "

JAMERSON Marvin	19 July 1902 03 Mar. 1977	Ragland Jamerson, Sam Lee	Yes

Other Info: Shares a headstone with her husband.

JAMERSON Mary E.	18 May 1868 20 Dec. 1952		Yes

LAST NAME First Name	Date of Birth Date of Death Age at Death	Maiden Name Spouse	Tombstone
	Inscription: "Our Dear Mother." Footstone inscribed: "M.E.J."		
JAMERSON Mattie R.	14 Aug. 1899 27 Aug. 1980	Jamerson, Frank	Yes
	Other Info: Shares a headstone with her husband.		
JAMERSON Phillis Ann	10 Aug. 1948 15 Feb. 1949		Yes
	Inscription: Footstone inscribed: "P.A.J."		
JAMERSON R. Claude	29 June 1913 23 Jan. 1969	Jamerson, Annie L.	Yes
	Inscription: "Married Mar. 30, 1935."		
	Other Info: Shares a headstone with his wife. Grave also marked by a funeral home metal marker inscribed: "Ruby Claude Jamerson 1913-1969."		
JAMERSON Reggie L.	12 Apr. 1896 23 Aug. 1986	Jamerson, Mary W.	Yes
	Inscription: "In Loving Memory ... Father."		
JAMERSON Robert Kary	01 Aug. 1926 02 Sep. 1951		Yes
JAMERSON Robert Mitchell	29 Sep. 1902 26 Nov. 1978	Jamerson, Berta Amos	Yes
	Inscription: "Father."		
JAMERSON Sam Lee	24 May 1898 07 Mar. 1976	Jamerson, Marvin R.	Yes
	Other Info: Shares a headstone with his wife.		
JAMERSON T. Ashby	10 Aug. 1910 21 Nov. 1993	Jamerson, Zanie May	Yes
	Inscription: "Father."		
JAMERSON Thomas Wilbur	16 Aug. 1937 16 Sep. 1962		Yes
	Inscription: "Gone But Not Forgotten." Footstone inscribed: "T.W.J."		
KERN Charles	17 Feb. 1920 03 Jan. 1992	Kern, Christine H. J.	Yes
	Other Info: Shares a headstone with his wife.		

LAST NAME First Name	Date of Birth Date of Death Age at Death	Maiden Name Spouse	Tombstone
KERN Christine H.	21 June 1932 19 Feb. 1979	Kern, Charles	Yes

Inscription: Shares a headstone with her husband.

Other Info: Grave also marked by a funeral home metal marker inscribed: "Christine J. Kern 1932 - 1979."

NICHOLS Isabelle V.	1928 1984	Nichols, Robert L.	Yes
RAGLAND Charlie E.	04 Nov. 1886 24 July 1946		Yes

Inscription: Footstone inscribed: "C.E.R."

SHARP S. E.	1856 1947		Yes

Inscription: "At Rest."

WRIGHT Maggie L.	08 Oct. 1893 05 Oct. 1917		Yes

Inscription: Footstone inscribed: "M.L.W."

Gilliam Family at "Millcote" - Hwy 612 (Cole Forest Road)

GILLIAM William Edward	20 July 1843 18 May 1897	Gilliam,	Yes

Inscription: Footstone inscribed: "W.E.G."

Other Info: After the death of William, his wife and children moved to Richmond, Va., and are buried in Hollywood Cemetery there. There are approximately thirty-six graves here all marked by fieldstones.

Gunter Family - Hwy 601

GUNTER Robert C.	1839 (circa)	Gunter, Elizabeth	Yes

Inscription: Robert served as inscribed: "C.S.A."

Other Info: Robert C. was the son of Jane Gunter, and had at least six sisters and brothers. He was married to Elizabeth, and they were the parents of at least six children. Any of this extended family could be buried in this cemetery, as there are many more graves all marked by fieldstones.

LAST NAME	Date of Birth	Maiden Name	Tombstone
First Name	Date of Death	Spouse	
	Age at Death		

Hocker Family Slave Plot - Black - Hwy 708

Other Info: This property belonged to one of the Hocker families who lived in the area. It is believed to be the slave burying ground. There are approximately three rows with 14 - 16 graves in each row. About 45 - 48 graves. This cemetery is located about 500 yards north of the Powell Family Cemetery cited in a separate survey.

Holman/Jones Family at "Oak Hill" - Hwy 642

| BONDURANT | | | No |
| Virginia Baker | 1860s | | |

Other Info: She died young. Her grave is marked by fieldstones only.

| HOLMAN | 1844 | | Yes |
| Hartwell J. | 1863 | | |

Inscription: Hartwell served as inscribed: "CO A 57th VA INF (C.S.A.)"

Other Info: Son of Tandy Holman and Judith H.S. Holman. Hartwell and his brother, James, went to fight in the Civil War, but died in camp of some disease; both were brought back home for burial.

| HOLMAN | 1834 | | No |
| James S. | 1863 | | |

Other Info: James served as follows: "CO A 57th VA INF (C.S.A.)" James and his brother, Hartwell, went to fight in the Civil War, but died in camp of some disease; both were brought back home for burial. Son of Tandy Holman and Judith H.S. Holman.

HOLMAN	1830 (circa)		No
Jane Elizabeth	1854 (circa)		
	18 yr.		

Other Info: Eldest child of Tandy and Judith H. S. Holman. She died before 1854 at around 18 yrs. of age. Grave marked with fieldstones only.

| HOLMAN | 1813 (circa) | Spencer | No |
| Judith Hales | | Holman, Tandy | |

Other Info: Known to be buried here beside her husband. Most of the graves are marked by fieldstones only.

| HOLMAN | 1838 (circa) | | No |
| Martha Ellen "Barley" | | | |

Other Info: Known to be buried here. Grave marked by fieldstones only. Daughter of Tandy and Judith H. S. Holman.

LAST NAME First Name	Date of Birth Date of Death Age at Death	Maiden Name Spouse	Tombstone
HOLMAN Tandy	1810 (circa)	Holman, Judith H. S.	No

Other Info: He is known to be buried at this cemetery on his homeplace. Most of the graves are marked by fieldstones only.

JONES James Wiley "Jimmy"	1871		No

Other Info: Grave marked by fieldstones only. Son of Wiley T. and Mary L.H. Jones.

JONES Matilda C.	1821 (circa)	Jones, Tazwell	No

Other Info: Known to be buried here beside her husband. Grave marked by fieldstones only.

JONES Tazwell	1823 (circa)	Jones, Matilda Caroline	Yes

Inscription: Tazwell served as inscribed: "CO C 25 VA INF C.S.A."

JONES Wiley T.	1846 (circa) 1874	Jones, Mary L. H.	Yes

Inscription: Wiley served as inscribed: "CO D VA ART (C.S.A.)"

Other Info: Son of Tazwell and Matilda C. Jones.

SPENCER Judith	1768 (circa) 1850 (to 1860)	Hales	No

Other Info: Known to be buried here where her daughter is buried. Mother of Judith H. S. Holman.

Horsley family - Hwy 604

HORSLEY Bluefield			No

Other Info: Known to be buried here. Cemetery not found. He was the son of Jennie Horsley.

HORSLEY Charles			No

Other Info: Known to be buried here. Son of Jennie Horsley.

HORSLEY Jean	1933		No

LAST NAME	Date of Birth	Maiden Name	Tombstone
First Name	Date of Death	Spouse	
	Age at Death		

Other Info: Known to be buried here. Jean and Claudine Horsley were the daughters of "Goat" Horsley. Jean was buried here in 1933/34. Claudine married and left the area.

HORSLEY   No
John "Goat"

Other Info: Son of Jennie Horsley. This family cemetery on the Horsley place that adjoined "Yellow Gravel" cannot be found at this time; it might have been destroyed.

HORSLEY   No
"Trig"

Other Info: Died as a young boy. Son of Jennie Horsley.

WILKERSON   No
William   1916

Jamerson/Sharpe Family - Hwy 650

DEAN   1825 (circa)   Yes
William R.

Inscription: William served as inscribed: "CO C 3 VA RES C.S.A."

HARRIS   1822 (circa)   Yes
Willliam R.

Inscription: William served as inscribed: "CO C 3 VA RES C.S.A."

JAMISON   1824 (circa)   Yes
William J.

Inscription: William served as inscribed: "CO K 2 VA ARTY C.S.A."

MANN   Nov. 1762   Yes
Lucy   26 Feb. 1856

Other Info: On the handcarved inscription on the fieldstone, it looks like "LIAM", but it's believed to be this lady who was alive in the 1850 U.S. Census, age 85; but does not appear in the 1860 U.S. Census. It is probably "LTM" as she was Lucy Thomas Mann, wife of John Mann.

Kyle/Davis Family Cemetery - Hwy 637

KYLE   25 Apr. 1846   Yes
Mildred Perkins   01 Dec. 1849
Inscription: "Sacred To the Memory of ...Only daughter of W. P. and M. M. Kyle...She Sleeps In Jesus, Sweet Innocent, Of Such Is the Kingdom Of Heaven."

LAST NAME First Name	Date of Birth Date of Death Age at Death	Maiden Name Spouse	Tombstone
KYLE William P.	05 Oct. 1862 18 yr		Yes

Inscription: ""... In His 18 Year. Rest In Heaven, Soldier Boy." He served as inscribed in the Civil War.

| KYLE William P. | 02 June 1862 44 yr | Kyle, M. M. | Yes |

Inscription: "... In His 44 Year. Blessed Are the Dead, Who Die In the Lord."

| PERKINS Sarah P. | 24 Nov. 1817 01 Nov. 1836 | | Yes |

Inscription: "...Daughter of Samuel and Sally Perkins of Williamson County, Kentucky..."

Laury - Dora Laury Family - Black - Hwy 660

| LAURY Dora | | | No |

Other Info: The general location of this cemetery is known. There is no longer any evidence that there was ever a cemetery here. But it is known that this lady and several of her small children were buried here.

Mann Family (Mann Tract Road) - Hwy 636

| BAGBY Verna M. | 02 Sep. 1892 21 Dec. 1913 | | Yes |

Other Info: This headstone and footstone exactly match those in the Austin Family Cemetery located nearby.

MANN A. W.	03 Apr. 1857 17 Mar. 1924	Mann, Susan Ellen	Yes
MANN J. T.	17 Dec. 1888		Yes
MANN Lewis D.	31 May 1901 09 June 1958	Mann, Mildred T. C.	Yes

Inscription: Footstone inscribed: "L.D.M."

Other Info: Shares a headstone with his wife.

| MANN Massie Watson | 08 Jan. 1890 30 Dec. 1940 | | Yes |

LAST NAME First Name	Date of Birth Date of Death Age at Death	Maiden Name Spouse	Tombstone

Inscription: "He Was the Sunshine Of Our Home." Footstone inscribed: "M.W.M."

| MANN Mildred T. | 14 Oct. 1908 27 Aug. 1988 | Coleman Mann, Lewis D. | Yes |

Inscription: Footstone inscribed: "Mildred T. Coleman October 14, 1908 August 27, 1988."

Other Info: Shares a headstone with her husband.

| MANN Robert E. | 11 Apr. 1895 13 July 1945 | | Yes |

Inscription: Robert E. served as inscribed: "Virginia CPL 518 Inf. 80 Div. "

| MANN S. E. | 16 Sep. 1866 18 June 1937 70 yr. 09 mo. | Mann, A. W. | Yes |

Other Info: Grave is also marked by a funeral home metal marker inscribed: "Mrs. Susan Ellen Mann Died June 18, 1937 70 yrs. 9 mos. __ dys. J. Dunkum & Bro. Funeral Directors."

| PETTIE James U. | 03 Dec. 1875 09 Jan. 1936 | Pettie, Minnie M. | Yes |

Inscription: Footstone inscribed: "J.U.P."

Other Info: Shares a headstone with his wife.

| PETTIE Mary O. | 22 Dec. 1925 21 June 1931 | | Yes |

Inscription: Footstone inscribed: "M.O.P."

| PETTIE Minnie M. | 30 Oct. 1884 26 Feb. 1962 | Pettie, James U. | Yes |

Inscription: Footstone inscribed: "M.M.P."

Other Info: Shares a headstone with her husband.

| SIMPSON Carrie | 21 June 1907 09 Feb. 1962 | Mann | Yes |

Inscription: "Mother." Footstone inscribed: "C.M.S."

Maxey - G. W. Maxey Family - Hwy 705

| AGEE Georgie Ellen | 27 Sep. 1890 1903 - 1910 | | No |

LAST NAME	Date of Birth	Maiden Name	Tombstone
First Name	Date of Death	Spouse	
	Age at Death		

Other Info: Daughter of Robert M. and Nannie L. Maxey Agee. Nannie Maxey Agee was the daughter of G.W. and M.J.F. Maxey and sister of George Albert Maxey. Either two or three other infants of R. M. and N. L. M. Agee are buried at this cemetery also.

| HARRIS | 21 Oct. 1858 | Maxey | No |
| Mary Ellen | 27 Oct. 1885 | | |

Other Info: Daughter of G.W. and M.J.F. Maxey.

| HARRIS | 03 Aug. 1876 | | No |
| Mary Lula | 22 Dec. 1891 | | |

Other Info: Daughter of Mary Ellen M. Harris.

| MAXEY | 03 Oct. 1827 | | No |
| George William | 30 Dec. 1890 | Maxey, Mary Jane F. | |

Other Info: Son of Abraham Maxey. This cemetery was destroyed. All information was given by a great-granddaughter of the family.

| MAXEY | 18 Oct. 1863 | | No |
| James Ballard "Ball" | 1930s | | |

Other Info: Son of G. W. and M.J.F. Maxey.

| MAXEY | 23 June 1823 | Ferguson | No |
| Mary Jane | 19 June 1903 | Maxey, George William | |

McKinney/Jones Family Slave Cemetery - Hwy 636 (at New Store)

HARRIS			Yes
Lucy Jane (Mrs.)	25 May 1935		
	62 yr.		

Other Info: After the 1860s, this cemetery continued to be used as a black community cemetery.

| WOODSON | | | Yes |
| Coleman | 13 June 1937 | | |

Inscription: "At Rest."

Other Info: After the 1860s, this cemetery continued to be used as a black community cemetery.

LAST NAME	Date of Birth	Maiden Name	Tombstone
First Name	Date of Death	Spouse	
	Age at Death		

Miller Family/Poor House Farm - Hwy 659

COBBS
Sue
No

Other Info: Grave marked by fieldstones only.

HACKETT
Milly
No

Other Info: Grave marked by fieldstones only.

MILLER   1823 (circa)
Catharine   Miller, William Thomas
No

Other Info: Known to be buried here beside her husband. Graves marked by fieldstones only.

MILLER   1815 (circa)
William Thomas   Miller, Catharine
No

Other Info: General location of this cemetery is known. Graves marked by fieldstones only.

STATON
Ellen
No

Other Info: Grave marked by fieldstones only.

WOMACK (Mr.)
No

Other Info: Grave marked by fieldstones only.

Mt. Zion Baptist Church - Hwy 610

AGEE   1862
Francis Lee   1943   Agee, Irene Dunkum
Yes

Other Info: Shares a headstone with his wife.

AGEE   1860   Dunkum
Irene   1936   Agee, Francis Lee
Yes

Other Info: Shares a headstone with her husband.

AGEE   13 Sep. 1855   Dunkum
Susie Putney   03 Apr. 1913   Agee, L. R.
Yes

Inscription: "The Lord Is My Shepherd. In Memory of ... Wife of L. R. Agee. None Knew Thee But To Love Thee."

ANDERSON   02 Nov. 1918
Andrew W.   11 Aug. 1919
Yes

LAST NAME First Name	Date of Birth Date of Death Age at Death	Maiden Name Spouse	Tombstone

Inscription: "Son of T. B. & Virginia Anderson."

Other Info: Shares a headstone with his brother, Herbert.

ANDERSON Bessie	31 Aug. 1894 14 May 1972		Yes
ANDERSON Brenda P.	31 Jan. 1938 08 Apr. 1938		Yes
ANDERSON Ella	13 May 1853 25 Aug. 1925	Boatwright Anderson, John W.	Yes

Inscription: "Our Mother. Her Christian Influence Still Lives."

ANDERSON Fannie D.	1889 1968	Anderson, Herbert B.	Yes

Other Info: Shares a headstone with her husband.

ANDERSON Hazel Martin	08 July 1925 12 Sep. 1993	Anderson, William Bryant	Yes
ANDERSON Herbert B.	1884 1972	Anderson, Fannie D.	Yes

Other Info: Shares a headstone with his wife.

ANDERSON Herbert M.	11 Dec. 1911 23 Apr. 1913		Yes

Inscription: "Son of T. B. & Virginia Anderson."

Other Info: Shares a headstone with his brother, Andrew.

ANDERSON Irma	11 June 1918 22 Mar. 1986	Bickford Anderson, Robert B.	Yes

Inscription: "Mother. In God's Care."

ANDERSON Jennie	20 July 1859 30 Mar. 1945	Goodman Anderson, Oly Louis	Yes

Other Info: Shares a headstone with her husband.

ANDERSON John P. Jr.	20 May 1916 14 Mar. 1982		Yes

Inscription: "Your Memory Is Dear To Us."

ANDERSON John Penick	26 Apr. 1888 05 Jan. 1969	Anderson, Lucy Wootten	Yes

Other Info: Shares a headstone with his wife.

LAST NAME First Name	Date of Birth Date of Death Age at Death	Maiden Name Spouse	Tombstone
ANDERSON John W.	03 June 1851 15 Jan. 1897	 Anderson, Ella Boatwright	Yes

Inscription: "Father. Prepared To Meet God." (Masonic Symbol)

ANDERSON Lucy	18 Jan. 1890 06 Oct. 1960	Wootten Anderson, John Penick	Yes

Other Info: Shares a headstone with her husband.

ANDERSON Luther A.	1900 1959		No

Other Info: Grave marked by a funeral home metal marker.

ANDERSON Maitland Hilston	1913 1914		Yes

Inscription: "Baby."

ANDERSON Mary Ellen	15 May 1893 16 Oct. 1985		Yes

Inscription: "God Is Love."

ANDERSON Nannie Louise	01 Sep. 1889 30 June 1969		Yes

Inscription: "At Home With Her Lord."

ANDERSON O. W.	21 Sep. 1896 17 Feb. 1919		Yes

Inscription: "Our Son. He Was Ever Ready To Do His Best."

ANDERSON Oly Louis	10 Sep. 1853 13 Apr. 1941	 Anderson, Jennie Goodman	Yes

Other Info: Shares a headstone with his wife.

ANDERSON Robert B.	05 July 1911 20 Jan. 1989	 Anderson, Irma B.	Yes

Inscription: "Father. In God's Care."

ANDERSON Sallie	1860 1934	Harris	Yes

Inscription: "Mother."

ANDERSON Stuart Granville	03 Aug. 1929 25 Oct. 1990	 Anderson, Shelva Jean Christian	Yes

ANDERSON Thomas Bernice	26 Feb. 1877 24 Nov. 1955	 Anderson, Virginia Davis	Yes

LAST NAME	Date of Birth	Maiden Name	Tombstone
First Name	Date of Death	Spouse	
	Age at Death		

Inscription: "To Live In Hearts We Leave Behind Is Not To Die."

Other Info: Shares a headstone with his wife.

| ANDERSON | 08 Oct. 1909 | | Yes |
| Vera Preston | 08 Apr. 1983 | | |

Inscription: "Wife of Carl Fredrick Mertz MI, William Joseph Beall LA, Elias Athol Butler VA. "

| ANDERSON | 02 Nov. 1877 | Davis | Yes |
| Virginia | 27 Dec. 1963 | Anderson, Thomas Bernice | |

Inscription: "To Live In Hearts We Leave Behind Is Not To Die."

Other Info: Shares a headstone with her husband.

| APPERSON | 02 Dec. 1879 | Anderson | Yes |
| Ada | 05 Apr. 1954 | Apperson, Lemuel W. Sr. | |

Other Info: Shares a headstone with her husband.

| APPERSON | 23 Apr. 1868 | | Yes |
| Braxton Lee Sr. | 03 Nov. 1963 | Apperson, Ruby A. | |

Inscription: On the back of the headstone is inscribed: "Father & Mother of: Braxton Lee Jr., Samuel Wertley, Ruby Pearl. Made by Edward Wayne Apperson Grandson."

Other Info: Shares a headstone with his wife.

| APPERSON | | | Yes |
| (Infant Boy) | 13 Feb. 1914 | | |

| APPERSON | 28 Jan. 1910 | | Yes |
| John Werna | 20 June 1910 | | |

| APPERSON | 31 July 1875 | | Yes |
| Lemuel W. Sr. | 10 July 1958 | Apperson, Ada Anderson | |

Other Info: Shares a headstone with his wife.

| APPERSON | 26 Sep. 1918 | | Yes |
| Lemuel Wertley Jr. | 01 Sep. 1993 | Apperson, Dorothy Whitlow | |

| APPERSON | 15 Apr. 1908 | Apperson | Yes |
| Ruby | 15 June 1987 | Apperson, Braxton Lee Sr. | |

Inscription: On the back of the headstone is inscribed: "Father & Mother of Braxton Lee Jr., Samuel Wertley, Ruby Pearl Made By Edward Wayne Apperson Grandson."

Other Info: Shares a headstone with her husband.

LAST NAME First Name	Date of Birth Date of Death Age at Death	Maiden Name Spouse	Tombstone
APPERSON Virginia T.	15 Dec. 1863 04 May 1925	Apperson, B. L.	Yes

Inscription: "Wife of B. L. Apperson. Blessed Are the Pure In Heart For They Shall See God."

APPERSON Winnie H.	02 Dec. 1842 18 Mar. 1922	Apperson, B. L.	Yes

Inscription: "Death Is Eternal Life. Why Should We Weep? Stand Up For Jesus. Wife of B. L. Apperson."

BABER Agness	24 Mar. 1882 19 July 1925	Baber, W. H.	Yes

Inscription: " Wife of ... She Was A Kind and Affectionate Wife, A Fond Mother and A Friend To All."

BABER Mary Jane	21 Feb. 1880 01 June 1955		Yes

Inscription: "Gone, But Not Forgotten."

BABER William H.	26 Oct. 1872 29 May 1952	Baber, Agness	Yes

Inscription: "We Will Gather At the River."

BAGBY Callie P.	1895 1979		Yes

BAGBY Loniel (sic) B.	1891 1969		Yes

BAILEY Edward M.	1873 1937	Bailey, Elizabeth E.	Yes

Inscription: "Let Our Father's Will Be Done."

Other Info: Shares a headstone with his wife.

BAILEY Elizabeth E.	1864 19__	Bailey, Edward M.	Yes

Inscription: "Let Our Father's Will Be Done."

Other Info: Shares a headstone with her husband. Her death date was never inscribed on this headstone.

BELCHER Jimper B.	01 Oct. 1901 21 Feb. 1978		Yes

BERSCH John Christian	1846 1930	Bersch, Virginia Dunkum	Yes

LAST NAME First Name	Date of Birth Date of Death Age at Death	Maiden Name Spouse	Tombstone

Inscription: A second tombstone shows he served as inscribed: "John Christian Bersch Co B 18th VA Reg. C.S.A."

Other Info: Shares a headstone with his wife.

| BERSCH
Virginia | 1853
1914 | Dunkum
Bersch, John Christian | Yes |

Other Info: Shares a headstone with her husband.

| BICKFORD
Bobby | 22 Nov. 1929
13 Feb. 1966 | | Yes |

Inscription: "This Is the Promise the Life Everlasting." Footstone inscribed: "Father."

| BICKFORD
Debbie T. | 20 Feb. 1960
09 May 1990 | | Yes |

Inscription: "In Loving Memory..."

| BICKFORD
Dovie C. | 13 Jan. 1895
11 Aug. 1962 | | Yes |

Inscription: "Faith Is the Victory.' Footstone inscribed: "Mother."

| BICKFORD
James Oral | 1921
1985 | Bickford, Louise Davidson | Yes |

Inscription: "In God's Care."

| BICKFORD
Vernon E. | 17 Aug. 1920
06 May 1960 | | Yes |

Inscription: "There Will Be Peace In the Valley For Me." Footstone inscribed: "Son."

| BLACKWELL
Emmett Lee | 15 Feb. 1872
06 Dec. 1956 | | Yes |

| BOATWRIGHT
Annie Elizabeth | 10 Aug. 1845
12 July 1934 | Sibley
Boatwright, Wm. G. | Yes |

Inscription: "Our Mother. Wife of Wm. G. Boatwright. Peace, Perfect Peace."

| BOATWRIGHT
Benjamin S. | 21 June 1877
08 May 1968 | Boatwright, Edna Marion | Yes |

Inscription: "Resting In Hope Of A Glorius (sic) Resorection (sic)."

| BOATWRIGHT
Carlton F. | 1906
1972 | | Yes |

| BOATWRIGHT
Edna | 11 Feb. 1875
18 Apr. 1966 | Marion
Boatwright, Benjamin S. | Yes |

LAST NAME First Name	Date of Birth Date of Death Age at Death	Maiden Name Spouse	Tombstone
	Inscription: "At Rest With the Lord."		
BOATWRIGHT Ellen J.	23 Sep. 1844 08 Jan. 1928	Hudgins Boatwright, P. P.	Yes

Inscription: "Wife of P. P. Boatwright. There Remaineth A Rest For the Children Of God."

| BOATWRIGHT
Eva | 01 Apr. 1886
05 Aug. 1976 | Anderson
Boatwright, George Carlton | Yes |

Inscription: "Blessed Are They That Die In the Lord Rev. 14:13."

Other Info: Shares a headstone with her husband.

| BOATWRIGHT
George Carlton | 06 July 1871
16 Apr. 1962 | Boatwright, Eva Anderson | Yes |

Inscription: "Blessed Are They That Die In the Lord Rev 14:13."

Other Info: Shares a headstone with his wife.

BOATWRIGHT Grace Leolene	23 July 1880 03 Oct. 1942		Yes
BOATWRIGHT James Franklin	20 July 1920 22 Sep. 1973		Yes
BOATWRIGHT Norma	07 Mar. 1913 26 Oct. 1979	Putney Boatwright, Reuben Curtis	Yes
BOATWRIGHT P. P.	21 July 1846 05 Mar. 1930	Boatwright, Ellen J. H.	Yes

Inscription: "Prepare To Meet Thy God." Footstone shows he served as inscribed: "Sgt. P. P. Boatwright Co C 3 Regt. VA. Res. C.S.A."

| BOGGS
Clarence W. | 21 Apr. 1901
18 Oct. 1973 | Boggs, Kathleen Taylor | Yes |
| BREED
George Frederick | 25 Aug. 1929
29 Nov. 1977 | Breed, Jeanne Riddle | Yes |

Inscription: "Together Forever."

| BROOKS
Florence | 23 Dec. 1886
24 Oct. 1978 | Boatwright | Yes |
| BROWN
Amanda M. | 10 June 1830
15 Dec. 1919 | | Yes |

Inscription: "Died ... In Lynchburg. Her End Was Peace."

| BRYANT
Andrew J. | 1858
1942 | Bryant, Bettie G. | Yes |

LAST NAME First Name	Date of Birth Date of Death Age at Death	Maiden Name Spouse	Tombstone

Inscription: "From the Red House Farm."

Other Info: Shares a headstone with his wife.

BRYANT Bettie G.	1868 1957	Bryant, Andrew J.	Yes

Inscription: "From the Red House Farm."

Other Info: Shares a headstone with her husband.

BRYANT "Pelham"	1935 1948		Yes

Other Info: Engraving of a dog's head. This is the grave of the pet dog of Andrew and Bettie Bryant.

BRYANT Richard L. Sr.	29 Dec. 1909 11 Sep. 1992	Bryant, Verna Stinson	Yes

Other Info: Shares a headstone with his wife.

BRYANT Thomas William	28 Nov. 1932 15 Feb. 1979		Yes

Inscription: He served as inscribed: "SP4 US Army Korea."

BRYANT Verna	27 Oct. 1913 20 May 1972	Stinson Bryant, Richard L. Sr.	Yes

Other Info: Shares a headstone with her husband.

BUTLER Elias Athol	12 Dec. 1896 13 Jan. 1967	Anderson, Vera Preston	Yes

CANN Mary Anderson	08 Dec. 1889 27 Apr. 1980		Yes

CARRINGTON Robert Bernard	20 Oct. 1917 27 May 1974	Carrington, Estelle Mahon	Yes

CARTER Alice W.	16 Sep. 1858 28 Apr. 1928		Yes

Inscription: Footstone inscribed: "A.W.C."

CARTER Gay Bradley	11 Nov. 1871 24 July 1965		Yes

CARTER James H.	15 July 1824 28 Dec. 1908	Carter, Mary B.	Yes

Inscription: Footstone shows he served as inscribed: "James H. Carter Co K 4 VA CAV C.S.A."

LAST NAME First Name	Date of Birth Date of Death Age at Death	Maiden Name Spouse	Tombstone
CARTER M. Eddie	16 Oct. 1853 13 July 1929		Yes
CARTER Mary B.	15 July 1828 10 Jan. 1912	Carter, James H.	Yes

Inscription: Footstone inscribed: "M.B.C."

CASE Ann D.	27 Apr. 1863 17 June 1875		Yes

Inscription: "Little Desie"

CASE Tatum			Yes

Other Info: No dates inscribed on this headstone.

CAVE Bessie	30 Aug. 1902 19 Dec. 1985	Hurt Cave, Charles Wesley	Yes

Other Info: Shares a headstone with her husband.

CAVE Charles Wesley	11 Mar. 1901 06 Jan. 1976	Cave, Bessie Hurt	Yes

Other Info: Shares a headstone with his wife.

CHILDRESS Albert K.	07 Oct. 1899 14 Jan. 1970	Childress, Mayme N.	Yes

Other Info: Shares a headstone with his wife.

CHILDRESS Maree			Yes

Inscription: "I Am the Resurrection and the Life."

Other Info: No dates are inscribed on this headstone. Shares a headstone with Princess Childress.

CHILDRESS Mayme N.	19 Sep. 1903 21 Feb. 1982	Childress, Albert K.	Yes

Other Info: Shares a headstone with her husband.

CHILDRESS Princess			Yes

Inscription: "I Am the Resurrection and the Life."

Other Info: Shares a headstone with Maree Childress.

CHILDRESS Walter F.	14 June 1920 18 Oct. 1993		Yes

LAST NAME First Name	Date of Birth Date of Death Age at Death	Maiden Name Spouse	Tombstone

Inscription: He served as inscribed: "CoX US Navy World War II."

CHILDRESS Wealthia	11 Mar. 1886 15 Apr. 1967	Davis Childress, William Thomas	Yes

Inscription: "This Is the Promise, the Life Everlasting."

Other Info: Shares a headstone with her husband.

CHILDRESS William Harrison	1922 1968		Yes

CHILDRESS William Thomas	25 Apr. 1886 03 Dec. 1955	Childress, Wealthia Davis	Yes

Inscription: "This Is the Promise, the Life Everlasting."

Other Info: Shares a headstone with his wife.

CHRISTIAN C. Viola	17 Sep. 1905 03 Feb. 1986	Christian, G. Norman	Yes

Other Info: Shares a headstone with her husband.

CHRISTIAN Clarice H.	10 Aug. 1912 06 Jan. 1994	Christian, John M.	Yes

Inscription: "Our Precious Mother."

Other Info: Grave is also marked by a funeral home metal marker inscribed: "Clarice Boatwright 1912-1994 Age 81 yr."

CHRISTIAN G. Norman	22 Oct. 1905 07 Nov. 1963	Christian, C. Viola	Yes

Inscription: Footstone inscribed: "Father."

Other Info: Shares a headstone with his wife.

CHRISTIAN James Oscar	09 Oct. 1891 29 Apr. 1939	Christian, Nellie Davis	Yes

Inscription: "In God's Care."

Other Info: Shares a headstone with his wife.

CHRISTIAN John M.	21 June 1910 14 July 1954	Christian, Clarice H.	Yes

Inscription: "This Is the Promise the Life Everlasting."

CHRISTIAN Laura C.	1888 1975	Christian, Thomas L.	Yes

Other Info: Shares a headstone with her husband.

LAST NAME First Name	Date of Birth Date of Death Age at Death	Maiden Name Spouse	Tombstone
CHRISTIAN Lillian Hudgins	29 Mar. 1896 07 June 1927		Yes
CHRISTIAN Nellie	28 Apr. 1889 02 Aug. 1960	Davis Christian, James Oscar	Yes

Inscription: "In God's Care."

Other Info: Shares a headstone with her husband.

CHRISTIAN Thomas Ashby	1908 1923		Yes

Inscription: Footstone inscribed: "T.A.C."

CHRISTIAN Thomas L.	1880 1939	Christian, Laura C.	Yes

Other Info: Shares a headstone with his wife.

CLAYTON John Stuart	15 Aug. 1910 05 Dec. 1989		Yes
COLE A. P.	23 Nov. 1837 19 Sep. 1917	Cole, Cornelia B.	Yes

Inscription: "Father. Native of Smyth Co., VA. Asleep In Jesus."

COLE Andrew Howard	12 June 1882 03 Jan. 1970		Yes
COLE Cornelia	13 Apr. 1845 07 Aug. 1931	Boatwright Cole, A. P.	Yes
COLE Edward Sidney Sr.	25 Aug. 1885 22 Jan. 1949	Cole, Grace West	Yes

Other Info: Shares a headstone with his wife, and his brother, T. W. Cole.

COLE Estelle Mahon	08 Nov. 1887 12 Jan. 1968		Yes
COLE Grace	26 July 1896 08 Dec. 1979	West Cole, Edward Sidney Sr.	Yes

Other Info: Shares a headstone with her husband and her husband's brother.

COLE Thomas William			Yes

Inscription: "Brother."

Other Info: No dates inscribed on the tombstone for T. W. Cole. Shares a headstone with Edward S. Cole, Sr. and his wife, Grace West Cole.

LAST NAME First Name	Date of Birth Date of Death Age at Death	Maiden Name Spouse	Tombstone
DANIEL John William	02 May 1898 02 Feb. 1965	Daniel, Willis Alice	Yes

Other Info: Shares a headstone with his wife.

DANIEL Willis Alice	22 July 1906	Daniel, John William	Yes

Inscription: "Willie."

Other Info: Shares a headstone with her husband.

DAVIDSON John I.	16 May 1894 18 Mar. 1973	Davidson, Sarah B.	Yes

Inscription: Footstone shows he served as inscribed: "Virginia PVT US Army World War I."

Other Info: Shares a headstone with his wife.

DAVIDSON Sarah B.	05 June 1904 29 July 1979	Davidson, John I.	Yes

Other Info: Shares a headstone with her husband.

DAVIDSON William H.			Yes

Other Info: No dates inscribed on this headstone.

DAVIES Carl Wm.	1907 1992		Yes

DAVIS Annie E.	26 Dec. 1871 06 Feb. 1904		Yes

Inscription: "In Memory of ... She Is Not Dead But Sleepeth."

DAVIS Edna	1897 1975	Christian Davis, Frank Lee	Yes

Inscription: "Mother."

Other Info: Shares a headstone with her husband.

DAVIS Edward Melvin	14 Sep. 1902 15 Mar. 1905		Yes

DAVIS Frank Lee	1891 1958	Davis, Edna Christian	Yes

Inscription: "Father." Footstone shows he served as inscribed: "Virginia PVT US Army World War I."

Other Info: Shares a headstone with his wife.

LAST NAME	Date of Birth	Maiden Name	Tombstone
First Name	Date of Death	Spouse	
	Age at Death		

DAVIS
George F.   Davis, Willie A.   Yes

Inscription: He served as inscribed: "Co C 44th VA Reg. C.S.A."

Other Info: No dates inscribed on this headstone.

DAVIS   12 Sep. 1902   Yes
Grafton Gates   26 Jan. 1981

Inscription: He served as inscribed: "PVT. US Army World War II."

DAVIS   18 Feb. 1871   Painter   Yes
Hettie   10 May 1964   Davis, Jefferson

Inscription: Footstone inscribed: "Mother."

Other Info: Shares a headstone with her husband, her daughter, W. D. Hooe, and her son, S. F. Davis."

DAVIS   14 Sep. 1853   Yes
Janie M. Mrs.   20 June 1894   Davis, William A.

Inscription: "In Memory of ... Take The Bible For Your Guide."

DAVIS   03 Mar. 1861   Yes
Jefferson   12 Dec. 1922   Davis, Hettie Painter

Inscription: Footstone inscribed: "Father."

Other Info: Shares a headstone with his wife, a daughter, W. D. Hooe, and his son, S. F. Davis.

DAVIS   1938   Yes
Jerry Leroy   1940

Inscription: "Our Son."

DAVIS   1911   Yes
John Thomas   1992   Davis, Mae Snoddy

Inscription: Footstone shows he served as inscribed: "John T. Davis PVT US Army World War II."

DAVIS   19 Apr. 1881   Yes
Katie F.   29 May 1955   Davis, Merrill K.

Inscription: "Earth Has No Sorrow That Heaven Cannot Heal."

Other Info: Shares a headstone with her husband.

DAVIS   12 Feb. 1882   Yes
Leslie L.   23 Apr. 1959   Davis, Mattie D.

Inscription: "Married April 27, 1915."

LAST NAME First Name	Date of Birth Date of Death Age at Death	Maiden Name Spouse	Tombstone

Other Info: Shares a headstone with his wife.

| DAVIS
Mary F. | 1872
1963 | | Yes |

Inscription: "Asleep In Jesus."

| DAVIS
Mattie D. | 10 Jan. 1892
19 Feb. 1964 | Davis, Leslie L. | Yes |

Inscription: "Married April 27, 1915."

Other Info: Shares a headstone with her husband.

| DAVIS
Melvin L. | 27 June 1870
09 Feb. 1905 | | Yes |

| DAVIS
Merrill K. | 20 Oct. 1879
09 Dec. 1969 | Davis, Katie F. | Yes |

Inscription: "Earth Has No Sorrow That Heaven Cannot Heal."

Other Info: Shares a headstone with his wife.

| DAVIS
Nancy C. | 1896
1969 | Davis, William J. | Yes |

Other Info: Shares a headstone with her husband.

| DAVIS
Ora | 09 May 1910
28 Nov. 1984 | Newton
Davis, Roy Mahlon | Yes |

Inscription: "Mother. Married Apr. 4, 1929."

Other Info: Shares a headstone with her husband.

| DAVIS
Roy Mahlon | 14 Sep. 1896
28 Nov. 1979 | Davis, Ora Newton | Yes |

Inscription: "Father. Married Apr. 4, 1929."

| DAVIS
Russell L. | 1881
1949 | | Yes |

| DAVIS
Samuel Rufus | 09 July 1902
01 Dec. 1930 | | Yes |

Inscription: Footstone inscribed: "Son."

Other Info: Shares a headstone with his father and mother, Jefferson and Hettie P. Davis, and his sister, W. D. Hooe."

| DAVIS
Wesley Thompson | Nov. 1958 | | Yes |

LAST NAME First Name	Date of Birth Date of Death Age at Death	Maiden Name Spouse	Tombstone
	Other Info: Grave also marked with a funeral home metal marker inscribed: "Wesley T. Davis 1958-1958."		
DAVIS William A.	08 Oct. 1842 29 July 1909	Davis, Janie M.	Yes
	Inscription: "In Loving Memory Of ... Father. A Devoted Husband and Father. Bless My Little Children, Bless Every One Of Their Dear Hearts. I Want You All To Meet Me In Heaven. At Rest."		
DAVIS William J.	1887 1933	Davis, Nancy C.	Yes
	Inscription: Footstone inscribed: "W.J.D."		
	Other Info: Shares a headstone with his wife.		
DAVIS Willie A.	14 May 1844 03 Feb. 1903	Davis, George F.	Yes
	Inscription: "In Memory of ... A Dutiful Wife and Parent. Christ Became the First Fruits Of Them That Slept. 1 Cor. XV 15."		
DEANE Edythe Mae	05 Aug. 1917 27 June 1938		Yes
DEANE Joseph T.	24 Oct. 1917 30 Sep. 1992		Yes
	Inscription: He served as inscribed: "PVT US Army World War II."		
DEANE Lillian	19 Oct. 1891 19 July 1973	Johnson Deane, Myrtle Emmett	Yes
	Other Info: Shares a headstone with her husband.		
DEANE Myrtle Emmett	26 Apr. 1886 21 Jan. 1980	Deane, Lillian Johnson	Yes
	Other Info: Shares a headstone with his wife.		
DUNKUM S. Willie	17 Apr. 1857 08 Jan. 1883		Yes
	Inscription: "In Memory Of Our Darling Sister Willie. Though Gone, Yet Not Forgotten. Asleep In Jesus."		
FISHER Ella T.	01 Dec. 1907 16 Aug. 1978		Yes
	Inscription: "Mother."		
FLIPPEN Edward Wesley	29 May 1882 17 Sep. 1946	Flippen, Edward Wesley	Yes

LAST NAME First Name	Date of Birth Date of Death Age at Death	Maiden Name Spouse	Tombstone

Inscription: "Loving Memory of ... In God's Care."

| FLIPPEN
Mariah C. | 28 Sep. 1891
07 July 1963 | | Yes |

Inscription: "Loving Memory Of ..."

| FLIPPEN
Nettie F. | 22 Jan. 1892
13 Feb. 1916 | Flippen, Edward Wesley | Yes |

Inscription: "To My Wife ... A Tender Mother and A Faithful Friend."

| FLURRY
Blanch L. | 18 Aug. 1913
28 Aug. 1987 | Flurry, John H. | Yes |

Inscription: "Nearer My God To Thee."

| GENTRY
A. Estelle Mrs. | 25 Feb. 1881
05 June 1903 | | Yes |

Inscription: "In Memory Of ... Meet Me In Heaven."

| GOODE
Martha J. | 1852
1927 | Goode, Wm. J. C. | Yes |

Inscription: Footstone inscribed: "M.J.G."

Other Info: Shares a headstone with her husband.

| GOODE
Wm. J. C. | 1848
1927 | Goode, Martha J. | Yes |

Inscription: Foostone inscribed: "Wm. J. C. G." A second stone inscribed: "William J. C. Goode Co. 1 1st VA Reg. C.S.A."

Other Info: Shares a headstone with his wife.

| GOODMAN
Ada | 1872
1956 | Toler
Goodman, Edward A. | Yes |

Inscription: "Mother."

Other Info: Shares a headstone with her husband; also with a daughter and son - Ava G. and L. Layton Goodman.

| GOODMAN
Ava G. | 1895
1935 | | Yes |

Inscription: "Daughter."

Other Info: Shares a headstone with her father and mother, Edward A. and Ada T. Goodman; also with her brother, L. Layton Goodman.

| GOODMAN
Edward A. | 1868
1935 | Goodman, Ada Toler | Yes |

LAST NAME	Date of Birth	Maiden Name	Tombstone
First Name	Date of Death	Spouse	
	Age at Death		

Inscription: "Father."

Other Info: Shares a headstone with his wife; also with his daughter, Ava G. and a son, L. Layton Goodman.

| GOODMAN | 1908 | | Yes |
| L. Layton | 1962 | | |

Inscription: "Son."

Other Info: Shares a headstone with his father and mother, Edward A. and Ada T. Goodman; also with his sister, Ava G. Goodman.

| GOODMAN | 30 Apr. 1858 | | Yes |
| M. W. | 21 Aug. 1927 | Goodman, Nannie F. | |

Other Info: Shares a headstone with his wife.

| GOODMAN | 08 Feb. 1859 | | Yes |
| Nannie F. | 03 Feb. 1953 | Goodman, M. W. | |

Other Info: Shares a headstone with her husband.

| HANRAHAN | 19 Feb. 1907 | | Yes |
| Charles Patrick | 05 Dec. 1992 | | |

Inscription: (Masonic Symbol)

Other Info: Grave also marked by a funeral home metal marker.

| HARDING | 26 Mar. 1905 | Garrett | Yes |
| Bessie | 28 Feb. 1983 | Harding, Lawrence W. | |

Other Info: Shares a headstone with her husband.

| HARDING | 10 Mar. 1886 | | Yes |
| Comma C. | 08 May 1974 | Harding, John W. | |

Inscription: Footstone inscribed: "C.C.H."

Other Info: Shares a headstone with her husband.

| HARDING | 15 Apr. 1875 | | Yes |
| John W. | 04 May 1958 | Harding, Comma C. | |

Inscription: Footstone inscribed: "J.W.H."

Other Info: Shares a headstone with his wife.

| HARDING | 14 May 1905 | | Yes |
| Lawrence W. | 18 Sep. 1987 | Harding, Bessie Garrett | |

Other Info: Shares a headstone with his wife.

LAST NAME First Name	Date of Birth Date of Death Age at Death	Maiden Name Spouse	Tombstone
HARRIS Julian Newton	09 Jan. 1905 03 Mar. 1989		Yes
HARRIS R. W.	15 Sep. 1863 12 Sep. 1899		Yes

Inscription: "He Died At His Post."

HARRISON Janie Thompson	11 Dec. 1876 01 Jan. 1981		Yes
HAYDEN Edna H.	1904 1937	Hayden, John W.	Yes

Inscription: "The Faithful Are Certain Of Their Reward."

Other Info: Shares a headstone with her husband.

HAYDEN John W.	1901	Hayden, Edna H.	Yes

Inscription: "The Faithful Are Certain Of Their Reward."

Other Info: Shares a headstone with his wife.

HERNDON Henry W.	17 June 1923 10 Aug. 1951		Yes
HERNDON Joan Hawkins	1925 1995		No

Other Info: Grave marked by a funeral home metal marker.

HERNDON Rosa L.	08 May 1897 26 Nov. 1979	Herndon, T. Douglas	Yes

Inscription: "May They Rest In Peace."

Other Info: Shares a headstone with her husband.

HERNDON T. Douglas	03 Apr. 1886 28 Apr. 1948	Herndon, Rosa L.	Yes

Inscription: "Doubs." "May They Rest In Peace."

Other Info: Shares a headstone with his wife.

HODGES Jesse J.	06 Apr. 1911 13 July 1977	Hodges, Vearnie S.	Yes
HOOE Winnie	09 Apr. 1895 14 June 1971	Davis Hooe,	Yes

Inscription: Footstone inscribed: "Daughter."

LAST NAME First Name	Date of Birth Date of Death Age at Death	Maiden Name Spouse	Tombstone

Other Info: Shares a headstone with her father and mother, Jefferson and Hettie P. Davis, and her brother, S.F. Davis.

HUDGINS A. S.	04 Feb. 1842 03 Apr. 1901	Hudgins, Mary A.	Yes

Inscription: "In Memory of Father ..." He served as inscribed: "C.S.A. 1861 - 1865."

HUDGINS Abner Lee	01 Aug. 1880 08 Apr. 1956	Hudgins, Emma C.	Yes

Inscription: "Married Aug. 31, 1904. This Is the Promise, the Life Everlasting." Footstone inscribed: "Husband."

Other Info: Shares a headstone with his wife.

HUDGINS Alma	19 Dec. 1908 29 Sep. 1991	Martin Hudgins, Thomas Lee	Yes

Other Info: Shares a headstone with her husband.

HUDGINS Ashby H.	28 Aug. 1905 26 Dec. 1940		Yes

HUDGINS Bessie Lee	1892 1945	Patteson Hudgins, Reuben B.	Yes

Inscription: "Wife of Reuben B. Hudgins."

HUDGINS Blanche S.	1914 1992	Hudgins, Howard A.	Yes

Other Info: Shares a headstone with her husband.

HUDGINS Burley	07 Mar. 1904 03 Oct. 1962	Hudgins, Cassie L.	Yes

Inscription: Footstone inscribed: "Father."

Other Info: Shares a headstone with his wife.

HUDGINS Cassie L.	25 Dec. 1914 27 July 1993	Hudgins, Burley	Yes

Inscription: "Mother."

Other Info: Shares a headstone with her husband.

HUDGINS Edner Putney	01 Jan. 1873 06 Oct. 1937	Hudgins, Edna Lee	Yes

HUDGINS Eliza B.	10 Oct. 1830 09 Apr. 1908		Yes

LAST NAME	Date of Birth	Maiden Name	Tombstone
First Name	Date of Death	Spouse	
	Age at Death		

Inscription: "In Memory of ... Mother."

| HUDGINS | 01 Dec. 1883 | | Yes |
| Emma C. | 10 Dec. 1970 | Hudgins, Abner Lee | |

Inscription: "Married Aug. 31, 1904. This Is the Promise, the Life Everlasting." Footstone inscribed: "Wife."

Other Info: Shares a headstone with her husband.

| HUDGINS | 02 May 1898 | | Yes |
| Flossie B. | 12 Jan. 1989 | Hudgins, George R. | |

Inscription: "A Nurse. Widow of George R. Hudgins."

| HUDGINS | 1908 | | Yes |
| Howard A. | 1970 | Hudgins, Blanche S. | |

Other Info: Shares a headstone with his wife.

| HUDGINS | 21 Mar. 1915 | | Yes |
| L. Allison | 11 Oct. 1994 | Hudgins, Elizabeth B. | |

Inscription: He served as inscribed: " S. Sgt. US Army World War II."

| HUDGINS | 06 Apr. 1919 | Stinson | Yes |
| Lucille | 22 May 1990 | Hudgins, Woodrow | |

Inscription: "Mother. Married Apr. 15, 1937."

Other Info: Shares a headstone with her husband.

| HUDGINS | 25 Dec. 1852 | Wren | Yes |
| Lucy J. | 22 Feb. 1937 | Hudgins, Robert Henry | |

Inscription: " ... His wife. Yea, Though I Walk Through the Valley Of the Shadow of Death, I Will Fear No Evil; For Thou Are With Me; Thy Rod and Thy Staff They Comfort Me." Footstone inscribed: "L.J.H."

Other Info: Shares a headstone with her husband.

| HUDGINS | 01 July 1894 | Davis | Yes |
| Mary | 27 Feb. 1981 | Hudgins, Tom Henry | |

Inscription: "Till We Meet Again." Footstone inscribed: "Mother."

Other Info: Shares a headstone with her husband.

| HUDGINS | 19 Apr. 1840 | | Yes |
| Mary A. | 20 Sep. 1917 | Hudgins, A. S. | |

Inscription: "In Memory of ... Wife of ... Gone But Not Forgotten."

LAST NAME First Name	Date of Birth Date of Death Age at Death	Maiden Name Spouse	Tombstone
HUDGINS Milton F.	08 May 1860 12 Sep. 1893		Yes

Inscription: "Darling Thou Art Gone From Me Sleep Dear One Sleep. Though At Thy Grave I Kneel and Weep, It Is Sweet Dear One, To Know There Is Rest For Thee."

HUDGINS Nola Davis	05 Oct. 1878 10 Nov. 1954		Yes
HUDGINS Olive E.	1895 1984		Yes
HUDGINS R. B. Mr.	31 Mar. 1836 18 Sep. 1900	Hudgins, Sarah S.	Yes

Inscription: "Precious In the Sight Of the Lord Is the Death Of His Saints." Footstone inscribed: "R.B.H." A second stone shows that he served as inscribed: "Reuben B. Hudgins Co C 44 VA. INF C.S.A."

HUDGINS Reuben B. Sr.	1885 1975	Hudgins, Bessie L. P.	Yes

Other Info: Grave also marked by a funeral home metal marker.

HUDGINS Robert F.	1861 1946	Hudgins, Willie O.	Yes

Other Info: Shares a headstone with his wife.

HUDGINS Robert Henry	04 Feb. 1847 31 Oct. 1915	Hudgins, Lucy J. Wren	Yes

Inscription: "Yea, Though I Walk Through the Valley Of the Shadow Of Death, I Will Fear No Evil; For Thou Are With Me; Thy Rod and Thy Staff They Comfort Me." Footstone inscribed: "R.H.H."

Other Info: Shares a headstone with his wife.

HUDGINS Sarah S.	09 June 1842 14 Dec. 1929	Hudgins, R. B.	Yes

Inscription: "Mother. Wife of R. B. Hudgins. Tis Sweet To Be With Loved Ones Gone Before."

HUDGINS Thomas Harold	Feb. 1937 Dec. 1937		Yes

Inscription: "Son of Tommy and Alma Hudgins."

HUDGINS Thomas Lee	29 Oct. 1902 25 Jan. 1991	Hudgins, Alma Martin	Yes

Other Info: Shares a headstone with his wife.

LAST NAME First Name	Date of Birth Date of Death Age at Death	Maiden Name Spouse	Tombstone
HUDGINS Tom Henry	03 Aug. 1882 22 Oct. 1965	Hudgins, Mary Davis	Yes

Inscription: "We Will Meet Again." Footstone inscribed: "Father."

Other Info: Shares a headstone with his wife.

HUDGINS Willie O.	1871 1930	Hudgins, Robert F.	Yes

Other Info: Shares a headstone with her husband.

HUDGINS Willy Martain (sic)	27 Dec. 1907 12 Aug. 1918		Yes

Inscription: "Safely, Safely, Gathered In Far From Sorrow, Pain and Sin. God Knoweth Best." Footstone inscribed: "W.M.H."

HUDGINS Woodrow	10 Oct. 1914 29 Jan. 1978	Hudgins, Lucille Stinson	Yes

Inscription: "Jerry." "Father. Married Apr. 15, 1937."

Other Info: Shares a headstone with his wife.

HURT Minnie G.	11 Aug. 1874 23 May 1932	Hurt, Mitchell H.	Yes

Inscription: "She Was the Sunshine Of Our Home."

HURT Mitchell H.	28 May 1857 03 July 1928	Hurt, Minnie G.	Yes

Inscription: "There Is Rest In Heaven."

JACKSON Bessie	1896 1984	Thompson Jackson, James F.	Yes

Inscription: "In God's Care."

Other Info: Shares a headstone with her husband.

JACKSON James F.	1885 1932	Jackson, Bessie T.	Yes

Inscription: "In God's Care."

Other Info: Shares a headstone with his wife.

JAMERSON Andrew Lawrence	23 July 1903 06 Nov. 1966	Jamerson, Ruby Harris	Yes

Other Info: Shares a headstone with his wife.

LAST NAME First Name	Date of Birth Date of Death Age at Death	Maiden Name Spouse	Tombstone
JAMERSON Ruby	19 Sep. 1909 20 May 1990	Harris Jamerson, Andrew Lawrence	Yes

Other Info: Shares a headstone with her husband.

JOHNSON Goode W.	26 Aug. 1887 24 May 1958		Yes
JOHNSON James W.	10 Oct. 1955 07 Nov. 1962		Yes

Inscription: "Bubs."

JOHNSON Janette Glenn	06 Apr. 1923 26 June 1993	Johnson, Maynard Kenneth	Yes
JOHNSON Joseph R.	05 Nov. 1851 10 Jan. 1900		Yes

Inscription: "In Memory of ... We Shall Meet Beyond the Skies Some Sweet Day, Some Sweet Day." Footstone inscribed: "J.R.J."

JOHNSON Louise M.	14 May 1904 09 Nov. 1979		Yes
JOHNSON Nannie	06 Sep. 1864 19 Dec. 1931	Griffith	Yes

Inscription: "Our Mother ... She Kept The Faith."

JOHNSON Robert H.	29 Nov. 1811 11 Dec. 1897		Yes

Inscription: "Father, At Rest..." Foostone inscribed: "R.H.J."

Other Info: Headstone is signed at bottom as inscribed: " J. L. Miller & Co."

JONES Betty H.	04 Dec. 1884 13 Apr. 1965	Jones, Samuel L.	Yes

Inscription: Footstone inscribed: "Mother."

Other Info: Shares a headstone with her husband.

JONES Clifford Avington	23 Sep. 1901 19 Dec. 1992	Jones, Annie Davis	Yes

Inscription: "Married 65 years."

JONES Edward Avington	10 Mar. 1880 07 June 1955		Yes
JONES John Robert	1911 1991	Jones, Katherine A.	Yes

LAST NAME First Name	Date of Birth Date of Death Age at Death	Maiden Name Spouse	Tombstone

Inscription: "Together Forever."

Other Info: Shares a headstone with his wife.

JONES Myrtle Edwin	14 May 1910 11 Oct. 1912		Yes
JONES Nettie Johnson	20 Mar. 1882 19 Apr. 1964		Yes
JONES Roy Berkley	29 July 1906 25 Mar. 1968	Jones, Mary Harding	Yes

Inscription: Footstone inscribed: "Father."

| JONES
Samuel L. | 07 June 1878
03 July 1960 | Jones, Betty H. | Yes |

Inscription: Footstone inscribed: "Father."

Other Info: Shares a headstone with his wife.

| KEATING
Carrie B. | 01 Oct. 1907
09 Apr. 1990 | Woodfin
Keating, | Yes |

Other Info: Grave also marked by a funeral home metal marker.

| KENDALL
Nancy J. | 18 May 1888
22 Jan. 1957 | Kendall, Thomas O. | Yes |

Other Info: Shares a headstone with her husband.

| KENDALL
Raleigh T. | 29 Dec. 1915
25 July 1965 | | Yes |

Inscription: He served as inscribed: "Virginia S. Sgt. Coast Arty Corps World War II."

| KENDALL
Thomas O. | 29 July 1886
18 June 1955 | Kendall, Nancy J. | Yes |

Other Info: Shares a headstone with his wife.

| KING
Doris Eleanor | 06 Oct. 1920
03 Aug. 1989 | Newton
King, | Yes |

Inscription: "In God's Care."

Other Info: Grave also marked by a funeral home metal marker.

| KOENIG
Louis | 1891
1942 | | Yes |
| LeSUER
Clarence Overton | 23 Oct. 1912
13 Apr. 1993 | LeSueur, Caroline Yancey | Yes |

LAST NAME First Name	Date of Birth Date of Death Age at Death	Maiden Name Spouse	Tombstone
	Inscription: "Wed June 11, 1934."		
MAHON Alexander Lee	20 Feb. 1857 27 Feb. 1927		Yes
	Other Info: Shares a headstone with Ashby Turner Mahon.		
MAHON Ashby Turner	25 May 1862 05 May 1950		Yes
	Other Info: Shares a headstone with Alexander Lee Mahon.		
MAHON Blanche P.	1893 1977		Yes
MAHON Everett B.	1885 1950		Yes
MAHON Everett Brown	13 Aug. 1919 22 Feb. 1989		Yes
	Inscription: He served as inscribed: "US. Army World War II."		
MARCH Marian Anderson Riddle	29 Oct. 1907 09 Mar. 1954		Yes
MARION Richard D.	11 Aug. 1959 22 Nov. 1981		Yes
	Inscription: "Beloved Son."		
MARTIN A. Hamilton	1880 1963	Martin, Lillie D.	Yes
	Other Info: Shares a headstone with his wife.		
MARTIN Alexander H. Jr.	10 Oct. 1923 04 June 1989		Yes
	Inscription: He served as inscribed: "Sgt. US Army World War II."		
MARTIN Connie	26 Nov. 1905 07 Mar. 1984	Davis Martin, Russell Algie	Yes
	Inscription: "In God's Care."		
	Other Info: Shares a headstone with her husband.		
MARTIN Julien D.	13 Mar. 1902 04 Apr. 1967		Yes
MARTIN Lillie D.	1884 1961	Martin, A. Hamilton	Yes
	Other Info: Shares a headstone with her husband.		

LAST NAME First Name	Date of Birth Date of Death Age at Death	Maiden Name Spouse	Tombstone
MARTIN Olivia Goode	03 Sep. 1874 15 July 1949		Yes
MARTIN Orson Watts	1886 1966		Yes

Inscription: "Botts."

| MARTIN
Russell Algie | 11 Nov. 1907
03 Mar. 1986 | Martin, Connie Davis | Yes |

Inscription: "In God's Care."

Other Info: Shares a headstone with his wife.

| MERTZ
Carl Fredrick Lt. | 15 May 1910
23 June 1943 | Anderson, Vera Preston | Yes |

Inscription: "Born in Saginaw, Mich. Died in Monogram, VA."

| MESSENGER
Alpha E. | 1862
1939 | Messenger, Belle P. | Yes |

Other Info: Shares a headstone with his wife.

| MESSENGER
Belle P. | 1860
1946 | Messenger, Alpha E. | Yes |

Other Info: Shares a headstone with her husband.

| MILLER
R. H. Capt. | 19 Oct. 1833
01 Oct. 1915 | | Yes |

Inscription: He served as inscribed: "He Was A Confederate Soldier, and A Member Of Mt. Zion Baptist Church. Gone But Not Forgotten. Asleep In Jesus."

| MILLIKIN
Mary Jane | 1935
1975 | Millikin, James E. | Yes |

Inscription: "Together Forever."

| MITCHELL
Birdie M. | 27 May 1889
24 June 1973 | | Yes |
| MITCHELL
John Mason | 30 July 1870
03 Oct. 1955 | | Yes |

Inscription: Footstone inscribed: "J.M.M."

| MITCHELL
John W. | 1908
1994 | | No |

Other Info: Grave marked by a funeral home metal marker.

LAST NAME First Name	Date of Birth Date of Death Age at Death	Maiden Name Spouse	Tombstone
MITCHELL Pearl Newton	1914 1978		No

Other Info: Grave marked by a funeral home metal marker.

| MITCHELL
Thomas G. | 09 Jan. 1952
10 May 1952 | | Yes |

Inscription: "Gone So Soon."

MITCHELL Walter Herman	22 Oct. 1915 03 Dec. 1990		Yes
MYERS Marjorie Putney	23 Oct. 1923 17 Sep. 1960		Yes
NEWTON Eleanora D.	06 Apr. 1884 07 Sep. 1955	Newton, Emmett T.	Yes

Other Info: Shares a headstone with her husband.

| NEWTON
Emmett T. | 10 June 1880
20 May 1955 | Newton, Eleanora D. | Yes |

Other Info: Shares a headstone with his wife.

| NEWTON
Frank L. | 21 Aug. 1882
10 Feb. 1962 | | Yes |
| NEWTON
Katie | 07 Mar. 1912
07 Sep. 1991 | Newton
Newton, Emmett Leake | Yes |

Inscription: "Married April 26, 1933."

| NIXON
Miles Archie | 1927
1979 | Nixon, Ann Page | Yes |

Inscription: He served as inscribed: "PFC US Army Korea."

| NOBLE
Bertice | 12 Dec. 1911
02 Nov. 1965 | Jones
Noble, John Weldon | Yes |

Inscription: "Mother." Footstone inscribed: "Mother."

Other Info: Shares a headstone with her husband.

| NOBLE
John Weldon | 25 June 1904
20 Jan. 1967 | Noble, Bertice Jones | Yes |

Inscription: "Father." Footstone inscribed: "Father."

Other Info: Shares a headstone with his wife.

| NOBLE
Weldon Bruce | 1935
1971 | | Yes |

LAST NAME First Name	Date of Birth Date of Death Age at Death	Maiden Name Spouse	Tombstone

Inscription: He served as inscribed: "Sgt. US Marine Corps Korea."

| OLIVER
Baxter C. Jr. | 1981
1981 | | No |

Other Info: Grave marked by a funeral home metal marker.

| OLIVER
Bettie | 1856
1931 | Miller
Oliver, William Edgar | Yes |

Inscription: "Christ Is Our Hope."

Other Info: Shares a headstone with her husband.

| OLIVER
Charles Keel | 18 Nov. 1900
19 Jan. 1974 | | Yes |

| OLIVER
Claude Irvin | 25 July 1915
17 May 1939 | | Yes |

| OLIVER
Florence D. | 25 July 1875
05 Sep. 1954 | Oliver, John H. | Yes |

Other Info: Shares a headstone with her husband.

| OLIVER
Grace F. | 1898
1970 | Oliver, John C. Sr. | Yes |

Other Info: Shares a headstone with her husband.

| OLIVER
Herman L. | 1925
1984 | | No |

Other Info: Grave is marked by a funeral home metal marker.

| OLIVER
Horace Gordon | 04 Nov. 1908
03 Sep. 1979 | | Yes |

| OLIVER
Jane Claudette | 23 Aug. 1939
21 Oct. 1939 | | Yes |

| OLIVER
John C. Sr. | 1888
1959 | Oliver, Grace F. | Yes |

Other Info: Shares a headstone with his wife.

| OLIVER
John H. | 10 Dec. 1870
17 June 1946 | Oliver, Florence D. | Yes |

Other Info: Shares a headstone with his wife.

| OLIVER
John Perkins | 20 Apr. 1903
19 July 1945 | | Yes |

LAST NAME First Name	Date of Birth Date of Death Age at Death	Maiden Name Spouse	Tombstone
OLIVER Louise Wingfield	11 Nov. 1918 02 June 1976		Yes
OLIVER Robbie Franklin	14 July 1890 05 July 1979		Yes
OLIVER Virginia G.	1979 1979		No

Other Info: Grave is marked by a funeral home metal marker.

OLIVER William Edgar	1860 1942	Oliver, Bettie Miller	

Inscription: "Christ Is Our Hope."

Other Info: Shares a headstone with his wife.

OLIVER William Fitzhugh	1887 1928		Yes

Inscription: "The Lord Is My Shepherd."

PARKER Annie V.	19 Nov. 1876 02 May 1929		Yes

Inscription: "Our Loved One ... May She Find Joy In the Life Everlasting."

PARKER Jessie C.	03 Nov. 1901 13 Oct. 1925		Yes

Inscription: "Gone But Not Forgotten."

PARKER Luther W.	1874 1947		Yes
PARKER Mary V.	21 Oct. 1844 11 Aug. 1921		Yes

Inscription: "In Memory of ... "

PARKER Maude W.	1894 1939		Yes
PARKER Oscar W.	1879 1970		Yes
PARKER Rufus I.	1881 1941		Yes
PARKER W. J.	29 Feb. 1827 25 Nov. 1905		Yes

Inscription: He served as inscribed: "William J. Parker Co C 3 VA CAV. C.S.A."

LAST NAME First Name	Date of Birth Date of Death Age at Death	Maiden Name Spouse	Tombstone
PATTERSON Ann C.	05 May 1817 08 Sep. 1899		Yes

Inscription: "In Memory Of Our Dear ... Mother ... Though Lost To Sight To Memory Dear."

PATTERSON Irene E.	14 Feb. 1869 23 Dec. 1930		Yes

Inscription: "God Be With You Till We Meet Again."

PATTERSON J. Edgar	04 Feb. 1875 24 July 1901		Yes

Inscription: "Death Loves A Shining Mark."

Other Info: Bottom of headstone is signed as inscribed: " J. L. Miller & Co."

PATTERSON Kate Miss	05 May 1856 10 Mar. 1920		Yes
PATTERSON Robert S.	28 July 1872 28 June 1902		Yes

Inscription: "Rest To the Weary Soul."

Other Info: Bottom of headstone is signed as inscribed: " J. L. Miller & Co."

PATTERSON Sally P.	23 Sep. 1885 05 June 1975	Patterson, Willie M.	Yes

Other Info: Shares a headstone with her husband.

PATTERSON Sarah E.	28 Apr. 1843 29 Feb. 1936	Patterson, Thomas W.	Yes

Inscription: "Prepare To Meet Thy God."

PATTERSON Thomas W.	16 Mar. 1843 18 July 1906	Patterson, Sarah E.	Yes

Inscription: "Calmly Sleeps This Brave Soldier of 1861." A second headstone shows he served as inscribed: "Thomas Wakefield Patteson (sic) C.S.A."

PATTERSON Willie M.	11 Mar. 1878 27 Dec. 1968	Patterson, Sally P.	Yes

Other Info: Shares a headstone with his wife.

PATTERSON Wm. Eldon	1907 1977	Patterson, Louise A.	Yes
PENDLETON Donald K.	1929 1993	Pendleton, Ruby D.	Yes

LAST NAME First Name	Date of Birth Date of Death Age at Death	Maiden Name Spouse	Tombstone
PERRIN Charles Nelson	18 Sep. 1918 20 Nov. 1983		Yes

Other Info: Grave is also marked by a funeral home metal marker.

PHILLIPS Andrew J.	1925 1938		Yes
PHILLIPS Bernice B.	1895 1973	Phillips, John R.	Yes

Other Info: Shares a headstone with her husband.

PHILLIPS Durward B.	1887 1945		Yes
PHILLIPS John R.	1889 1980	Phillips, Bernice B.	Yes

Other Info: Shares a headstone with his wife.

PHILLIPS Richard Randolph	15 Sep. 1900 23 Dec. 1960		Yes
PHILLIPS Thomas M.	14 Oct. 1849 24 Jan. 1932		Yes

Inscription: "He Was Faithful To Every Duty."

PHILLIPS VA. Bagby	05 Jan. 1860 08 Feb. 1947		Yes

Inscription: "At Rest."

PHILLIPS Willie B.	1890 1927		Yes
PIERCY Ellis Walter	09 Jan. 1910 22 Mar. 1938		Yes

Inscription: "At Rest."

PIERCY Nancy C.	1879 1980	Piercy, Walter R.	Yes

Other Info: Shares a headstone with her husband.

PIERCY Walter R.	1876 1958	Piercy, Nancy C.	Yes

Other Info: Shares a headstone with his wife.

PIPPIN H. Cecil	11 July 1900 04 Mar. 1952		Yes

LAST NAME First Name	Date of Birth Date of Death Age at Death	Maiden Name Spouse	Tombstone
	Inscription: "Gone, But Not Forgotten."		
PIPPIN Otis S.	11 July 1911 14 Mar. 1948		Yes
PITTS (Infant Girl)	20 Sep. 1922		Yes
PITTS Mattie Winston	23 Apr. 1902 23 May 1938		Yes
PUTNEY (Baby)	1917 1917		Yes
PUTNEY Edna Phillips	1884 1969	Putney, Wm. Thornton	Yes
	Other Info: Shares a headstone with her husband.		
PUTNEY Elizabeth Hyde	19 Jan. 1866 10 July 1945		Yes
PUTNEY Etta	23 Dec. 1892 12 Oct. 1985	Stinson Putney, James Norman	Yes
	Other Info: Shares a headstone with her husband.		
PUTNEY James Norman	20 Feb. 1889 16 Jan. 1980	Putney, Etta Stinson	Yes
	Other Info: Shares a headstone with his wife.		
PUTNEY Julian E.	1866 1930		Yes
PUTNEY Maude Goode	03 May 1872 30 Sep. 1961		Yes
PUTNEY Richard	15 Apr. 1842 04 Oct. 1928		Yes
	Inscription: "Sacred to the Memory of ... " "Resurgam." Footstone shows he served as inscribed: "Richard Putney Co C 44th VA Regt. C.S.A."		
PUTNEY S. C.	Nov. 1910		Yes
	Inscription: Footstone inscribed: "S.C.P."		
	Other Info: This is a slate headstone - face of the front of the slate is mostly flaked off making it impossible to decipher the inscription.		
PUTNEY Va. Elizabeth	1923 1924		Yes

LAST NAME First Name	Date of Birth Date of Death Age at Death	Maiden Name Spouse	Tombstone
PUTNEY Wm. Thornton	1890 1961	Putney, Edna Phillips	Yes

Other Info: Shares a headstone with his wife.

RAGLAND Maude Phillips	1898 1939		Yes
RIDDLE Kate Evlyn (sic)	16 June 1875 05 Feb. 1958		Yes
ROBERTS Claude S.	13 July 1905 24 Sep. 1981	Roberts, Ruby S.	Yes

Other Info: Shares a headstone with his wife.

| ROBERTS
Robert S. | 02 Oct. 1934
20 Mar. 1982 | Roberts, Doris C. | Yes |

Inscription: "In God's Care."

| ROBERTS
Ruby S. | 04 Feb. 1912
27 Nov. 1971 | Roberts, Claude S. | Yes |

Other Info: Shares a headstone with her husband.

| SHUMAKER
Gladys S. | 1924
1975 | Shumaker, Richard H. | Yes |

Other Info: Shares a headstone with her husband.

| SHUMAKER
Richard H. | 1921
1979 | Shumaker, Gladys S. | Yes |

Other Info: Shares a headstone with his wife.

| SIMANSKE
Mamie | 1909
1935 | Yancey
Simanske, Fred M. | Yes |

Inscription: "A Little Time On Earth She Spent Till God For Her His Angel Sent." Footstone inscribed: "M.Y.S."

| SMITH
Luther L. | 06 Jan. 1943
28 May 1981 | | Yes |
| SNODDY
Albert Flemming (sic) | 09 Jan. 1879
07 Apr. 1956 | Snoddy, Blanche Wootten | Yes |

Other Info: Shares a headstone with his wife.

| SNODDY
Albert Wilford | 07 May 1928
02 Dec. 1981 | | Yes |

Inscription: He served as inscribed: "Sgt. US Army Korea."

LAST NAME	Date of Birth	Maiden Name	Tombstone
First Name	Date of Death	Spouse	
	Age at Death		

| SNODDY | 04 Sep. 1913 | | Yes |
| Aubrey Fleming | 11 July 1974 | | |

Inscription: Footstone inscribed: "Husband."

| SNODDY | 02 Sep. 1892 | Wootten | Yes |
| Blanche | 21 Sep. 1961 | Snoddy, Albert Flemming | |

Other Info: Shares a headstone with her husband.

| SNODDY | 07 Apr. 1811 | | Yes |
| James C. | 11 Mar. 1899 | | |

Inscription: "In Memory of ... Happy Is He Whose Hope Is In the Lord."

| SNODDY | 1880 | | Yes |
| Robert Marion | 1935 | Snoddy, Sydney Hudgins | |

Inscription: Footstone inscribed: "R.M.S."

Other Info: Shares a headstone with his wife.

| SNODDY | | | Yes |
| Sammie P. | | | |

Other Info: No dates inscribed on this headstone.

| SNODDY | 1878 | Hudgins | Yes |
| Sydney | 1934 | Snoddy, Robert Marion | |

Inscription: Footstone inscribed: "S.H.S."

Other Info: Shares a headstone with her husband.

| STANSBERRY | 05 June 1883 | | Yes |
| Emma C. | 01 May 1952 | | |

| STINSON | | | Yes |
| (Baby) | 12 Dec. 1943 | | |

Inscription: "Daughter of Jack & Minnie Stinson."

| STINSON | 28 Dec. 1900 | Hudgins | Yes |
| Bettie | 25 Dec. 1972 | Stinson, John Willie | |

Inscription: "Till We Shall Meet and Never Part."

| STINSON | 21 Oct. 1910 | | Yes |
| David R. | 17 Aug. 1929 | | |

Inscription: "At Rest. Life's Work Well Done. He Rests In Peace."

| STINSON | 1880 | | Yes |
| George W. | 1942 | Stinson, Mattie H. | |

LAST NAME First Name	Date of Birth Date of Death Age at Death	Maiden Name Spouse	Tombstone
	Inscription: "Father. At Rest. Gone, But Not Forgotten."		
STINSON George W. Jr.	19 May 1921 04 June 1980		Yes
STINSON Ida	10 Jan. 1877 10 June 1921		Yes
	Inscription: "Our Mother. At Rest."		
STINSON James Carlton	31 Aug. 1909 18 Aug. 1943		Yes
	Inscription: "Gone, But Not Forgotten."		
STINSON John Thomas	05 Oct. 1866 29 Nov. 1946		Yes
STINSON John Willie	20 Feb. 1900 02 Mar. 1959	Stinson, Bettie Hudgins	Yes
	Inscription: "Till We Shall Meet and Never Part."		
STINSON Mattie H.	1894 1954	Stinson, George W.	Yes
	Inscription: "Mother. At Rest."		
STINSON Maureen Gordon	1918 1973		Yes
STINSON P. Hubert	17 Apr. 1922 27 July 1991		Yes
	Inscription: He served as inscribed: "SSgt. US Air Force World War II."		
STINSON Virginia D.	1896 1943	Stinson, William D.	Yes
	Other Info: Shares a headstone with her husband.		
STINSON William D.	1874 1943	Stinson, Virginia D.	Yes
	Other Info: Shares a headstone with his wife.		
TALLEY Elsie Newton	28 Oct. 1906 10 Mar. 1981		Yes
	Inscription: "The Lord Is My Shepherd."		
TATUM Thelma P.	03 Oct. 1907 19 June 1989		Yes

LAST NAME First Name	Date of Birth Date of Death Age at Death	Maiden Name Spouse	Tombstone
TATUM Willie E.	14 Oct. 1896 29 July 1986		Yes
TAYLOR W. H. Rev.	04 Aug. 1811 24 Oct. 1889		Yes

Inscription: "In Memory Of ... Prepare To Meet Thy God." Footstone inscribed: "W.H.T."

THOMAS Alma Gertrude	09 Oct. 1911 27 Apr. 1994	Thomas, J. Clarence	Yes

Inscription: "Together Forever."

Other Info: Shares a headstone with her husband.

THOMAS (Baby)	26 July 1929		Yes
THOMAS George V.	30 Nov. 1908 11 Apr. 1982	Thomas, Ruby Yancey	Yes

Inscription: "In God We Trust."

THOMAS J. Clarence	25 July 1906 16 July 1987	Thomas, Alma Gertrude	Yes

Inscription: "Together Forever." (Masonic Symbol)

Other Info: Shares a headstone with his wife.

THOMAS Mannie W.	27 May 1877 27 May 1914		Yes

Inscription: "Our Darling ... Resting Sweetly."

THOMAS Margaret Elizabeth	04 Oct. 1920 01 Aug. 1962		Yes

Inscription: "Mother."

THOMAS Robert V.	22 Dec. 1932 31 Aug. 1950		Yes

Inscription: He served as inscribed: "Virginia PFC 9 INF 2 INF DIV Korea PH."

THOMAS Ruby	08 Oct. 1911 12 Aug. 1943	Yancey Thomas, George V.	Yes

Inscription: "Mother."

THOMPSON Georgia	1873 1947	Yancey Thompson, Horace Clinton	Yes

Inscription: Footstone inscribed: "G.Y.T."

LAST NAME First Name	Date of Birth Date of Death Age at Death	Maiden Name Spouse	Tombstone

Other Info: Shares a headstone with her husband. Her daughter is Bessie Thompson Jackson.

| THOMPSON
Gladys R. | 24 Nov. 1910
23 Jan. 1976 | | Yes |

| THOMPSON
H. Clinton | 1871
1944 | Thompson, Georgia Y. | Yes |

Inscription: Footstone inscribed: "H.C.T."

Other Info: Shares a headstone with his wife.

| THOMPSON
James Andrew | 23 Dec. 1930
02 Oct. 1993 | | Yes |

Inscription: He served as inscribed: "A1C US Air Force Korea."

| THOMPSON
Judith Jane | 27 Nov. 1837
04 Oct. 1916 | | Yes |

Inscription: "Our Mother. Blessed Are the Pure In Heart, For They Shall See God. A True and Faithful Christian."

| THOMPSON
Wade H. | 06 Feb. 1905
14 Aug. 1972 | | Yes |

| TINSLEY
J. Walter | 25 Dec. 1855
09 July 1914 | | Yes |

Inscription: "Born ... at Holcomb Rock, Amherst Co., VA., on James River." "Asleep In Jesus."

| TONEY
Ethel R. | 1894
1982 | Toney, Marion E. | Yes |

Inscription: "God Doeth All Things Well."

Other Info: Shares a headstone with her husband.

| TONEY
Howard W. | 26 May 1915
05 Mar. 1963 | Toney, Rosa Pearl | Yes |

Inscription: "Gone But Not Forgotten."

Other Info: Shares a headstone with his wife.

| TONEY
John Leonard | 10 Jan. 1904
09 Jan. 1981 | Toney, Ressie Davis | Yes |

Other Info: Shares a headstone with his wife.

| TONEY
Kizzie Geneva | 05 Jan. 1881
04 Dec. 1933 | Toney, William Elmo | Yes |

LAST NAME / First Name	Date of Birth / Date of Death / Age at Death	Maiden Name / Spouse	Tombstone

Other Info: Shares a headstone with her husband.

| TONEY Lindsay G. | 28 May 1917 26 Nov. 1966 | | Yes |

| TONEY Marion E. | 1880 1954 | Toney, Ethel R. | Yes |

Inscription: "God Doeth All Things Well."

Other Info: Shares a headstone with his wife.

| TONEY Mary N. | 18 Aug. 1912 11 Apr. 1992 | Toney, Willie R. | Yes |

Inscription: "Married Oct. 27, 1927."

Other Info: Shares a headstone with her husband.

| TONEY Ressie | 08 Sep. 1899 30 Apr. 1987 | Davis Toney, John Leonard | Yes |

Other Info: Shares a headstone with her husband.

| TONEY Rosa Pearl | 18 May 1910 04 Jan. 1994 | Toney, Howard W. | Yes |

Inscription: "Gone But Not Forgotten."

Other Info: Shares a headstone with her husband.

| TONEY William Elmo | 08 May 1878 08 Nov. 1960 | Toney, Kizzie Geneva | Yes |

Other Info: Shares a headstone with his wife.

| TONEY Willie R. | 26 Dec. 1904 06 Sep. 1981 | Toney, Mary N. | Yes |

Inscription: "Married Oct. 27, 1927."

Other Info: Shares a headstone with his wife.

| TYSON Carroll Lee | 25 Sep. 1962 14 Feb. 1969 | | Yes |

Inscription: "Son."

Other Info: Grave also marked by a funeral home metal marker.

| TYSON Fred W. | 1916 1992 | Tyson, Dorothy | Yes |

| WALTERS Wilmer | 31 Mar. 1904 27 May 1980 | Walters, Louise Woodfin | Yes |

LAST NAME First Name	Date of Birth Date of Death Age at Death	Maiden Name Spouse	Tombstone
WEBER Anne Miller	06 Jan. 1950 10 Aug. 1983		Yes
WEBER Richard Joseph	03 Jan. 1918 16 May 1988	Weber, Ophelia Deane	Yes
WELLER Ida Kyle Davis	1855 1935		Yes
WELLER Thornton	09 Oct. 1849 28 June 1932.		Yes

Inscription: "In God's Care."

WHEELER Charles Joseph	29 Feb. 1896 18 May 1961	Wheeler, Mary Bransford	Yes

Other Info: Shares a headstone with his wife.

WHEELER Mary	22 Sep. 1892 08 May 1974	Bransford Wheeler, Charles Joseph	Yes

Other Info: Shares a headstone with her husband.

WHITE Arrianna M.	1860 1945		Yes

Inscription: "There Is Rest In Heaven."

WHITE Artie Hilston	1874 1943	White, Roberta Helen	Yes

Inscription: "The Faithful Are Certain Of Their Reward."

Other Info: Shares a headstone with his wife.

WHITE Bertha O.	20 Mar. 1881 09 Nov. 1905		Yes

Inscription: "In Memory of ... " Footstone inscribed: "B.O.W."

WHITE Chapman	1806 1887	White, Mary F.	Yes

Other Info: Shares a headstone with his wife and an infant daughter, Sarah J.

WHITE Fountain E.	24 May 1846 13 July 1918		Yes

Inscription: He served as inscribed: "Co C 44 Regt. VA INF CSA."

WHITE Mary F.	1815 1904	White, Chapman	Yes

LAST NAME First Name	Date of Birth Date of Death Age at Death	Maiden Name Spouse	Tombstone

Other Info: Shares a headstone with her husband and an infant daughter, Sarah J.

WHITE Roberta Helen	1877 1961	White, Artie Hilston	Yes

Inscription: "The Faithful Are Certain Of Their Reward."

Other Info: Shares a headstone with her husband.

WHITE Sarah J.	1834		Yes

Other Info: Shares a headstone with her father and mother, Chapman and Mary F. White.

WHITE Wesley T.	1853 1925		Yes

Inscription: "There'll Be No Night There."

WHITING Marguerite P.	02 Oct. 1910 25 Jan. 1993		Yes

WILKINSON Carroll H.	06 Apr. 1903 14 July 1949		Yes

WILKINSON Essie B.	05 Apr. 1869 30 July 1938		Yes

WOODFIN Donald Pierce	22 Nov. 1949 06 Apr. 1970		Yes

Inscription: "Those Who Knew Him Could Not Help Loving Him." Footstone shows he served as inscribed: "Virginia PFC CO A 31 INF 9 INF Div Vietnam BSM & OLC."

WOODFIN Edmund P.	11 Oct. 1863 20 Feb. 1946	Woodfin, Jennie Rebecca	Yes

WOODFIN Jennie Rebecca	1866 1950	Woodfin, Edmund P.	Yes

WOODFIN Meade Painter	18 Oct. 1902 10 Feb. 1979	Woodfin, Iva Ford	Yes

WOODFIN Ralph Pierce	1914 1988		Yes

Inscription: He served as inscribed: "PVT World War II."

WOODFIN Ray	12 May 1889 18 July 1962		Yes

LAST NAME First Name	Date of Birth Date of Death Age at Death	Maiden Name Spouse	Tombstone
WOODSON Anna May	02 Mar. 1903 24 Nov. 1990		Yes
WOODSON Drury Gilliam	22 Apr. 1862 18 Jan. 1940	Woodson, Willie Newton	Yes

Inscription: Footstone inscribed: "Father."

Other Info: Shares a headstone with his wife.

WOODSON E. Frank	09 Jan. 1859 17 May 1939		Yes
WOODSON Mary L.	20 Aug. 1898 14 Apr. 1980		Yes

Inscription: "Mittie."

WOODSON Polly W.	03 June 1868 05 Dec. 1930	Woodson, W. Lafayette	Yes

Other Info: Shares a headstone with her husband.

WOODSON W. Lafayette	16 Aug. 1855 27 Feb. 1936	Woodson, Polly W.	Yes

Other Info: Shares a headstone with his wife.

WOODSON William E.	18 June 1902 18 Oct. 1942		Yes
WOODSON Willie	24 Sep. 1875 02 June 1961	Newton Woodson, Drury Gilliam	Yes

Inscription: Footstone inscribed: "Mother."

Other Info: Shares a headstone with her husband.

WOOTTEN Archie P.	30 Mar. 1909 27 Oct. 1942		Yes
WOOTTEN D. Perkins	22 Oct. 1904 29 Apr. 1958	Wootten, L. Fleming	Yes

Inscription: Footstone inscribed: "Our Brother D. Perkins Wootten 1904-1958 Fellowship Bible Class."

Other Info: Shares a headstone with his wife.

WOOTTEN Garnette E. Sr.	02 Oct. 1913 04 Aug. 1960	Wootten, Virginia L.	Yes

Inscription: (Masonic Symbol)

Other Info: Shares a headstone with his wife.

LAST NAME First Name	Date of Birth Date of Death Age at Death	Maiden Name Spouse	Tombstone
WOOTTEN James B.	12 Nov. 1902 21 Nov. 1946		Yes
WOOTTEN L. Fleming	11 Apr. 1907 06 Jan. 1981	Wootten, D. Perkins	Yes
WOOTTEN Virginia L.	21 July 1921 30 Aug. 1970	Wootten, Garnette E. Sr.	Yes

Other Info: Shares a headstone with her husband.

WOOTTON Bessie J.	1895 1985	Wootton, Irving A.	Yes

Other Info: Shares a headstone with her husband.

WOOTTON Irving A.	1886 1967	Wootton, Bessie J.	Yes

Other Info: Shares a headstone with his wife.

WOOTTON Leland C.	30 Jan. 1930 09 Mar. 1935		Yes

Inscription: "Son. I Pray Thee Lord My Soul To Keep."

WOOTTON Lucy	25 Feb. 1853 19 Feb. 1932	Boatwright Wootton, Wiley H.	Yes

Inscription: Footstone inscribed: "L.B.W."

WOOTTON Wiley H.	24 July 1859 16 Oct. 1915	Wootton, Lucy Boatwright	Yes

Inscription: Footstone inscribed: "W.H.W."

YANCEY Bernard W.	29 July 1909 24 Feb. 1991		Yes

Inscription: He served as inscribed: "TEC 4 US Army World War II."

YANCEY Edward Smith	28 Jan. 1920 13 June 1994	Yancey, Martha Payne	Yes

Inscription: "The Lord Is My Shepherd." Footstone shows that he served as inscribed: "PFC US Army World War II."

Other Info: Shares a headstone with his wife.

YANCEY Elizabeth	1886 1942	Christian Yancey, William Thomas	Yes

Inscription: "Mother." Footstone inscribed: "E.C.Y."

Other Info: Shares a headstone with her husband.

LAST NAME First Name	Date of Birth Date of Death Age at Death	Maiden Name Spouse	Tombstone
YANCEY John G.	31 Mar. 1916 17 Apr. 1974	Yancey, Ernie Pearcy	Yes

Other Info: Shares a headstone with his wife.

YANCEY Joseph W.	08 Mar. 1917 24 Sep. 1986	Yancey, Rosa Payne	Yes
YANCEY Margaret A.	1869 1948	Yancey, Robert E.	Yes

Other Info: Shares a headstone with her husband.

YANCEY Martha	25 Mar. 1927 10 Sep. 1993	Payne Yancey, Edward Smith	Yes

Inscription: "The Lord Is My Shepherd."

Other Info: Shares a headstone with her husband.

YANCEY Robert E.	1869 1948	Yancey, Margaret A.	Yes

Other Info: Shares a headstone with his wife.

YANCEY Sallie D.	1891 1958	Yancey, Waverly G.	Yes

Inscription: "Gone But Not Forgotten."

Other Info: Shares a headstone with her husband.

YANCEY Waverly G.	1881 1962	Yancey, Sallie D.	Yes

Inscription: "Gone But Not Forgotten."

Other Info: Shares a headstone with his wife.

YANCEY William Thomas	1874 1957	Yancey, Elizabeth C.	Yes

Inscription: "Father." Footstone inscribed: "W.T.Y."

Other Info: Shares a headstone with his wife.

Murphey/Flood Family - Hwy 640

GREGORY Florence I.	08 Dec. 1858 19 July 1878		Yes

Inscription: "Our Sister ... Daughter of Obadiah & Maria E. Gregory. Sleep On, Thou Short Lived Love, Thy Grave Is Deep; Thy Life Was Bitter,

LAST NAME	Date of Birth	Maiden Name	Tombstone
First Name	Date of Death	Spouse	
	Age at Death		

But Thy Rest Is Sweet; Though O'er Thy Burial Place None PauseTo Weep; It Is Approached By None Save Unshod Feet." Footstone inscribed: "F.I.G."

Other Info: This place was called "Murpheytown" when three maiden Murphy sisters owned this place and an adjoining home. The name of this home was changed to "Locust Grove" when the Flood family purchased it around 1847.

New Store Presbyterian Church Cemetery - Hwy 609

ANDREWS			No
Fred			

Other Info: Known to be buried here on Feb. 8, 1921.

BALLOWE	11 Nov. 1863		Yes
Alice K.	20 May 1946	Ballowe, Alice K.	

Inscription: "Mother."

BALLOWE	09 Oct. 1900		Yes
Charles R.	23 July 1976		

BALLOWE	27 Mar. 1857		Yes
Charles S.	08 Dec. 1941	Ballowe, Alice K.	

Inscription: "Father."

BOOKER	28 Dec. 1885		Yes
Anderson W.	19 Mar. 1968	Booker, Annie Rosen	

Other Info: Shares a headstone with his wife.

BOOKER	06 Feb. 1880	Rosen	Yes
Annie	29 July 1954	Booker, Anderson W.	

Inscription: Footstone inscribed: "A.R.B."

Other Info: Shares a headstone with her husband.

BOOKER	05 Mar. 1889		Yes
Leake B.	18 May 1970	Booker, Myrtle	

Other Info: Shares a headstone with his wife.

BOOKER	13 Apr. 1887		Yes
Myrtle	17 May 1978	Booker, Leake B.	

Other Info: Shares a headstone with her husband.

BOWLING	10 Jan. 1889		Yes
Ernest H.	03 Dec. 1981	Bowling, Sarah Johns	

LAST NAME	Date of Birth	Maiden Name	Tombstone
First Name	Date of Death	Spouse	
	Age at Death		

Other Info: Shares a headstone with his wife.

| BOWLING | 24 May 1962 | | Yes |
| (infant) | 24 May 1962 | | |

Inscription: "Infant Son of Ernest & Rebecca Bowling Jr."

| BOWLING | 27 Feb. 1889 | Johns | Yes |
| Sarah | 21 June 1972 | Bowling, Ernest H. | |

Other Info: Shares a headstone with her husband.

| BROOKS | | | No |
| Ethel | | | |

Other Info: Grave marked with a Funeral Home metal marker.

| BROOKS | | | No |
| Lucy | | | |

Other Info: Grave marked with a Funeral Home metal marker.

| BROOKS | | | No |
| Richard | | | |

Other Info: Known to be son of Thomas Brooks. He was buried on Feb. 7, 1940. Grave marked with a Funeral Home metal marker.

| BROOKS | 29 Jan. 1857 | | Yes |
| T. S. | 11 Mar. 1922 | | |

Inscription: "At Rest." Footstone inscribed: "T.S.B."

| CARTER | 1863 | Young | Yes |
| Eva M. | 1964 | Carter, George W. | |

Inscription: Footstone inscribed: "Eva Young Carter 1863-1964."

Other Info: Shares a headstone with her husband.

| CARTER | 1860 | | Yes |
| George W. | 1933 | Carter, Eva M. Young | |

Inscription: Footstone inscribed: "Geo. W. Carter 1860-1933."

Other Info: Shares a headstone with his wife.

| CARTER | 09 Jan. 1894 | | Yes |
| James N. | 21 Sep. 1977 | Carter, Merrie V. Word | |

Inscription: Footstone inscribed: "Jim Nat Carter 1894--1977."

Other Info: Shares a headstone with his wife.

LAST NAME First Name	Date of Birth Date of Death Age at Death	Maiden Name Spouse	Tombstone
CARTER Merrie V.	11 July 1896 19 Jan. 1984	Word Carter, James N.	Yes

Inscription: Footstone inscribed: "Merrie Word Carter 1896-1984."

Other Info: Shares a headstone with her husband.

CARWILE Arthur P.	02 Oct. 1904 1986	Carwile, Beulah Garrett	Yes

Other Info: Shares a headstone with his wife. Grave marked with a Funeral Home metal marker.

CARWILE Beulah	1906 1963	Garrett Carwile, Arthur P.	Yes

Inscription: "In Loving Memory...Wife of Arthur P. Carwile."

Other Info: Shares a headstone with her husband.

CHAPPELL Graham	10 July 1888 07 May 1976	Trent Chappell, William H.	Yes

Inscription: "Rest In Peace."

Other Info: Shares a headstone with her husband.

CHAPPELL William H.	22 Apr. 1891 14 July 1971	Chappell, Graham T.	Yes

Inscription: "Rest In Peace."

Other Info: Shares a headstone with his wife.

COX Annie Jones	23 May 1869 05 Apr. 1950		Yes

Inscription: Footstone inscribed: "A.J.C."

COX Geneva Oakley	20 July 1904 19 Jan. 1969	Cox, George Henry	Yes

Other Info: Shares a headstone with her husband.

COX George Henry	10 June 1899 08 Mar. 1956	Cox, Geneva Oakley	Yes

Other Info: Shares a headstone with his wife.

DORRIER John William	1920 12 Nov. 1986 66 yr.	Dorrier, Alice Forbes	No

Other Info: Son of Walter E. and Goldie Smith Dorrier.

LAST NAME	Date of Birth	Maiden Name	Tombstone
First Name	Date of Death	Spouse	
	Age at Death		

| DOWDY | 14 Nov. 1870 | Wooten | Yes |
| Annie | 24 May 1955 | Dowdy, Shirley Preston | |

Inscription: Footstone inscribed: "A.W.D."

Other Info: Shares a headstone with her husband.

| DOWDY | 14 Sep. 1906 | | Yes |
| Floyd G. | 03 Nov. 1933 | | |

| DOWDY | 19 Oct. 1921 | | Yes |
| Herman L. | 22 Apr. 1984 | | |

Inscription: He served as inscribed: "TEC 5 US Army World War II."

| DOWDY | 13 Nov. 1877 | | Yes |
| Shirley Preston | 01 July 1953 | Dowdy, Annie Wooten | |

Inscription: Footstone inscribed: "S.P.D."

Other Info: Shares a headstone with his wife.

| EATON | | | No |

Other Info: Grave marked with a Funeral Home metal marker.

| FARRISH | 1906 | | Yes |
| Burney C. | 1977 | | |

Inscription: "Rest In Peace."

| FORBES | 08 Oct. 1866 | | Yes |
| Alexander | 03 Oct. 1955 | Forbes, Elizabeth Gilliam | |

Inscription: Footstone inscribed: "A.F."

Other Info: Shares a headstone with his wife.

| FORBES | 06 Apr. 1858 | | Yes |
| Charles Wm. | 01 Jan. 1927 | | |

| FORBES | 27 Aug. 1877 | Gilliam | Yes |
| Elizabeth | 01 Apr. 1957 | Forbes, Alexander | |

Inscription: Footstone inscribed: "E.G.F."

Other Info: Shares a headstone with her husband.

| FORBES | 22 May 1899 | Venable | Yes |
| Elizabeth | 18 Aug. 1984 | Forbes, James Henry Jr. | |

Inscription: Footstone inscribed: "E.V.F."

| FORBES | 14 Feb. 1864 | | Yes |
| James Henry | 04 Mar. 1934 | Forbes, Julia Gilliam | |

LAST NAME First Name	Date of Birth Date of Death Age at Death	Maiden Name Spouse	Tombstone

Inscription: Footstone inscribed: "J.H.F."

Other Info: Shares a headstone with his wife.

| FORBES
James Henry Jr. | 26 Sep. 1901
14 Nov. 1975 |
Forbes, Elizabeth Venable | Yes |

Inscription: Footstone inscribed: "J.H.F."

| FORBES
Julia | 08 May 1873
16 Mar. 1957 | Gilliam
Forbes, James Henry | Yes |

Inscription: Footstone inscribed: "J.G.F."

Other Info: Shares a headstone with her husband.

| HEBDITCH
J. W. | 1846
1919 |
Hebditch, Kate | Yes |

Inscription: "Erected by his son J.C.H. in fond memory of his father." Footstone inscribed: "J.W.H."

| HEBDITCH
Joseph B. | 04 Apr. 1895
28 June 1923 | | Yes |

Inscription: "At Rest." Footstone inscribed: "J.B.H."

| HEBDITCH
Kate |
25 Nov. 1913
52 yr |
Hebditch, J. W. | Yes |

Inscription: "In Memory of ... Wife of J. W. Hebditch Died 25th Nov. 1913 In her 52nd year. The Perfect Wife, The True Friend." Footstone inscribed: "K.H."

| HEBDITCH
William A. | 16 June 1919
16 June 1919 | | Yes |

| HOOPER
John | 19 May 1844
14 Jan. 1920 |
Hooper, Lucy | Yes |

Inscription: "Asleep In Jesus Rejoice In the Lord." Footstone inscribed: "J.H."

| HOOPER
Lucy | 25 May 1845
15 Mar. 1915 |
Hooper, John | Yes |

Inscription: "He Leadeth Me." Footstone inscribed: "L.H."

| KIDD
Annie B. | 23 July 1891
07 Jan. 1969 |
Kidd, William J. | Yes |

Inscription: "Mother."

| KIDD
Floyd L. Jr. | 12 Apr. 1823
08 May 1884 | | Yes |

LAST NAME First Name	Date of Birth Date of Death Age at Death	Maiden Name Spouse	Tombstone

Inscription: Footstone inscribed: "F.L.K. Jr."

| KIDD
Martha M. | 03 June 1839
08 Jan. 1924 | | Yes |

Inscription: "Mother."

| KIDD
(twin infants) | | | No |

Other Info: Grave marked with a Funeral Home metal marker.

| KIDD
William J. | 31 Mar. 1879
20 Mar. 1951 | Kidd, Annie B. | Yes |

Inscription: "Father."

| LIGON
Bessie | 20 Apr. 1877
31 Jan. 1951 | Booker
Ligon, David Greenhill | Yes |

Inscription: "At Rest." A second stone at the foot of her grave is inscribed: "Bessie B. Ligon Apr. 20, 1877 - Jan. 31, 1951 T.E.L. Bible Class Newbridge Baptist Ch."

Other Info: Shares a headstone with her husband.

| LIGON
David Greenhill | 16 Sep. 1878
04 Oct. 1947 | Ligon, Bessie Booker | Yes |

Inscription: "At Rest."

Other Info: Shares a headstone with his wife.

| MCCRAW
(infant) | | | No |

Other Info: Grave marked with a Funeral Home metal marker.

| MCCRAW
(infant) | | | No |

Other Info: Grave marked with a Funeral Home metal marker.

| MORRIS
Dorothy S. | 10 Nov. 1897
28 Sep. 1979 | Morris, Lacy Earl | Yes |

Other Info: Shares a headstone with her husband.

| MORRIS
Lacy E. | 05 May 1895
30 July 1977 | Morris, Dorothy S. | Yes |

Inscription: A second stone at the foot of his grave shows he served as inscribed: "Lacy Earl Morris PVT US Army World War I 1895-1977."

LAST NAME / First Name	Date of Birth / Date of Death / Age at Death	Maiden Name / Spouse	Tombstone

Other Info: Shares a headstone with his wife.

| NEWSOME Mabel | 29 Feb. 1880 / 05 May 1973 | Hebditch | Yes |

Inscription: "Ashes Buried on Father's Grave."

Other Info: Daughter of J. W. and Kate Hebditch.

| PARSONS Elizabeth "Annie" | 16 Dec. 1912 / 08 Mar. 1979 | Booker / Parsons, Jean Curtis | Yes |

Inscription: Grave also marked with a Funeral Home Metal Marker inscribed: "Annie Booker Parsons 1912-1979."

Other Info: Shares a headstone with her husband.

| PARSONS Jean Curtis | 30 Dec. 1901 / 15 June 1971 | Parsons, Elizabeth "Annie" Booker | Yes |

Other Info: Shares a headstone with his wife.

| PROFFITT Mattie E. | 22 June 1883 / 12 Dec. 1883 | | Yes |

Inscription: "In Memory of.... Footstone inscribed: "M.E.P."

| RANSON Evelina | 19 Aug. 1882 / 05 Aug. 1964 | Binford / Ranson, W. Malcolm G. | Yes |

Inscription: "Wife of W.M.G. Ranson." Footstone inscribed: "E.B.R."

| RANSON W. Malcolm G. | 1845 / 1920 | Ranson, Evelina Binford | Yes |

Inscription: "Son of Wm. D. and Eliza J. Ranson."

| RICHARDSON Earnest | 1919 / 1934 | | Yes |

| SENGER Annie B. | 1889 / 1966 | Senger, Daniel M. | Yes |

Inscription: "At Rest."

Other Info: Shares a headstone with her husband.

| SENGER Bessie | 15 Oct. 1895 / 01 June 1959 | Shull / Senger, Edward Roy | Yes |

Other Info: Shares a headstone with her husband.

| SENGER Daniel M. | 1863 / 1948 | Senger, Annie B. | Yes |

LAST NAME First Name	Date of Birth Date of Death Age at Death	Maiden Name Spouse	Tombstone

Inscription: "At Rest."

Other Info: Shares a headstone with his wife.

| SENGER
Daniel M. Jr. | 1921
1981 | | Yes |

Inscription: He served as inscribed: "U.S. Navy World War II."

| SENGER
Edward Roy | 31 Jan. 1891
20 Mar. 1980 | Senger, Bessie Shull | Yes |

Other Info: Shares a headstone with his wife.

| SENGER
Jessie W. | 05 Aug. 1914
20 Nov. 1979 | Senger, H. Paul | Yes |

| SENGER
Lula M. | 29 May 1920
13 Jan. 1923 | | Yes |

Inscription: Footstone inscribed: "L.M.S."

Other Info: Young child of Mr. Roy Senger.

| SENGER
T. Massey | 1910
1972 | Senger, Mary K. | Yes |

| SOUTHALL
Albert P. | 1869
1911 | | Yes |

| SOUTHALL
Edgar B. | 1897
1985 | Southall, Ora Duffy | Yes |

Other Info: Grave also marked with a Funeral Home Metal Marker inscribed: "Edgar Blair Southall." Shares a headstone with his wife.

| SOUTHALL
Henry A. | 1872
1942 | Southall, Sallie V. | Yes |

Other Info: Shares a headstone with his wife.

| SOUTHALL
L. Page | 1909
1910 | | Yes |

| SOUTHALL
Ora | 1898
1951 | Duffy
Southall, Edgar Blair | Yes |

Other Info: Shares a headstone with her husband.

| SOUTHALL
Sallie V. | 1875
1963 | Southall, Henry A. | Yes |

Other Info: Shares a headstone with her husband.

LAST NAME First Name	Date of Birth Date of Death Age at Death	Maiden Name Spouse	Tombstone
SOUTHALL Wm. D. "Billy"	13 Sep. 1912 04 Mar. 1945		Yes

Inscription: He served as inscribed: "Virginia CPL 51 Arm D Inf Bn World War II."

STANLEY Edith E.	1898	Stanley, Melvin G.	Yes

Inscription: "Mother."

Other Info: Shares a headstone with her husband.

STANLEY Melvin G.	1888 1937	Stanley, Edith E.	Yes

Inscription: "Father."

Other Info: Shares a headstone with his wife.

STANTON Robert Olon	27 Feb. 1908 17 July 1982		Yes

Inscription: "Not My Will But Thine Be Done." A second stone at the foot of his grave shows that he served as inscribed: "US Army World War II Korea."

TRENT Susie R.	1858 1949	Trent, William C.	Yes

Inscription: Footstone inscribed: "S.R.T."

Other Info: Shares a headstone with her husband.

TRENT William C.	1849 1913	Trent, Susie R.	Yes

Inscription: Footstone inscribed: "W.C.T."

Other Info: Shares a headstone with his wife.

TRENT William Malcolm	13 Mar. 1893 06 Dec. 1972		Yes

Inscription: He served as inscribed: "Virginia PVT U.S. Marine Corps World War I."

VAUGHAN Willie C.	28 Aug. 1905 25 Mar. 1962		Yes
WATKINS Milton E.	02 Nov. 1941 25 Aug. 1973		Yes

Inscription: "Now Cometh Eternal Rest."

LAST NAME First Name	Date of Birth Date of Death Age at Death	Maiden Name Spouse	Tombstone
WOOTEN (Mr.)			No

Other Info: Known to be buried here on Dec. 10, 1928.

Newton Family - Hwy 622 (At Int. with Hwy 729)

NEWTON Charles L.	1941		Yes

Inscription: "Baby"

NEWTON Kizzie C.	1849 1936	Guthrie Newton, W. W.	Yes

Other Info: Kizzie Guthrie Newton, the second wife of W. W. Newton, and the younger sister of his first wife, Nancy C. G. Newton.

NEWTON Nancy C.	1847 1901	Guthrie Newton, Willis Wade	Yes

Other Info: Her full name is Nancy Catherine Guthrie.

NEWTON R. E. Jr.	1938		Yes

Inscription: "Baby"

NEWTON Robbie W.	11 Aug. 1916 05 Jan. 1919		Yes

Other Info: Son of Joseph Nathan Newton and Sarah Elizabeth (Dunkum) Newton.

NEWTON Robert W.	1928 1931		Yes

Other Info: Son of Wade Lumsden Newton and Ada Lee (Dunkum) Newton.

NEWTON W. W.	1848 1902	Newton, Nancy C.G.	Yes

Other Info: His full name is Willis Wade Newton.

O'Brien Family - Hwy 640

O'BRIEN Amanda F.	19 Sep. 1840 12 Mar. 1882		Yes

Inscription: "Sacred To the Memory Of Our Mother ... Blessed Are the Dead Who Die In the Lord."

Other Info: Shares a headstone with her son, Charles H. O'Brien.

LAST NAME First Name	Date of Birth Date of Death Age at Death	Maiden Name Spouse	Tombstone
O'BRIEN Charles H.	03 May 1881 01 Nov. 1904		Yes

Inscription: "In Loving Memory of Our Brother ... Asleep In Jesus Blessed Sleep."

Other Info: Shares a headstone with his mother, Amanda F. O'Brien.

| O'BRIEN Hallie Clarke | 28 Oct. 1866 08 Aug. 1946 | | Yes |

Inscription: "I Know That My Redeemer Liveth." Footstone inscribed: "H.C.O."

| O'BRIEN Mary C. | 09 June 1849 02 Apr. 1912 | O'Brien, John H. | Yes |

Inscription: "... Wife of John H. O'Brien. Gone But Not Forgotten."

| O'BRIEN Percy H. | 20 Apr. 1890 30 Sep. 1906 | | Yes |

Inscription: "Blessed Are the Pure In Heart." Footstone inscribed: "P.H. O'B."

Oak Hill Baptist Church - Black - Hwy 633

| CAREY Ida P. | 18 June 1877 31 July 1968 | | Yes |

Other Info: Grave also marked with a Funeral Home metal marker.

| GARRETT John Henry | 18 June 1899 08 June 1975 | Garrett, Viola Louise | Yes |

Inscription: "Father...At Rest."

Other Info: Shares a headstone with his wife. Grave also marked with a Funeral Home metal marker.

| GARRETT Viola Louise | 06 Jan. 1901 16 Feb. 1980 | Garrett, John Henry | Yes |

Inscription: "Mother...At Rest."

Other Info: Shares a headstone with her husband. Grave also marked with a Funeral Home metal marker.

| HOLLAND Willie Jr. | | | Yes |

| HOLMES Estelle | 1911 1981 | | No |

Other Info: Grave marked with a Funeral Home metal marker.

LAST NAME First Name	Date of Birth Date of Death Age at Death	Maiden Name Spouse	Tombstone
JOHNSON Abram	28 Feb. 1881 23 May 1959	Johnson, Lula	Yes

Inscription: Footstone inscribed: "Father."

Other Info: Shares a headstone with his wife.

JOHNSON Lula	15 Nov. 1886 14 Oct. 1974	Johnson, Abram	Yes

Inscription: Footstone inscribed: "Mother."

Other Info: Shares a headstone with her husband.

JONES Lucile	1972		Yes
PERKINS Albert	06 Sep. 1884 22 Dec. 1943		Yes
PERKINS (Baby Girl)	1976		No

Other Info: Grave marked with a Funeral Home metal marker.

PERKINS Billie	11 Nov. 1955		No

Other Info: Grave marked with a Funeral Home metal marker.

PERKINS Charles	1907 1941		No

Other Info: Grave marked by a Funeral Home metal marker from Undertaker, C. D. Treat, Beckley, W. Va.

PERKINS Charles L. (Mrs.)	17 July 1964 35 yrs.	Perkins, Charles L.	No

Other Info: Grave marked with a Funeral Home metal marker.

PERKINS Lester Peyton			No

Other Info: Grave marked with a Funeral Home metal marker.

PERKINS Mollie	17 Sep. 1934 73 yrs.		Yes

Inscription: "Mother."

PERKINS Willie Edmund	1922 1943		No

LAST NAME First Name	Date of Birth Date of Death Age at Death	Maiden Name Spouse	Tombstone

Other Info: Grave marked with a Funeral Home metal marker.

| SPENCER Gilbert C. | 1917 1985 | | Yes |

Inscription: He served as inscribed: "PFC U.S. Army World War II."

| SPENCER Jennie Mae | 1883 1953 | | Yes |

Other Info: Grave also marked with a Funeral Home metal marker inscribed: "Jenny Spencer Died December 24, 1953 Aged 70 yrs." Monroe Spencer is her son.

| SPENCER Joseph | | | No |

Other Info: Marked with a Funeral Home metal marker. Brother of Thomas Spencer.

| SPENCER Nannie Smothers | | Spencer, Joseph | No |

Other Info: She is known to be buried in this cemetery.

| SPENCER Thomas | 09 July 1888 04 Nov. 1973 | | Yes |

Inscription: He served as inscribed: "Virginia Pvt. U.S. Army World War II."

| SPENCER William E. | 13 July 1917 24 Oct. 1965 | | Yes |

Inscription: He served as inscribed: "Maryland T. Sgt. U. S. Army World War II."

Other Info: Son of Joseph and Nannie Spencer and brother of Ruth Spencer Lewis.

| WORD Edith | 1954 | | Yes |

| WORD Hester C. | 15 June 1969 | Word, Howard | No |

Other Info: Grave marked with a Funeral Home metal marker.

| WORD Howard | 07 May 1982 | Word, Hester C. | No |

Other Info: Grave marked with a Funeral Home metal marker.

| WORD James N. | 12 July 1970 | | No |

LAST NAME	Date of Birth	Maiden Name	Tombstone
First Name	Date of Death	Spouse	
	Age at Death		

Other Info: Grave marked with a Funeral Home metal marker.

Oliver/Nixon/Gilliam/Snoddy Family at "Grass Dale" Hwy 20 (Near Int. with Hwy 15)

| SNODDY | 26 Mar. 1907 | | Yes |
| Baby R. | 07 Apr. 1907 | | |

Inscription: Infant of "Mr. and Mrs. W. T. Snoddy."

| SNODDY | 1830s | Thornhill | No |
| Harriet | | Snoddy, John Robert | |

Other Info: Grave marked by fieldstones only, but known to be buried here beside her husband.

| SNODDY | 11 Feb. 1836 | | Yes |
| J. R. | 24 Mar. 1900 | Snoddy, Harriet Thornhill | |

Inscription: "In Memory of ... Father ... (Engraving of crossed Confederate Flags)." Footstone inscribed: "J.R.S."

Other Info: Headstone is signed at bottom "M. R. Jones Arvonia, VA."

| SNODDY | | | No |
| Patty (Miss) | | | |

Other Info: Grave marked by fieldstones, but known to be buried in this cemetery. She died when a child.

Pleasant Grove Baptist Church Cemetery - Hwy 24

| AUSTIN | 17 Apr. 1930 | | Yes |
| Thomas T. | 30 Sep. 1930 | | |

| BRYANT | 25 Apr. 1910 | | Yes |
| Johnnie J. | 28 June 1983 | Bryant, Ethel B. | |

Inscription: "Rest In Peace." Footstone inscribed: "Daddy."

Other Info: Grave also marked with a Funeral Home metal marker inscribed: "Johnny James Bryant 1910--1983."

| CHILDRESS | 13 Sep. 1914 | | Yes |
| Robert C. | 26 Nov. 1964 | Childress, Hallie B. | |

Inscription: Footstone inscribed: "Father."

| DUNNEVANT | 23 May 1896 | | Yes |
| Horace E. | 19 Apr. 1977 | Dunnevant, Mildred W. | |

LAST NAME First Name	Date of Birth Date of Death Age at Death	Maiden Name Spouse	Tombstone

Inscription: "Father."

Other Info: Grave also marked with a Funeral Home metal marker.

| DUNNEVANT
Mildred W. | 02 Feb. 1894
28 Oct. 1978 | Dunnevant, Horace E. | Yes |

Inscription: "Mother."

Other Info: Grave also marked with a Funeral Home metal marker.

| GUNTER
Paul M. Jr. "Jasper" | 27 Feb. 1956
16 May 1983 | | Yes |

Inscription: "Beloved Only Son..." Footstone inscribed: "Bo."

| JAMERSON
Nellie G. | 1899
1984 | Jamerson, Raymond W. | Yes |

Inscription: "At Rest." Footstone inscribed: "Mother."

Other Info: Shares a headstone with her husband.

| JAMERSON
Raymond W. | 1900
1972 | Jamerson, Nellie G. | Yes |

Inscription: "At Rest." Footstone inscribed: "Father."

Other Info: Shares a headstone with his wife.

| JUSTUS
David Hubert | 19 Jan. 1916
13 Dec. 1972 | | Yes |

Inscription: He served as inscribed: "Indiana PVT Co D 272 Infantry World War II."

Other Info: Grave also marked with a Funeral Home metal marker.

| PERROW
C. Fitzhugh | 11 June 1868
03 Feb. 1956 | | Yes |

Inscription: "At Rest." Footstone inscribed: "C.F.P."

| STANLEY
J. E. | 1896
1966 | | Yes |

| WATSON
Bettie | 1892
1952 | Watson, Tom | Yes |

Inscription: "At Rest."

Other Info: Shares a headstone with her husband.

| WATSON
Cleveland Walker | 04 Mar. 1889
20 Feb. 1956 | | Yes |

LAST NAME First Name	Date of Birth Date of Death Age at Death	Maiden Name Spouse	Tombstone
WATSON George Richard	16 Dec. 1881 12 Sep. 1961		Yes
WATSON John R.	16 July 1887 28 Oct. 1956		Yes
WATSON Nannie E.	14 Oct. 1860 21 Dec. 1951		Yes
WATSON Tom	1887 1973	Watson, Bettie	Yes

Inscription: "At Rest."

Other Info: Shares a headstone with his wife.

| WATSON
William Robert | 11 Dec. 1883
15 July 1961 | | Yes |
| WOOTEN
Inez P. | 17 Mar. 1877
02 May 1966 | | Yes |

Poe Family - Hwy 664

AMOS Samuel			No

Other Info: Known to be buried here.

| AMOS
Tinker | | | No |

Other Info: Known to be buried here.

| BEASLEY
Nannie | | Poe | No |

Other Info: The general location of this cemetery is known. It could not be found at this time. All graves were marked by fieldstones only.

| POE
Jane | | - | No |

Other Info: Known to be buried here.

| POE
Lee | | | No |

Other Info: Known to be buried here.

| POE
Mary | | Amos | No |

LAST NAME	Date of Birth	Maiden Name	Tombstone
First Name	Date of Death	Spouse	
	Age at Death		

RAGLAND   No
Sally

Other Info: Known to be buried here.

Rocky Mount United Methodist Church - Hwy 15/669

ADERHOLD   28 Apr. 1925   Yes
Dewey Hubbard Jr. 17 Oct. 1948

    Inscription: "He Is Not Dead, This Friend; His Music Lingers In the Heart, His Kindness In the Soul." Footstone inscribed: "Slim Idaho."

ALLEN   18 Sep. 1895   Raikes   Yes
Emma   11 July 1977   Allen, Frank R.

    Inscription: "Rest In Peace"

    Other Info: Shares a headstone with her husband.

ALLEN   15 May 1891   Yes
Frank R.   07 May 1935   Allen, Emma Raikes

    Inscription: "Rest In Peace." Footstone inscribed: "F.R.A."

    Other Info: Shares a headstsone with his wife.

ALLEN   31 Mar. 1917   Yes
George Thomas   28 Nov. 1955

    Inscription: Footstone inscribed: "G.T.A."

ALLEN   17 Sep. 1930   Yes
Henry F.   11 May 1931

ALLEN   25 Sep. 1927   Yes
James C.   20 Nov. 1991   Allen, Doris T.

    Inscription: "Jimmy. Married Jan. 26, 1948."

ALLEN   15 Oct. 1977   Yes
Jamie Franklin   22 Oct. 1977

    Inscription: "Our Baby."

ALLEN   1942   Yes
Mary Barton   1961

ALLEN   24 Jan. 1980   Yes
Nicholaus Reed   30 Apr. 1980

    Inscription: "Our Angel. Little Ones To Him Belong."

LAST NAME First Name	Date of Birth Date of Death Age at Death	Maiden Name Spouse	Tombstone
APPERSON James L.	01 Aug. 1902 03 July 1974	Apperson, Margaret F.	Yes

Other Info: Shares a headstone with his wife.

| APPERSON
Margaret F. | 18 Nov. 1896
21 Jan. 1985 | Apperson, James L. | Yes |

Other Info: Shares a headstone with her husband.

| APPERSON
Paul L. | 18 Oct. 1908
08 Feb. 1970 | | Yes |

Inscription: "In God's Care. Our Beloved Son."

| APPERSON
S. Frances | 11 Oct. 1889
20 Apr. 1986 | | Yes |
| APPERSON
Thomas J. | 14 June 1892
26 Oct. 1974 | | Yes |

Inscription: He served as inscribed: "PFC US Army."

| AYERS
James Nathan | 13 Mar. 1879
17 Oct. 1950 | Ayers, Margarett L. | Yes |

Inscription: "Father."

Other Info: Shares a headstone with his wife.

| AYERS
Margarett L. | 08 Aug. 1886
18 Nov. 1978 | Ayers, James Nathan | Yes |

Inscription: "Mother."

Other Info: Shares a headstone with her husband.

| AYERS
Virginia T. | 06 June 1934
22 Mar. 1965 | | Yes |

Inscription: "Now Cometh Eternal Rest."

| AYRES
John James | 11 Mar. 1907
29 June 1958 | Ayres, Aileen Harris | Yes |

Inscription: "Father."

| AYRES
John McGuire | 13 Oct. 1883
10 May 1929 | Ayres, Sarah Allen | Yes |

Inscription: Footstone inscribed: "Father."

Other Info: Shares a headstone with his wife.

LAST NAME First Name	Date of Birth Date of Death Age at Death	Maiden Name Spouse	Tombstone
AYRES Sarah	09 Apr. 1889 01 Apr. 1959	Allen Ayres, John McGuire	Yes

Inscription: Footstone inscribed: "Mother."

Other Info: Shares a headstone with her husband.

| BOSLEY Margaret H. | 06 Feb. 1916 21 June 1993 | Bosley, Glenn | Yes |

Inscription: "Peggy."

| CALL James Daniel | 19 Mar. 1884 23 Mar. 1965 | Call, Willie Wooton | Yes |

Other Info: Shares a headstone with his wife.

| CALL Richard | 20 Feb. 1920 15 Aug. 1966 | | Yes |

Inscription: He served as inscribed: "Virginia PFC CO E 21 Infantry World War II."

| CALL Willie | 01 Oct. 1897 | Wooton Call, James Daniel | Yes |

Other Info: Shares a headstone with her husband.

| CHRISTIAN Bernice D. | 10 Jan. 1909 17 Feb. 1985 | Christian, H. Leslie | Yes |

Inscription: "Rest In Peace."

Other Info: Shares a headstone with her husband.

| CHRISTIAN Elsie D. | 05 July 1913 22 Apr. 1983 | Christian, Leonard | Yes |

Inscription: "Wed Mar. 28, 1939."

Other Info: Shares a headstone with her husband.

| CHRISTIAN H. Leslie | 20 July 1900 07 Oct. 1967 | Christian, Bernice D. | Yes |

Inscription: "Rest In Peace."

Other Info: Shares a headstone with his wife.

| CHRISTIAN James Wiley | 17 Mar. 1913 23 July 1974 | Christian, Shirley Worley | Yes |

Inscription: He served as inscribed: "PFC US Army." Footstone inscribed: "Father."

LAST NAME	Date of Birth	Maiden Name	Tombstone
First Name	Date of Death	Spouse	
	Age at Death		

Other Info: Shares a headstone with his wife.

| CHRISTIAN | 03 Nov. 1908 | | Yes |
| Leonard | 09 July 1985 | Christian, Elsie D. | |

Inscription: "Wed Mar. 28, 1939."

Other Info: Shares a headstone with his wife.

| CHRISTIAN | 09 Oct. 1865 | | Yes |
| Nancy V. | 18 Sep. 1945 | | |

Inscription: "Mother. We Will Meet Again."

| DRAKE | 19 June 1912 | | Yes |
| Francis Anderson | 07 Dec. 1967 | | |

Inscription: "Friend."

| DUNCAN | 20 Jan. 1911 | | Yes |
| Carlos A. | 06 Jan. 1966 | | |

Inscription: He served as inscribed: "PVT. Co. A 12 Bn IRTC World War II."

| DUNCAN | 22 June 1870 | | Yes |
| Church Hill | 26 Mar. 1959 | Duncan, Josie Lee | |

Inscription: "At Rest."

| DUNCAN | 21 Sep. 1947 | | Yes |
| Jeanette | 19 Dec. 1947 | | |

Inscription: "Daughter."

| DUNCAN | 17 Mar. 1875 | | Yes |
| Josie Lee | 11 Jan. 1944 | Duncan, Church Hill | |

Inscription: "A Tender Mother. And A Faithful Wife."

| DUNCAN | 03 Mar. 1915 | | Yes |
| Lonnie Mitchell | 12 Feb. 1983 | Duncan, Ruby Jamerson | |

Inscription: "Married Dec. 23, 1946. In God's Care. In Loving Memory Till We Meet Again."

| DUNKUM | 27 Nov. 1972 | | Yes |
| Brad Sterling | 20 June 1990 | | |

Inscription: "Our Darling Son."

| DUNKUM | 10 May 1905 | | Yes |
| Claude L. | 03 Oct. 1970 | Dunkum, Nannie L. | |

Other Info: Shares a headstone with his wife.

LAST NAME First Name	Date of Birth Date of Death Age at Death	Maiden Name Spouse	Tombstone
DUNKUM George Lumsden	1921 1978		Yes

Inscription: He served as inscribed: "MM2 US Navy World War II."

DUNKUM John J.	11 June 1905 04 Feb. 1983		Yes
DUNKUM Joshua Elijah	30 May 1906 07 July 1988	Dunkum, Annie Newton	Yes
DUNKUM Katie A.	18 Mar. 1912 08 Mar. 1971	Dunkum, Lennon J.	Yes

Inscription: "Mother."

DUNKUM Nannie L.	15 May 1904 24 Apr. 1980	Dunkum, Claude L.	Yes

Other Info: Shares a headstone with her husband.

FALLS Francis W.	17 Nov. 1913 01 Dec. 1981	Falls, Frances Wade	Yes

Inscription: "Rest In Peace."

GARRETT Annie O.	1884 1963	Garrett, Whitchomb (sic) P.	Yes

Other Info: Shares a headstone with her husband.

GARRETT Edward B.	07 Nov. 1923 20 Oct. 1977		Yes
GARRETT Herbert N.	25 Aug. 1919 03 Feb. 1992	Garrett, Virginia O.	Yes

Inscription: "In Loving Memory." Footstone shows he served as inscribed: "TEC5 US Army World War II."

GARRETT Whitchomb (sic) P.	1879 1961	Garrett, Annie O.	Yes

Other Info: Shares a headstone with his wife.

GARRETT William Pratt	31 Jan. 1912 06 Sep. 1985		Yes
GORMUS Douglas Forrest	1962 1963		Yes

Inscription: "Son."

GORMUS Frances T.	27 Sep. 1922 14 May 1989	Gormus, Robert W.	Yes

LAST NAME First Name	Date of Birth Date of Death Age at Death	Maiden Name Spouse	Tombstone

Inscription: "Loving Mother. Married Dec. 15, 1940." Footstone inscribed: "Mother."

Other Info: Shares a headstone with her husband.

| GORMUS
Georgia Lee G. | 06 Mar. 1922
27 Oct. 1984 | Gormus, Rosen Herman | Yes |

Other Info: Shares a headstone with her husband.

| GORMUS
Robert W. | 07 Apr. 1912
04 Feb. 1986 | Gormus, Frances T. | Yes |

Inscription: "Devoted Father. Married Dec. 15, 1940." Footstone inscribed: "Father."

Other Info: Shares a headstone with his wife.

| GORMUS
Rosen Herman | 06 Apr. 1907
13 Dec. 1966 | Gormus, Georgia Lee G. | Yes |

Other Info: Shares a headstone with his wife.

| HARRIS
Joseph Isaiah | 27 Aug. 1880
12 Aug. 1963 | | Yes |

| HARRIS
Mary Lillian | 12 Oct. 1889
25 June 1957 | Wade
Harris, J. Edgar | Yes |

Inscription: "Wife of ... At Rest." Footstone inscribed: "M.L.W.H."

| HARRIS
Raymond B. | 20 Aug. 1906
16 Oct. 1959 | Harris, Katherine D. | Yes |

Inscription: "Married Dec. 19, 1942."

| HART
Mary Thomas | 11 Jan. 1931
04 June 1979 | | Yes |

Inscription: "Forever In Our Hearts."

| HARVEY
Myrtie R. | 26 Oct. 1925
25 Dec. 1983 | Harvey, Sandy E. | Yes |

Other Info: Shares a headstone with her husband.

| HARVEY
Sandy E. | 16 Aug. 1914
05 Nov. 1986 | Harvey, Myrtie R. | Yes |

Other Info: Shares a headstone with his wife.

| JAMES
Floyd | | | No |

LAST NAME First Name	Date of Birth Date of Death Age at Death	Maiden Name Spouse	Tombstone

Other Info: Grave marked by a funeral home metal marker. Dates not readable.

| JONES
William Edward | 23 Nov. 1913
27 Apr. 1972 |
Jones, Ruth D. | Yes |

Inscription: "Father. In Precious Memory."

| KEY
Robert B. | 27 May 1910
13 Sep. 1973 |
Key, Annie W. | Yes |

Inscription: "Married Sept. 8, 1943."

| LeSUER
Ethel A. | 08 July 1894
22 Jan. 1967 | | Yes |

| LIPSCOMB
Elizabeth Duncan | 11 June 1906
11 July 1941 | | Yes |

Inscription: "Daughter & Sister. How Desolate Our Home Bereft Of Thee."

| NEWTON
Ada | 17 July 1889
22 Jan. 1970 | Dunkum
Newton, Wade Lumsden | Yes |

Inscription: "Married Dec. 28, 1908." Footstone inscribed: "Mother."

Other Info: Shares a headstone with her husband.

| NEWTON
Annie A. | 1911
1986 |
Newton, J. Hypes | Yes |

Other Info: Shares a headstone with her husband.

| NEWTON
Bobby E. | 30 July 1941
25 May 1991 | | Yes |

Inscription: "Rest In Peace."

| NEWTON
J. Hypes | 1908
1958 |
Newton, Annie A. | Yes |

Inscription: (Masonic Symbol.) Footstone inscribed: "Husband."

Other Info: Shares a headstone with his wife.

| NEWTON
Wade Lumsden | 27 Nov. 1887
22 Sep. 1963 |
Newton, Ada Dunkum | Yes |

Inscription: "Married Dec. 28, 1908." Footstone inscribed: "Father."

Other Info: Shares a headstone with his wife.

| O'BRYANT
Evelyn | 1911
1967 | Walker | Yes |

LAST NAME	Date of Birth	Maiden Name	Tombstone
First Name	Date of Death	Spouse	
	Age at Death		

Inscription: "Mother."

| O'BRYANT | 10 Oct. 1915 | | Yes |
| Ida Gertrude | 12 Nov. 1980 | O'Bryant, Joseph Benjamin | |

Other Info: Shares a headstone with her husband.

| O'BRYANT | 04 Feb. 1911 | | Yes |
| Joseph Benjamin | 24 July 1983 | O'Bryant, Ida Gertrude | |

Other Info: Shares a headstone with his wife.

| O'BRYANT | 1872 | | No |
| Mary Seay | 1961 | | |

Other Info: Grave marked by a funeral home metal marker.

| PERKINS | 05 Mar. 1914 | | Yes |
| Anna L. | 10 Nov. 1991 | Perkins, "Pete" T. D. | |

Other Info: Shares a headstone with her husband.

| PERKINS | 28 Feb. 1905 | | Yes |
| Charles E. | 30 Dec. 1973 | Perkins, Estelle J. | |

Inscription: "Thy Kingdom Come."

| PERKINS | 15 Aug. 1906 | | Yes |
| Theodore D. | 24 Sep. 1958 | Perkins, Anna L. | |

Inscription: "Pete."

Other Info: Shares a headstone with his wife.

| RAGLAND | 02 Oct. 1897 | | Yes |
| Richard B. | 13 Nov. 1986 | Ragland, Sallie F. | |

Inscription: "Devoted Father."

| RAKES | 12 Jan. 1890 | Wootton | Yes |
| Ada B. | 02 Nov. 1958 | Rakes, Thomas G. | |

Inscription: "Mother. Wife of ... Beyond the Sunset." Footstone inscribed: "Mother."

| RAKES | 16 June 1886 | | Yes |
| Thomas G. | 05 Nov. 1959 | Rakes, Ada B. Wootton | |

Inscription: "Father. Beyond the Sunset." Footstone inscribed: "Father."

| STEVENS | | | No |

Other Info: Grave marked by an unreadable funeral home metal marker.

LAST NAME First Name	Date of Birth Date of Death Age at Death	Maiden Name Spouse	Tombstone
TAYLOR Herman M.	09 Feb. 1924 30 Sep. 1977	Taylor, Fannie G.	Yes

Inscription: "Father."

| TAYLOR
Mannie Sue | 25 Sep. 1903
13 Jan. 1969 | Taylor, Matt | Yes |

Inscription: Footstone inscribed: "Mother."

| TAYLOR
Matt | 28 May 1892
11 June 1978 | Taylor, Mannie Sue | Yes |

Inscription: "Father." He served as inscribed on his footstone: "PVT US Army World War I."

| THOMAS
Carl Edwin | 15 Aug. 1922
04 Oct. 1945 | | Yes |

Inscription: "Blessed Are the Pure In Heart." He served as inscribed: "Virginia Staff Sgt. Air Corps."

| THOMAS
Elizabeth | 23 Dec. 1915
17 June 1990 | Pinnell
Thomas, Willard Archer | Yes |

Inscription: "At Rest."

| THOMAS
Henry B. | 13 Sep. 1893
22 July 1976 | Thomas, Nellie L. | Yes |

Other Info: Shares a headstone with his wife.

| THOMAS
Henry V. | 09 Mar. 1919
13 Dec. 1985 | Thomas, Thelma G. | Yes |

Inscription: Footstone inscribed: "Father."

Other Info: Shares a headstone with his wife.

| THOMAS
Howell L. | 22 Oct. 1895
07 Aug. 1978 | Thomas, Mary Lee H. | Yes |

Inscription: "Married June 8, 1919."

Other Info: Shares a headstone with his wife.

| THOMAS
Joseph B. | 08 June 1927
01 Jan. 1972 | | Yes |

Inscription: "Daddy." He served as inscribed: "Virginia PVT Co. C 70 TK BN World War II."

| THOMAS
Lottie A. | 11 Jan. 1903
22 Oct. 1960 | Thomas, Stuart E. | Yes |

LAST NAME First Name	Date of Birth Date of Death Age at Death	Maiden Name Spouse	Tombstone

Inscription: Footstone inscribed: "Mother."

Other Info: Shares a headstone with her husband.

| THOMAS
Mary Lee H. | 27 May 1898
21 Aug. 1958 |
Thomas, Howell L. | Yes |

Inscription: "Married June 8, 1919." Footstone inscribed: "M.L.H.T."

Other Info: Shares a headstone with her husband.

| THOMAS
Nellie L. | 22 June 1895
03 Jan. 1968 |
Thomas, Henry B. | Yes |

Other Info: Shares a headstone with her husband.

| THOMAS
Stuart E. | 25 Nov. 1891
30 Jan. 1971 |
Thomas, Lottie A. | Yes |

Inscription: Footstone inscribed: "Father."

Other Info: Shares a headstone with his wife.

| THOMAS
Thelma G. | 17 Apr. 1921
27 Sep. 1971 |
Thomas, Henry V. | Yes |

Inscription: Footstone inscribed: "Mother."

Other Info: Shares a headstone with her husband.

| THOMAS
Todd Baker | 23 Jan. 1961
27 May 1981 | | Yes |

Inscription: "Precious Lord Take My Hand."

| WADE
Alfred Byron | 06 Feb. 1896
20 May 1972 | | Yes |

Inscription: He served as inscribed: "Virginia PVT US Army World War I."

| WADE
Sarah H. | 25 Jan. 1899
27 Sep. 1982 | | Yes |

Inscription: "Mother. Always In Our Hearts."

| WOODS
Bertha | 17 Oct. 1919
21 Oct. 1993 | Smith
Woods, James W. | Yes |

Inscription: "Mother."

| WOODS
James W. Jr. | 09 Oct. 1949
21 Feb. 1969 | | Yes |

Inscription: He served as inscribed: "Virginia SP4 501 AG Admin Co."

LAST NAME First Name	Date of Birth Date of Death Age at Death	Maiden Name Spouse	Tombstone
WOOTTON J. Cliff	21 Feb. 1888 02 June 1920		Yes
WOOTTON Mary E.	15 Dec. 1861 14 Sep. 1954	LeSueur Wootton, Joseph W.	Yes
WOOTTON Minnie R.	05 Aug. 1895 28 Sep. 1978	Wootton, Samuel E.	Yes

Other Info: Shares a headstone with her husband.

WOOTTON Samuel E.	25 July 1900 05 Dec. 1984	Wootton, Minnie R.	Yes

Other Info: Shares a headstone with his wife.

WORLEY Ida	07 Jan. 1906 08 Sep. 1980	Hicks Worley, J. Cleve Sr.	Yes

Inscription: Footstone inscribed: "Mother."

Other Info: Shares a headstone with her husband.

WORLEY J. Cleve Sr.	09 May 1902 11 Feb. 1957	Worley, Ida Hicks	Yes

Inscription: Footstone inscribed: "Father."

Other Info: Shares a headstone with his wife.

WORLEY Ruby E.	1903 1976	Worley, S. William	Yes

Inscription: Footstone inscribed: "R.E.W."

Other Info: Shares a headstone with her husband.

WORLEY S. William	1900 1956	Worley, Ruby E.	Yes

Other Info: Shares a headstone with his wife.

"Rolfton" Homeplace - Hwy 749

Other Info: Indian Mound located near the Slate River. Local residents know where these old Indian burial mounds are located, and they should always be preserved.

Rush Family Cemetery - Hwy 642

FLOOD J. M.			Yes

LAST NAME	Date of Birth	Maiden Name	Tombstone
First Name	Date of Death	Spouse	
	Age at Death		

Other Info: Believed to be J. Monroe Flood. No dates inscribed on the tombstone.

| MAXEY | | | Yes |
| Mary Lula | | | |

Other Info: No dates inscribed on the tombstone.

| RUSH | 10 Feb. 1905 | Bryant | Yes |
| Alma | 21 July 1983 | Rush, Peter Walker | |

Inscription: "Mother."

Other Info: Shares a headstone with her husband.

| RUSH | 06 Oct. 1842 | | Yes |
| Ann E. | 18 Sep. 1883 | Rush, John S. | |

Inscription: " Asleep In Jesus! Peaceful Rest, Whose Waking Is Supremely Blest; No Fear, No Woe, Shall Dim That Hour That Manifests the Savior's Power." Footstone inscribed: "A.E.R."

| RUSH | | | Yes |
| Ben E. | | | |

Inscription: He served as inscribed: "TR. K. 4 VA. CAV. C.S.A."

Other Info: Born circa 1841. No dates inscribed on the headstone.

| RUSH | | | Yes |
| Eddie S. | | | |

Other Info: No dates inscribed on this headstone.

| RUSH | | | Yes |
| Eliza S. | | | |

Other Info: No dates inscribed on the headstone.

| RUSH | | | Yes |
| G. V. | 22 Dec. 1918 | | |

| RUSH | | | No |
| Mary F. | | | |

Other Info: Known to be buried here.

| RUSH | | | Yes |
| Mary S. | | Rush, Peter S. | |

Other Info: Born circa 1840. No dates inscribed on the headstone.

| RUSH | | | Yes |
| Peter S. | | Rush, Mary S. | |

LAST NAME First Name	Date of Birth Date of Death Age at Death	Maiden Name Spouse	Tombstone

Other Info: Born Circa 1828. No dates inscribed on the headstone.

| RUSH
Peter Walker | 23 July 1876
18 Jan. 1969 | Rush, Alma Bryant | Yes |

Inscription: "Father."

Other Info: Shares a headstone with his wife.

| RUSH
Sallie J. | | | Yes |

Other Info: No dates inscribed on the headstone.

| WOODSON
Olivia | 1988 | Rush | No |

Other Info: Known to be buried here, the daughter of John S. & Ella G. Rush, and the sister of Vincent P. Rush. She died around 1988, in her 90s.

Salem Baptist Church - Black - Hwy 627

| ANDERSON
Charlie Edward | 09 Feb. 1944
22 Dec. 1986
42 yr. | | No |

Other Info: Grave marked with a Funeral Home metal marker.

| HOCKER
Ned Edward | 1913
1987
74 yr | | No |

Other Info: Grave marked with a Funeral Home metal marker.

| JACKSON
Archer (Deacon) | 25 Nov. 1900
05 Sep. 1982 | | No |

Other Info: Grave marked with a Funeral Home metal marker.

| JACKSON
W. Ethel | 1917
1984 | Harris | Yes |

| JACKSON
Willie H. | 1906
1985 | | Yes |

| JONES
Fannie Courtney | 14 Aug. 1927
28 July 1982 | Lee
Jones, James L. | Yes |

Inscription: "Daughter of the late Clarence and Virginia Lee...the Beloved Wife of James L. Jones."

Other Info: Grave also marked with a Funeral Home metal marker.

LAST NAME First Name	Date of Birth Date of Death Age at Death	Maiden Name Spouse	Tombstone
JONES Ruth	28 Aug. 1905 12 Aug. 1976	Amos	Yes
JONES William H. Jr. "Shag"	1892 1976		Yes

Inscription: He served as inscribed: "Pvt. U.S. Army World War I."

| KENNEY
Mary | 28 June 1905
21 Feb. 1982 | Smith | Yes |

Inscription: "Mother."

| LEWIS
Eliza | 04 Apr. 1937
82 yr 3 mo | | No |

Other Info: Grave marked with a Funeral Home metal marker. She was the mother of Minerva Lewis and grandmother of Irving Lewis, both of whom lived with her.

| PERKINS
Minerva | 11 Jan. 1918 | | Yes |

Inscription: "Gone But Not Forgotten."

| PERKINS
Robert | 22 Apr. 1875
01 Apr. 1927 | | Yes |

Inscription: "A.G. Thompson Lodge - 7. I. O. King David." Footstone inscribed: "Robt. E. Perkins, Died April 1, 1927, Friendship Lodge - 3816. G.U.O.O.F."

Salem United Methodist Church Cemetery - Hwy 632

| ATWATER
William Bulluck (sic) | 1933
1972 | | Yes |

Inscription: "Rest In Peace."

| BAILEY
(Infants) | 1910-1912 | | No |

Other Info: Graves marked by fieldstones - no inscriptions. Three baby girls - all died as infants and were not named. Sisters of William Allen "Buck" Bailey.

| BAILEY
Nancy H. | 1878
1961 | Bailey, William A. Sr. | Yes |
| BAILEY
William A. Sr. | 1853
1932 | Bailey, Nancy H. | Yes |

LAST NAME First Name	Date of Birth Date of Death Age at Death	Maiden Name Spouse	Tombstone
BAIRD John Robert	25 May 1889 04 Nov. 1946		Yes
BANTON David A.	29 Jan. 1876 09 Apr. 1955	Banton, Ida Virginia	Yes

Inscription: Shares a headstone with his wife.

BANTON Decker	15 Aug. 1888 02 Aug. 1970		Yes
BANTON George W.	1851 21 Feb. 1924		Yes

Inscription: "Father Into Thy Hands I Commend My Spirit." Footstone inscribed: "G.W.B."

BANTON Ida Virginia	25 Dec. 1884 03 Jan. 1960	Banton, David A.	Yes

Other Info: Shares a headstone with her husband.

BANTON Letcher L.	23 Dec. 1905 27 Oct. 1974		Yes
BANTON (Male)			No

Other Info: Unreadable funeral home metal marker, but known to be a male member of the Banton family.

BANTON Murray "Shortie"	25 July 1922 20 Jan. 1972		Yes
BANTON Percy J.	10 Aug. 1901 23 Mar. 1992	Banton, Ada B.	Yes

Other Info: Grave also marked by a funeral home metal marker.

BANTON Shirley Mae	06 Jan. 1937 07 May 1983		Yes

Inscription: "Dau. of Sidney & Ruth Banton."

BANTON Wallace Woodrow Sr.	23 Dec. 1916 19 Apr. 1990		Yes

Inscription: "Rest In Peace."

Other Info: Grave is also marked by a funeral home metal marker.

BANTON William A.	29 Mar. 1896 24 Jan. 1977		Yes

LAST NAME First Name	Date of Birth Date of Death Age at Death	Maiden Name Spouse	Tombstone
BOLLINGER (Male)	1931-1933		No

Other Info: Grave marked by an unreadable funeral home metal marker. Known to have died between 1931-1933.

BOSTAIN Edward J.	09 Aug. 1915 28 Nov. 1988	Bostain, Ruth Baird	Yes
BOYD Wade Glenwood	02 July 1939 26 Apr. 1940		Yes

Inscription: "Son of John and Eliza Boyd."

CARRUTHERS Emma	1864 1957	Carter Carruthers, John Aden	Yes

Inscription: "Together On Earth, Together In the Tomb, At the Resurrection Morn, We Will Make Heaven Our Home."

Other Info: Shares a headstone with her husband.

CARRUTHERS John Aden	1866 1956	Carruthers, Emma Carter	Yes

Inscription: "Together On Earth, Together In the Tomb, At the Resurrection Morn, We Will Make Heaven Our Home."

Other Info: Shares a headstone with his wife.

CARTER George W.	1870 1949		Yes
CHANCE Terry Lynn	20 Feb. 1955 25 Feb. 1955		Yes

Inscription: "Son of Howard & Jewell Chance." Footstone inscribed: "T.L.C."

CHINN Dee L.	1915 1975		Yes
CHRISTIAN Anna	20 June 1885 10 Sep. 1967	Sharp Christian,	Yes

Inscription: "Mother."

CHRISTIAN Thomas Reeves	08 Apr. 1927 08 Sep. 1971		Yes
CROW Charles Ferdinand	1884 1955	Crow, Myrtle A.	Yes
CROW (Infant)	26 Aug. 1917		Yes

LAST NAME First Name	Date of Birth Date of Death Age at Death	Maiden Name Spouse	Tombstone

Inscription: "Infant Daughter Of J. S. & C. F. Crow."

| CROW
(Infants) | 15 Mar. 1927 | | Yes |

Inscription: "Infant Sons of Robt. J. H. & Maude S. Crow. Born Mar. 15, 1927 and Born Nov. 9, 1930."

| CROW
James C. | 23 May 1851 | Crow, Sue Harrison | Yes |

Other Info: Shares a headstone with his wife. His date of death was never inscribed on the headstone.

| CROW
Julia | 06 Apr. 1887
27 Sep. 1921 | Stokes
Crow, C. F. | Yes |

Inscription: Footstone inscribed: "J.S.C."

| CROW
Maude | 30 Oct. 1895
25 Dec. 1969 | Shepard
Crow, Robert J. H. | Yes |

Other Info: Shares a headstone with her husband.

| CROW
Myrtle | 1892
1980 | Anderson
Crow, Charles Ferdinand | Yes |

Other Info: Grave marked by a funeral home metal marker also.

| CROW
R. J. H. Jr. | 1917
1943 | | Yes |

Inscription: He served as inscribed: "Lt. R.J.H. Crow, Jr. Lost in South Pacific World War II."

| CROW
Robert J. H. | 02 Oct. 1890
19 July 1971 | Crow, Maude Shepard | Yes |

Other Info: Shares a headstone with his wife.

| CROW
Sue | 26 Feb. 1850
22 July 1928 | Harrison
Crow, James C. | Yes |

Other Info: Shares a headstone with her husband.

| DAVIS
Josephine S. | 28 July 1868
13 Sep. 1952 | Davis, Mathew M. | Yes |

Inscription: "Earth Has No Sorrow That Heaven Cannot Heal." Footstone inscribed: "Mother."

Other Info: Shares a headstone with her husband.

| DAVIS
Mathew M. | 13 June 1867
14 Jan. 1957 | Davis, Josephine S. | Yes |

LAST NAME	Date of Birth	Maiden Name	Tombstone
First Name	Date of Death	Spouse	
	Age at Death		

Inscription: "Earth Has No Sorrow That Heaven Cannot Heal." Footstone inscribed: "Father."

Other Info: Shares a headstone with his wife.

| DENICOURT | 22 Sep. 1907 | Shepard | Yes |
| Agnes | 10 Jan. 1988 | Denicourt, Gerald M. | |

Inscription: Footstone inscribed: "A.S.D."

| DENICOURT | 24 Apr. 1902 | | Yes |
| Gerald M. | 20 May 1966 | Denicourt, Agnes Shepard | |

Inscription: Footstone inscribed: "G.M.D."

| DENISON | 1886 | | Yes |
| Barbara C. | 1974 | Denison, Raymond | |

Other Info: Shares a headstone with her husband.

| DENISON | 1885 | | Yes |
| Raymond | 1943 | Denison, Barbara C. | |

Other Info: Shares a headstone with his wife.

| DOWDY | 26 Feb. 1844 | | Yes |
| Kate C. | 05 Feb. 1936 | Dowdy, Thomas H. | |

Inscription: "Gone, But Not Forgotten."

DOWDY			Yes
Thomas H.	14 Aug. 1908	Dowdy, Kate C.	
	72 yr.		

Inscription: "Gone But Not Forgotten. C.S.A." Footstone inscribed: "T.H.D." A second stone shows that he served as inscribed: "Thomas H. Dowdy Co. E. 25 VA. Inf. C.S.A."

| DUNCAN | 29 June 1898 | | Yes |
| Harve Curtis | 27 Nov. 1965 | | |

Inscription: "Jack."

| ELAM | 23 May 1920 | | Yes |
| Irma C. | 08 Oct. 1926 | | |

Inscription: "Our Darling Baby."

| ELAM | 10 Nov. 1886 | Guthrie | Yes |
| Mattie | 09 Sep. 1972 | Elam, William Archer | |

Inscription: "Beyond the Sunset." Footstone inscribed: "Mother."

Other Info: Shares a headstone with her husband.

LAST NAME First Name	Date of Birth Date of Death Age at Death	Maiden Name Spouse	Tombstone
ELAM William Archer	09 Mar. 1884 03 Apr. 1957	Elam, Mattie Guthrie	Yes

Inscription: "Beyond the Sunset." Footstone inscribed: "Father."

Other Info: Shares a headstone with his wife.

EMERSON Lelia	30 Sep. 1915 27 Dec. 1969	Bailey	Yes
FARRIS Mary Elizabeth (Huddleston)	1896 	Wright 1982	No

Other Info: Grave marked by a Funeral Home Metal Marker. It is said that she is buried in the same spot as Robert "Bob" Huddleston. (She was a former wife.)

FERGUSON (Male)		Ferguson, (Female) Banton	No

Other Info: No grave markers, but known to be a husband and wife buried here. No inscriptions. Christian names not known.

FIELDS Harold W. Jr.	1944 1983		Yes

Inscription: He served as inscribed: "MM2 US Navy Vietnam."

FIELDS Harold W. Sr.	26 May 1921 27 Nov. 1982	Fields, Zanie T.	Yes

Other Info: Shares a headstone with his wife. Grave is also marked by a funeral home metal marker inscribed: "Harold Willard Fields."

FIELDS Zanie	06 Feb. 1921 31 Jan. 1980	Trent Fields, Harold W. Sr.	Yes

Other Info: Shares a headstone with her husband. Grave is also marked by a funeral home metal marker inscribed: "Zanie Trent Fields."

FONES Joseph William	25 Nov. 1880 19 Apr. 1940		Yes

Inscription: "A Life Like His Has Left A Record Sweet For Memory To Dwell Upon."

FONES William S.	30 Aug. 1920 11 May 1954		Yes

Inscription: Footstone inscribed: "W.S.F."

FORBES Cleveland Jr.	29 May 1892 05 Mar. 1977	Forbes, Ruth Shepard	Yes

Other Info: Shares a headstone with his wife.

LAST NAME First Name	Date of Birth Date of Death Age at Death	Maiden Name Spouse	Tombstone
FORBES Cleveland Owen III	18 Nov. 1918 25 Dec. 1947	Forbes, Elizabeth Hall	Yes

Inscription: Footstone inscribed: "C.O.F."

FORBES Dorothy	29 Jan. 1914 15 Dec. 1914		Yes

Inscription: "Safe In the Arms Of Jesus."

FORBES Elizabeth H.	17 Aug. 1914 01 Mar. 1945	Hall Forbes, Cleveland Owen III	Yes

Inscription: Footstone inscribed: "E.H.F."

FORBES Ruth	19 Dec. 1891 17 Apr. 1987	Shepard Forbes, Cleveland Jr.	Yes

Other Info: Shares a headstone with her husband.

FOSTER A. Courtney	1881 1938	Foster, Martha O.	Yes

Inscription: Footstone inscribed: "A.C.F."

Other Info: Shares a headstone with his wife.

FOSTER Martha O.	1888 1964	Foster, A. Courtney	Yes

Inscription: Footstone inscribed: "M.O.F."

Other Info: Shares a headstone with her husband.

GANNAWAY Eula	07 Nov. 1897 22 Apr. 1988	Gary Gannaway, Richard W.	Yes

Inscription: Shares a headstone with her husband.

GANNAWAY Richard Winston	07 Oct. 1892 15 Feb. 1976	Gannaway, Eula Gary	Yes

Other Info: Shares a headstone with his wife.

GARLAND Frances W.	1910 1985	Garland, Joseph L.	Yes

Other Info: Shares a headstone with her husband.

GARLAND G. P. Dr.	02 Oct. 1866 12 July 1914	Garland, Mary R.	Yes

Inscription: "Thy Trials Ended, Thy Rest Is Won." Footstone inscribed: "G.P.G."

LAST NAME First Name	Date of Birth Date of Death Age at Death	Maiden Name Spouse	Tombstone
GARLAND Joseph L.	1910 1974	Garland, Frances W.	Yes

Other Info: Shares a headstone with his wife.

GARLAND Mary R.	29 Oct. 1872 01 Oct. 1936	Garland, Dr. G. P.	Yes

Inscription: "Thy Trials Ended, Thy Rest Is Won." Footstone inscribed: "M.R.G."

GILBERT Martha	25 July 1887 08 June 1919	Stinson Gilbert,	Yes

Inscription: "At Rest." Footstone inscribed: "M.S.G."

Other Info: Shares a headstone with her father and mother, John J. & Elizabeth B. Stinson.

GOODMAN Hubert Coleman	1911 1992	Goodman, Georgia Putney	Yes
GOODMAN Pocahontas Coleman	1870 1946		Yes
GOODMAN William Ivey	1911 1974		Yes
GRIGG Elijah H.	1872 1940	Grigg, Minnie G. Wise	Yes

Other Info: Shares a headstone with his wife.

GRIGG Inez H.	03 Aug. 1878 17 July 1913	Grigg, Philip Edward	Yes

Inscription: "In Memory of Mrs. ... They Shall Be Mine, Saith the Lord... In That Day ..." The front of the slate headstone is flaking off, making it impossible to read the full inscription. Footstone inscribed: "I.H.G."

GRIGG (Infant)	20 Apr. 1912		Yes

Inscription: "Infant Child Of P. E. and I. H. Grigg. Budded On Earth To Bloom In Heaven."

GRIGG Julia Inez	25 Apr. 1913 14 Aug. 1913		Yes

Inscription: "In Memory Of ... ..." The front of this slate headstone is flaking off making in impossible to read the full inscription.

GRIGG Minnie G.	1894 1982	Wise Grigg, Elijah H.	Yes

LAST NAME First Name	Date of Birth Date of Death Age at Death	Maiden Name Spouse	Tombstone

Other Info: Shares a headstone with her husband.

| GRIGG Philip Edward | 13 Apr. 1867 06 June 1935 | Grigg, Inez H. | Yes |

Inscription: Footstone inscribed: "P.E.G."

| GUTHRIE Annie H. | 1863 1924 | Guthrie, Thomas G. | Yes |

Inscription: "A Tender Mother. A Faithful Friend. Mother." Footstone inscribed: "A.H.G."

| GUTHRIE Blythe Samuel | 13 Oct. 1896 28 Nov. 1982 | Guthrie, Elizabeth G. | Yes |

Inscription: "In God's Keeping."

Other Info: Shares a headstone with his wife.

| GUTHRIE Charles Roy | 17 Dec. 1885 23 June 1945 | Guthrie, Margaret Kent | Yes |

Other Info: Shares a headstone with his wife.

| GUTHRIE Elizabeth | 23 Aug. 1904 | Guthrie Guthrie, Blythe Samuel | Yes |

Inscription: "In God's Keeping."

Other Info: Shares a headstone with her husband.

| GUTHRIE Forrest | 14 Oct. 1864 15 Feb. 1939 | Guthrie, Mary F. S. | Yes |

Inscription: (Masonic Symbol.) "Born Mt. Pleasant ... Died Rosny ..." Footstone inscribed: "Father."

Other Info: Shares a headstone with his wife.

| GUTHRIE Forrest Jr. | 23 Nov. 1899 28 Nov. 1936 | | Yes |

Inscription: "Born Rosny ... Died Buckingham C.H. ..." Footstone inscribed: "Son."

| GUTHRIE James Rappe | 12 Nov. 1892 13 Mar. 1921 | | Yes |

Inscription: (Masonic Symbol.) "At Rest. Member of Richmond Fire Dept. Killed in Jurgens & Hopkins Fire." Footstone inscribed: "J.R.G."

| GUTHRIE Leonard | 02 Sep. 1904 22 Oct. 1905 | | Yes |

LAST NAME	Date of Birth	Maiden Name	Tombstone
First Name	Date of Death	Spouse	
	Age at Death		

Inscription: "Son Of Thomas and Annie Guthrie."

| GUTHRIE | 18 Oct. 1888 | | Yes |
| Margaret Kent | 23 Aug. 1986 | Guthrie, Charles Roy | |

Other Info: Shares a headstone with her husband.

| GUTHRIE | 03 Aug. 1876 | Spencer | Yes |
| Mary Frances | 17 Apr. 1946 | Guthrie, Forrest | |

Inscription: "Born Dixie ... Died Rosny ..." Footstone inscribed: "Mother."

Other Info: Shares a headstone with her husband.

| GUTHRIE | 01 Sep. 1935 | Butrem | Yes |
| Paula Ann | 17 Mar. 1972 | Guthrie, | |

Inscription: "Born Neenah, Wis. ... Died Mt. Gilead, VA. ..."

| GUTHRIE | 1852 | | Yes |
| Thomas G. | 1924 | Guthrie, Annie H. | |

Inscription: "He Died As He Lived. A Christian." Footstone inscribed: "T.G.G."

| GUTHRIE | 29 Sep. 1956 | | Yes |
| Thomas Wills | 10 June 1993 | | |

Inscription: He served as inscribed: "US Navy."

| HAMMOND | 31 Dec. 1901 | | Yes |
| Betty Shepard | 27 Nov. 1967 | | |

| HAMMONDS | 13 May 1899 | | Yes |
| Mattie Baird | 02 Sep. 1987 | | |

| HUDDLESTON | | | No |
| A. Lee | | | |

Other Info: No grave markers, but known to be buried here. He is the son of Peter Huddleston.

| HUDDLESTON | 25 Oct. 1907 | | Yes |
| Annie Pearl | 02 Feb. 1971 | Huddleston, Rees Jeff | |

Inscription: "Beyond the Sunset."

Other Info: Shares a headstone with her husband.

| HUDDLESTON | 21 Apr. 1903 | | Yes |
| Chas. A. | 13 Sep. 1943 | | |

Inscription: "At Rest." Footstone inscribed: "C.A.H."

| HUDDLESTON | | | No |
| (Child) | | | |

LAST NAME	Date of Birth	Maiden Name	Tombstone
First Name	Date of Death	Spouse	
	Age at Death		

Other Info: Known to be buried here. Field stone marker only. The daughter of Peter Huddleston.

| HUDDLESTON | | | No |
| Daisy | | | |

Other Info: Grave marked by a fieldstone. She died Mar. 3, 1930.

| HUDDLESTON | 09 Aug. 1878 | | Yes |
| Drewey W. | 27 Apr. 1957 | | |

Inscription: "Father. At Rest."

| HUDDLESTON | | | No |
| Forest | | | |

Other Info: Grave marked by a fieldstone. He died March 4, 1925.

| HUDDLESTON | | | No |
| Gladys | | | |

Other Info: No grave markers, but known to be buried here.

| HUDDLESTON | | | No |
| (Infant) | | | |

Other Info: No grave markers, but this infant daughter of Peter Huddleston is known to be buried here.

| HUDDLESTON | | | No |
| John | | | |

Other Info: Grave marked by an unreadable funeral home metal marker. John was the son of Peter Huddleston and his second wife, Virginia Farris Huddleston.

| HUDDLESTON | 04 June 1954 | | Yes |
| John Morton III | 11 Dec. 1983 | | |

Inscription: "In Loving Memory of Our Son, Brother, Husband, Friend."

Other Info: Grave is also marked by a funeral home metal marker.

| HUDDLESTON | 1896 | Wright | No |
| Mary Elizabeth | 1982 | Huddleston, Robert | |

Other Info: No grave markers, but known to be buried here. She married again to a Ferris after the death of her first husband.

| HUDDLESTON | 18 Aug. 1875 | | Yes |
| Mary Sue | 24 May 1942 | | |

Inscription: "Asleep In Jesus."

LAST NAME First Name	Date of Birth Date of Death Age at Death	Maiden Name Spouse	Tombstone
HUDDLESTON (Mrs.)		Huddleston, Charles	No

Other Info: No grave markers, but known to be buried here.

| HUDDLESTON
Peter | 03 May 1931 | | No |

Other Info: No grave markers, but known to be buried here. Married first to Virginia Catlett Huddleston, secondly to Virginia Farris Huddleston.

| HUDDLESTON
Rees (sic) Jeff | 14 Nov. 1902 | Huddleston, Annie Pearl | Yes |

Inscription: "Beyond the Sunset."

Other Info: Shares a headstone with his wife.

| HUDDLESTON
Reese Jeff Jr. | 13 June 1933
27 Apr. 1994 | | Yes |

Inscription: "Have Faith In God."

| HUDDLESTON
Robert | | | No |

Other Info: No grave markers, but known to be buried here. He died around 1962.

| HUDDLESTON
Robert Wesley | 21 June 1920
22 June 1985 | | Yes |

Inscription: He served as inscribed: "PVT US Army World War II."

| HUDDLESTON
Samuel Allen | | | No |

Other Info: Grave marked by a fieldstone - no inscriptions.

| HUDDLESTON
Sarah Farris | | | No |

Other Info: No grave markers, but known to be buried here. She is the sister of Virginia Farris Huddleston.

| HUDDLESTON
Thomas | Dec. 1928 | | No |

Other Info: No grave marker, but known to be buried here.

| HUDDLESTON
Thomas C. | 1926
1978 | | No |

LAST NAME First Name	Date of Birth Date of Death Age at Death	Maiden Name Spouse	Tombstone

Other Info: Grave marked by a funeral home metal marker. Son of Peter Huddleston and his second wife, Virginia Farris Huddleston.

HUDDLESTON Thomas H.	04 Sep. 1876 19 Nov. 1958		Yes

HUDDLESTON Tom			No

Other Info: Grave marked by a fieldstone. He died Dec. 1928.

HUDDLESTON Virginia		Farris Huddleston, Peter	No

Other Info: No grave markers, but known to be buried here. She was the second wife of Peter, and the sister of Sarah Farris Huddleston.

HUDDLESTON Virginia	Feb. 1928	Catlett Huddleston, Peter	No

Other Info: No grave markers, but known to be buried here. She was the first wife of Peter H.

HUDDLESTON Walter L.	07 Nov. 1927 16 Jan. 1992		Yes

Inscription: "Our Father."

HUDDLESTON William (Robert)			Yes

Inscription: He served as inscribed: "C.S.A."

HUGHES D. E.	17 Mar. 1862 20 Apr. 1920	Hughes, Louise G. R.	Yes

Inscription: "He Is Not Dead But Sleepeth." Footstone inscribed: "D.E.H."

HUGHES John Cabble	31 Mar. 1896 09 Oct. 1947		Yes

HUGHES Louise Gates	22 Feb. 1868 14 Dec. 1953	Richardson Hughes, D. E.	Yes

Inscription: "Rest In Peace."

JAMERSON Ellie Irene	1917 1957	Jamerson, Henry L.	No

Other Info: Grave marked by a funeral home metal marker.

JAMERSON Henry L.	1914 1972	Jamerson, Ellie Irene	No

Other Info: Grave marked by a funeral home metal marker.

LAST NAME First Name	Date of Birth Date of Death Age at Death	Maiden Name Spouse	Tombstone

JENKS   1922-1923   No

Other Info: No Christian name remembered. He was a man from the state of Michigan, here in Buckingham County to cut timber. He died in the fire that burned his cabin down; around 1922-1923. Grave marked at head and foot by fieldstones.

LAWTON   1910   Yes
Mary Frances   1990

Inscription: "Proverbs 31: 10 - 31."

LAWTON   Yes
Robert Phillip

Other Info: No dates inscribed on the headstone.

MAKI   03 Apr. 1913   Yes
Elmer Leimo   23 Apr. 1983   Maki, Mary E. G.

Inscription: "Born Chassell, Michigan ... Died Rosny ..."

Other Info: Shares a headstone with his wife.

MAKI   19 Jan. 1902   Guthrie   Yes
Mary Eliza   04 Mar. 1983   Maki, Elmer Leimo

Inscription: "Born Rosny ... Died Rosny ..."

Other Info: Shares a headstone with her husband.

MORING   1904   Yes
LeRoy D.   1979   Moring, Vesta G.

Inscription: "Thy Kingdom Come."

MURPHY   03 Mar. 1955   Yes
Sandra Kay   26 Aug. 1957

Inscription: "Safe In the Arms of Jesus." Footstone inscribed: "S.K.M."

MURRAY   19 July 1904   Yes
Mattie A.   21 June 1978

PATTERSON   11 Oct. 1906   Yes
Elwood G.   02 Mar. 1962

Inscription: Footstone inscribed: "E.G.P."

PATTERSON   08 June 1908   Yes
John Dabney   10 July 1972

Inscription: He served as inscribed: "Virginia Cpl Btry B. 314 FA BN World War II."

LAST NAME First Name	Date of Birth Date of Death Age at Death	Maiden Name Spouse	Tombstone
PATTERSON Kemper Withers	03 Apr. 1918 27 Mar. 1981		Yes

Inscription: He served as inscribed: "PFC US Army."

| PATTERSON
William Henry | 06 June 1911
21 Apr. 1930 | | Yes |

Inscription: Footstone inscribed: "W.H.P."

| PATTESON [sic]
Frank T. | 28 Oct. 1874
29 Mar. 1948 | | Yes |

Inscription: He served as inscribed: "Virginia Sgt. 67 Co. Coast Arty."

| PATTESON [sic]
Rosa L. | 17 Dec. 1877
01 Apr. 1959 | | Yes |

| PURVIS
Charles Jefferson | 16 Nov. 1891
19 Mar. 1974 | Purvis, Mary Shepard | Yes |

| PURVIS
Mary | 13 June 1890
13 Aug. 1972 | Shepard
Purvis, Charles Jefferson | Yes |

Inscription: "At Rest."

| PUTNEY
Daisy Ruth | 15 Mar. 1880
03 Sep. 1912 | | Yes |

Inscription: To My Wife ... A Devoted Wife, A Loving Mother, A True Christian. Precious In the Sight Of the Lord Is the Death Of His Saints." Footstone inscribed: "D.R.P."

| RAGLAND
James T. | 1910
1992 | | No |

Other Info: Grave marked by a funeral home metal marker.

| RAGLAND
Mary V. | 12 Oct. 1872
09 Dec. 1955 | Jamerson
Ragland, Nathaniel E. | Yes |

Inscription: "Mother. Wife of Nathaniel E. Ragland."

| RAGLAND
Nathaniel E. | 16 Oct. 1899
22 Jan. 1947 | | Yes |

Inscription: "Son. Gone But Not Forgotten."

| REESE
Charles Edward | 14 May 1854
21 Jan. 1925 | Reese, Nealie Thacker | Yes |

Inscription: Footstone inscribed: "C.E.R."

Other Info: Shares a headstone with his wife.

LAST NAME First Name	Date of Birth Date of Death Age at Death	Maiden Name Spouse	Tombstone
REESE (child)			Yes

Inscription: A marker, but no inscription. Known to be a child of the Reese's who died young.

| REESE
Nealie | 25 Feb. 1878
14 May 1945 | Thacker
Reese, Charles Edward | Yes |

Inscription: Footstone inscribed: "N.T.R."

Other Info: Shares a headstone with her husband.

| RICHARDSON
James R. | 08 Aug. 1914
24 July 1973 | | Yes |

Inscription: He served as inscribed: "U.S. Army."

RICHARDSON Raymond Allen	1909 1979		Yes
RICHARDSON Roland McKenny	1879 1960		Yes
RICHARDSON Vivian Allen	1878 1947		Yes
ROZELL Ida S.	1892 1962	Rozell, Joseph J.	Yes

Other Info: Shares a headstone with her husband.

| ROZELL
Joseph J. | 1888
1964 | Rozell, Ida S. | Yes |

Other Info: Shares a headstone with his wife.

| SHARP
Daniel | 05 Feb. 1847
01 Jan. 1923 | Sharp, Nannie Stinson | Yes |

Inscription: "Father. Kind Father Of Love Thou Art Gone To Thy Rest." He served as inscribed on his footstone: "Daniel Sharp Co C 3rd VA Regt. C.S.A."

| SHARP
Nannie | 1855
1931 | Stinson
Sharp, Daniel | Yes |
| SHARPE
John W. | 1874
1937 | | Yes |

Inscription: "Father."

| SHEPARD
Alice Burwell | 1873
1966 | | Yes |

LAST NAME First Name	Date of Birth Date of Death Age at Death	Maiden Name Spouse	Tombstone
	Inscription: Footstone inscribed: "A.B.S."		
SHEPARD E. A.	1850 1920		Yes
	Inscription: "In God We Trust."		
SHEPARD Edith Loveline	05 Jan. 1894 10 Sep. 1975	Shepard, Edward Miller	Yes
	Inscription: "Foster." Footstone inscribed: "E.L.S."		
SHEPARD Edward Bossieux	25 July 1869 06 Nov. 1957	Shepard, Mattie Purvis	Yes
	Inscription: Footstone inscribed: "Father."		
SHEPARD Edward Miller	15 July 1894 20 Nov. 1990	Shepard, Edith Loveline	Yes
	Inscription: Footstone inscribed: "E.M.S."		
SHEPARD Edward Poindexter	1840 1935	Shepard, Georgia J.	Yes
	Inscription: He served as inscribed: "C.S.A."		
SHEPARD Everette Edward	03 June 1881 30 Aug. 1968	Shepard, Lula F. H.	Yes
	Inscription: Footstone inscribed: "Father."		
SHEPARD Georgia J.	24 Aug. 1841 20 Nov. 1910	Shepard, Edward P.	Yes
	Inscription: "To My Wife ... Let Her Own Works Praise Her In the Gates." Footstone inscribed: "G.J.S."		
SHEPARD (Infants)			Yes
	Inscription: "Our Darling Children ... Of Mr. and Mrs. E. E. Shepard. Christ Loved Them and Took Them Home." Two uninscribed footstones, and one footstone inscribed: "Lula L."		
	Other Info: Note: Lula L. Shepard is also included on the headstone of her mother, Lula F. H. Shepard.		
SHEPARD James Wilson	1870 1932		Yes
SHEPARD Janice S.	07 Dec. 1903 15 Jan. 1985		Yes

LAST NAME	Date of Birth	Maiden Name	Tombstone
First Name	Date of Death	Spouse	
	Age at Death		

| SHEPARD | 1901 | | Yes |
| John W. | 1981 | | |

Other Info: Grave also marked by a funeral home metal marker.

| SHEPARD | 29 June 1871 | | Yes |
| Lula Agnes | 17 June 1904 | | |

Inscription: " At Rest. A Precious One From Us Has Gone, A Voice We Loved Is Stilled, A Place Is Vacant In Our Home, Which Never Can Be Filled." Footstone inscribed: "L.A.S."

| SHEPARD | 08 Aug. 1882 | Harper | Yes |
| Lula F. | 29 July 1921 | Shepard, Everette Edward | |

Inscription: "Wife Of ... Gone But Not Forgotten." Footstone inscribed: "Mother."

Other Info: Shares a headstone with her daughter, Lula L. Also buried here with their mother and father are two other unnamed children: "Our Darling Children of Mr. and Mrs. E. E. Shepard. Christ Loved Them and Took Them Home."

| SHEPARD | 21 Apr. 1916 | | Yes |
| Lula L. | 11 Mar. 1918 | | |

Inscription: "Gone But Not Forgotten."

Other Info: Shares a headstone with her mother, Lula F.H. Shepard.

| SHEPARD | 18 May 1861 | | Yes |
| Martha A. | 30 July 1907 | | |

Inscription: "In Memory Of ... Thy Memory Shall Ever Be A Guiding Start To Heaven. Sister." Footstone inscribed: "M.A.S."

Other Info: Botton of headstone is signed: "M. R. Jones."

| SHEPARD | 03 Nov. 1845 | Guthrie | Yes |
| Martha J. | 23 Jan. 1924 | Shepard, W. B. | |

Inscription: "Wife of ... She Was the Sunshine Of Our Home. Mother." Footstone inscribed: "M.J.G.S."

| SHEPARD | 11 Jan. 1880 | Purvis | Yes |
| Mattie | 16 Dec. 1962 | Shepard, Edward Bossieux | |

Inscription: Footstone inscribed: "Mother."

| SHEPARD | 09 Apr. 1862 | | Yes |
| Miller Jones | 01 Mar. 1936 | Shepard, Sarah J. G. | |

Inscription: Footstone inscribed: "M.J.S."

LAST NAME First Name	Date of Birth Date of Death Age at Death	Maiden Name Spouse	Tombstone
SHEPARD Otis A.	16 Oct. 1899	Shepard, Pearl G.	Yes

Other Info: Shares a headstone with his wife. His death date was never inscribed.

SHEPARD Pearl G.	23 Nov. 1900 23 Feb. 1985	Shepard, Otis A.	Yes

Other Info: Shares a headstone with her husband.

SHEPARD Sarah Jane	26 Jan. 1868 19 May 1941	Gannaway Shepard, Miller Jones	Yes

Inscription: "NEC Timeo, Nec Sperno." Footstone inscribed: "S.J.G.S."

SHEPARD William B.	16 Feb. 1827 02 Nov. 1904	Shepard, Martha J. G.	Yes

Inscription: "In Memory of ... A Precious One From Us Has Gone, A Voice We Loved Is Stilled." He served as inscribed on his footstone: "W. B. Shepard Co. G 3rd VA Reg. C.S.A."

SHEPARD William R.	1903 1972	Shepard, Rebecca R.	Yes

Other Info: Grave also marked by a funeral home metal marker inscribed: "William Russell Shepard."

SHIELDS Gayle	29 Apr. 1912 06 Sep. 1962	Denison	Yes

Inscription: Footstone inscribed: "G.D.S."

SILVEY Agnes Beryl	06 Sep. 1902 26 June 1927		Yes

Inscription: "Daughter of William Russell and Eubelia (sic) Mayo Cabell Silvey. Blessed Are the Pure In Heart; For They Shall See God."

SILVEY Dorothy Filer	06 Sep. 1898 07 Jan. 1977	Silvey, W. Russell	Yes

SILVEY Eubelya Richardson	1880 1956		Yes

Inscription: "Mother. At Rest."

SILVEY W. Russell	1898 1976	Silvey, Dorothy Filer	Yes

Inscription: He served as inscribed: "Col. US Army World War I & II."

SILVEY William R.	17 Oct. 1853 23 Apr. 1908		Yes

LAST NAME	Date of Birth	Maiden Name	Tombstone
First Name	Date of Death	Spouse	
	Age at Death		

Inscription: (Masonic Symbol .) "Thy Loss We Dearly Feel." Footstone inscribed: "W.R.S."

| SLOAN | 22 Mar. 1901 | | Yes |
| Mattie Lou | 10 Mar. 1983 | | |

| SLOAN | 15 Sep. 1889 | | Yes |
| Spencer L. | 12 Sep. 1970 | | |

Inscription: He served as inscribed: "Virginia Pvt. US Army World War I."

| SMITH | | | No |
| Jackson | 1934 | | |

Other Info: Grave marked by unreadable funeral home metal marker. Son of Mary Bailey Smith.

| SMITH | | Bailey | No |
| Mary | 1950 | | |

Other Info: A visible grave, but no markers. She is known to be buried here, as remembered by a current church member. Mary was the mother of Jackson Smith.

| SPENCER | 30 Aug. 1889 | | Yes |
| A. Sidney Jr. | 27 Jan. 1916 | | |

Inscription: "In Memory Of ... Son Of A.S. & H.A. Spencer. We Trust In God To Meet Thee Again." Footstone inscribed: "A.S.S."

| SPENCER | 30 June 1862 | | Yes |
| Albert Sidney | 02 Dec. 1940 | Spencer, Hattie Abner | |

Inscription: Footstone inscribed: "A.S.S."

| SPENCER | 13 Aug. 1887 | | Yes |
| Bettie Kish | 21 Mar. 1903 | | |

Inscription: "Our Loved Ones ... Daughter ... Thy Memory Shall Ever Be A Guiding Star To Heaven."

Other Info: At the bottom of the back of the headstone is signed: "M. R. Jones, Arvonia, Va." Shares a headstone with her mother, Hattie A. Spencer.

| SPENCER | 29 Dec. 1883 | | Yes |
| Gelia S. | 25 May 1973 | Spencer, Wm. Abner | |

Inscription: "God Is and All Is Well."

Other Info: Shares a headstone with her husband.

| SPENCER | 28 Aug. 1907 | | Yes |
| H. Willard | 28 Nov. 1986 | Spencer, Virginia B. | |

LAST NAME	Date of Birth	Maiden Name	Tombstone
First Name	Date of Death	Spouse	
	Age at Death		

Other Info: Shares a headstone with his wife.

| SPENCER | 07 Aug. 1863 | | Yes |
| Hattie Abner | 17 June 1903 | Spencer, Albert Sidney | |

Inscription: "Our Loves Ones ... Wife ... Faithful To Her Trust, Even Unto Her Death." Footstone inscribed: "H.A.S."

Other Info: Shares a headstone with her daughter, B. K. Spencer. At the bottom on the back of the headstone is signed: "M.R. Jones, Arvonia, Va."

| SPENCER | | | Yes |
| Henrietta Virginia | 28 June 1943 | | |

Inscription: "Dau. of H. W. & Virginia B. Spencer."

| SPENCER | 20 May 1877 | | Yes |
| Jennie Corson | 07 Feb. 1946 | | |

| SPENCER | 05 June 1866 | | Yes |
| John Y. | 15 Nov. 1917 | | |

Inscription: (Masonic Symbol.) "Our Brother. In God We Trust." Footstone inscribed: "J.Y.S."

| SPENCER | 12 Sep. 1904 | | Yes |
| Katherine Fraser | 04 Dec. 1938 | | |

| SPENCER | 1894 | | Yes |
| Otell ... iston | 1911 | | |

Inscription: "She slee ... ... And near ... ... Her you ... ... In her ..." Footstone inscribed: "O.W.S."

Other Info: The front of the slate stone is flaking off, and the full inscription cannot be read.

| SPENCER | 19 Sep. 1918 | | Yes |
| Ruth E. | 22 Oct. 1960 | | |

| SPENCER | 25 Dec. 1908 | | Yes |
| Virginia B. | 22 May 1988 | Spencer, H. Willard | |

Other Info: Shares a headstone with her husband.

| SPENCER | 10 Mar. 1885 | | Yes |
| Wm. Abner | 04 Nov. 1951 | Spencer, Gelia S. | |

Inscription: (Masonic Symbol.) "God Is and All Is Well."

Other Info: Shares a headstone with his wife.

| STINSON | 11 May 1904 | | Yes |
| Elijah M. | 03 Dec. 1968 | Stinson, Nannie A. | |

LAST NAME First Name	Date of Birth Date of Death Age at Death	Maiden Name Spouse	Tombstone
STINSON Elizabeth B.	13 May 1859 20 Nov. 1954	Stinson, John J.	Yes

Inscription: "At Rest." Footstone inscribed: "E.B.S."

Other Info: Shares a headstone with her husband and a daughter, Martha S. Gilbert.

| STINSON
James Lewis | 05 June 1932
25 Apr. 1965 | | Yes |

Inscription: He served as inscribed; "Virginia PFC US Army Korea."

| STINSON
John J. | 15 June 1853
19 Dec. 1923 | Stinson, Elizabeth B. | Yes |

Inscription: "At Rest."

Other Info: Shares a headstone with his wife and daughter, Martha S. Gilbert.

STINSON Junius J.	05 Sep. 1875 13 Aug. 1958		Yes
STINSON Junius S.	11 May 1911 13 Mar. 1980		Yes
STINSON Lelia B.	12 June 1892 16 Feb. 1949	Stinson, Thomas E.	Yes

Inscription: "At Rest."

Other Info: Shares a headstone with her husband.

STINSON Mary L.	08 Apr. 1882 29 May 1955		Yes
STINSON Nannie A.	15 June 1915 27 Dec. 1975	Stinson, Elijah M.	Yes
STINSON Thomas E.	12 Aug. 1894 22 Nov. 1966	Stinson, Lelia B.	Yes

Inscription: "At Rest."

Other Info: Shares a headstone with his wife.

| STOUT
Novil E. | 27 Aug. 1914
27 Mar. 1980 | Stout, Rosa A. | Yes |

Inscription: (Masonic Symbol.) "Father."

| TOYLES
Mary Helen | 1898
5 yr. | | No |

LAST NAME First Name	Date of Birth Date of Death Age at Death	Maiden Name Spouse	Tombstone

Other Info: Grave marked by a fieldstone at head and foot. This young child, from Richmond, Va., was visiting at the home of John Randolph Coleman (the Peter Francisco House). While visiting, she died from pneumonia and was buried here at Salem. The name and dates were remembered by a current member of the church community.

| TRENT
Katie H. | 22 Apr. 1892
04 June 1985 | Trent, Robert L. | Yes |

Inscription: "Mother."

Other Info: Shares a headstone with her husband.

| TRENT
Robert L. | 04 July 1888
07 Apr. 1976 | Trent, Katie H. | Yes |

Inscription: "Father."

Other Info: Shares a headstone with his wife.

TRENT Robert Lee Jr.	01 Dec. 1923 09 June 1981		Yes
TURPIN Evelyn	1894 1927	Hughes Turpin, Johnson	Yes
TURPIN Florence Louise	07 Oct. 1927 14 Oct. 1927		Yes
(Unknown) (children)			No

Other Info: Two visible graves - no markers. The family of these children lived and worked at the Reese place (Hickory Hill - Buckingham Co.). One child died in 1925, and was buried at Salem Church while the men were working at building a new church. The second child died a while later.

| WALTON
John C. | 07 Jan. 1902
03 Jan. 1986 | Walton, Ruby Davis | Yes |
| WASH
Marvin Bruce | 10 Mar. 1906
26 Feb. 1960 | Wash, Alice Reese | Yes |

Inscription: "God Is Our Refuge and Strength." Footstone inscribed: "Husband."

| WILKERSON
Joshua Holmes | 11 June 1913
06 June 1973 | Wilkerson, Fletcher Smith | Yes |

LAST NAME	Date of Birth	Maiden Name	Tombstone
First Name	Date of Death	Spouse	
	Age at Death		

Scruggs - John & Eliz. Scruggs Family - Hwy 636

| SCRUGGS | 13 Feb. 1913 | | Yes |
| George Edward | 21 Nov. 1989 | | |

Inscription: He served as inscribed: "TEC 5 US Army World War II."

Other Info: Grave also marked by a funeral home metal marker.

| SCRUGGS | | | Yes |
| John T. | | Scruggs, Eliz. | |

Inscription: He served as inscribed: "Co. E. 21 VA. INF. C.S.A."

Other Info: No dates inscribed on headstone.

| SCRUGGS | 22 Oct. 1852 | | Yes |
| Lucy R. | 05 June 1938 | | |

Inscription: "At Rest." Footstone inscribed: "L.R.S."

| SCRUGGS | 07 Feb. 1841 | | Yes |
| Nannie A. | 20 Apr. 1926 | | |

Inscription: "She Was Faithful To Her Trust." Footstone inscribed: "N.A.S."

| SCRUGGS | 15 June 1868 | | Yes |
| William M. | 26 Feb. 1944 | | |

Inscription: "At Rest."

| WINGO | 11 Feb. 1854 | | Yes |
| C. B. | 14 Apr. 1932 | Wingo, Mary S. Scruggs | |

Inscription: "At Rest."

| WINGO | 27 Sep. 1844 | Scruggs | Yes |
| Mary S. | 11 Feb. 1879 | Wingo, C. B. | |

Inscription: "... Wife of C. B. Wingo ... At Rest." Footstone inscribed: "M.S.W."

Second Liberty Baptist Church (Black) - Hwy 640

| AUSTIN | 1882 | | No |
| Harrison | 1952 | | |

Other Info: Grave marked with a funeral home metal marker.

| AUSTIN | 21 July 1912 | | Yes |
| James E. | 25 Sep. 1977 | | |

LAST NAME First Name	Date of Birth Date of Death Age at Death	Maiden Name Spouse	Tombstone

Inscription: "Gone Home."

| AUSTIN
Margaret | 1884
1967 | | Yes |

| AUSTIN
Samuel | 15 Sep. 1956 | | No |

Other Info: Grave marked with a funeral home metal marker.

| AYERS
Annie | 19 Mar. 1965 | | No |

Other Info: Grave marked with a funeral home metal marker.

| BAGBY
Charles | 1935 | | Yes |

| BAGBY
Charles W. | 05 May 1917
04 July 1974 | | Yes |

Inscription: Charles served as inscribed: "TEC 5 US Army."

| BAGBY
Elizabeth | 1934 | | Yes |

| BAGBY
Floyd | 1946 | | Yes |

| BAGBY
(Infant Twins) | | | Yes |

| BAGBY
James | 12 Mar. 1890
07 Aug. 1913 | | Yes |

| BAGBY
John | 1935 | | Yes |

| BAGBY
Josephine | | | Yes |

Other Info: Just her name on her headstone.

| BAGBY
Katie | 1930 | | Yes |

Inscription: "Katie Bagby At Rest." Footstone inscribed: "1930"

| BAGBY
Matilda | 02 Dec. 1957 | | No |

Other Info: Grave marked with a funeral home metal marker.

| BAGBY
Mattie | | | Yes |

LAST NAME	Date of Birth	Maiden Name	Tombstone
First Name	Date of Death	Spouse	
	Age at Death		

Other Info: Just her name on her headstone.

| BAGBY | | | Yes |
| Phyllis | | | |

Other Info: Just her name on her headstone.

| BAGBY | 05 Sep. 1893 | | Yes |
| Wiley | 20 Feb. 1955 | | |

Inscription: Wiley served as inscribed: "Virginia US Army World War I."

| BARRETT | | | No |
| Lucy | 1981 | | |

Other Info: Grave is marked with a funeral home metal marker. Difficult to read the dates.

| BOLDEN | | | No |
| John | 03 Mar. 1961 | | |

Other Info: Grave marked with a funeral home metal marker.

| BOLDING | 1878 | Smith | Yes |
| Lorena | 1966 | | |

Inscription: "At Rest."

Other Info: She is the mother of Larry Smith, who took me to this cemetery.

| BOOKER | 1914 | | No |
| Ernest R. | 1982 | | |

Other Info: Grave is marked with a funeral home metal marker.

| BOOKER | 01 July 1916 | | Yes |
| John C. Jr. | 04 Aug. 1984 | Booker, Mattie V. | |

Other Info: Grave also marked with a funeral home metal marker inscribed: "John Booker 1916-1984."

| BOOKER | 1884 | | Yes |
| John Randolph | | Booker, Virginia Pearl | |

Other Info: Shares a headstone with his wife.

| BOOKER | 1890 | | Yes |
| Virginia Pearl | 1970 | Booker, John Randolph | |

Other Info: Shares a headstone with her husband.

BROWN			Yes
Amy Queen	21 Dec. 1956		
	95 yr.		

LAST NAME First Name	Date of Birth Date of Death Age at Death	Maiden Name Spouse	Tombstone

Inscription: Footstone inscribed: "A.Q.B."

Other Info: She is the grandmother of Larry Smith, who took me to this cemetery.

| BROWN
Fred | 1890
1960 | Brown, Jennette | Yes |

Inscription: "Loving Father."

| BROWN
Ida A. | 1892
1980 | | Yes |

Inscription: "Loving Mother."

| BROWN
Jennette | 1892
1973 | Brown, Fred | Yes |

Inscription: "Loving Mother."

| BROWN
Sally Daisy | 1902
1961 | | No |

Other Info: Grave is marked with a funeral home metal marker.

| BROWN
Wilson | | | Yes |

Other Info: Slate marker which is very difficult to read.

| COBBS
Sultania | 1888
1960 | | Yes |

| COLEMAN
Carrie | 1911
1985 | | No |

Other Info: Grave marked with a funeral home metal marker.

| COLEMAN
John E. | 07 June 1914
29 Jan. 1974 | | Yes |

| COTTMAN
Clarissa G. | 1954
1955 | | No |

Other Info: Grave is marked with a funeral home metal marker.

| DAVIS
Patty | 1912
1961 | | Yes |

Inscription: "Wife."

| EDMONDS
George | 29 July 1903
18 Mar. 1928 | | Yes |

Inscription: "Weep Not He Is At Rest." Footstone inscribed: "G.E."

LAST NAME First Name	Date of Birth Date of Death Age at Death	Maiden Name Spouse	Tombstone
EDMONDS Louis			Yes

Other Info: Grave is marked with a slate stone. Difficult to read.

EDMONDS Phil More	1879 1963		No

Other Info: Grave is marked with a funeral home metal marker.

EDMONDS Susan	1848 05 Oct. 1919		Yes

Inscription: "Faithful To Her Trust Even Unto Death." Footstone inscribed: "S.E."

EDMUNDS James	11 Nov. 1903 11 Sep. 1923		Yes

Inscription: "Weep Not He Is At Rest." Footstone inscribed: "J.E."

GILES Emma	28 Feb. 1911 10 Nov. 1969	Word Giles, Joshua A.	Yes
GILES Joshua A.	25 Mar. 1908 02 Oct. 1975	 Giles, Emma Word	No

Other Info: Grave is marked with a funeral home metal marker.

GORDON Henry W.	1897 1975		Yes

Other Info: Grave also marked with a funeral home metal marker inscribed: "Henry W. Gordon 1897-1975."

GORDON Josh	1910 1976	 Gordon, Elizabeth	Yes
GORDON Lila	29 Aug. 1884 11 May 1978		Yes

Other Info: Grave also marked with a funeral home metal marker inscribed: "Lila Gordon 1885-1978."

HARVEY Julia	1848 1962		Yes

Inscription: "At Rest." Footstone inscribed: "Julia P. Harvey."

Other Info: Grave also marked with a funeral home metal marker inscribed: "J. P. Harvey 9 - 18 - 1962."

JILES Ivanhoe Anderson	1931 1974		No

LAST NAME First Name	Date of Birth Date of Death Age at Death	Maiden Name Spouse	Tombstone
	Other Info: Grave is marked with a funeral home metal marker.		
JILES Sam Edward	1941 1970		No
	Other Info: Grave is marked with a funeral home metal marker.		
JOHNSON Emma Mrs.	19 Aug. 1967 55 yr.		Yes
JONES Annie Lee	1884 11 Oct. 1923 39 yrs.		Yes
	Inscription: Footstone inscribed: "A.L.J."		
JONES John P.	09 Jan. 1925 02 Dec. 19_8		Yes
	Inscription: Foootstone inscribed: "At Rest."		
	Other Info: Dates are difficult to read.		
LANGHORNE Bettie	1904 1977		No
	Other Info: Grave is marked with a funeral home metal marker.		
LANGHORNE Floyd	02 Aug. 1911 06 Feb. 1975		Yes
LANGHORNE Laura	1981		No
	Other Info: Grave is marked with a funeral home metal marker. Difficult to read the dates.		
LANGHORNE Willie	1864 19_6		No
	Other Info: Grave is marked with a funeral home metal marker. Difficult to read the dates.		
LASSENBARRY E.	1964 1983		No
	Other Info: Grave marked with a funeral home metal marker.		
LEWIS A. B.			Yes
	Other Info: Grave is marked with a slate stone and a funeral home metal marker. Both are difficult to read.		

LAST NAME First Name	Date of Birth Date of Death Age at Death	Maiden Name Spouse	Tombstone
MATHIS Alois	03 May 1926 22 Oct. 1973	Bagby	Yes

Inscription: "Mother...Forever In Our Hearts."

Other Info: Grave also marked with a funeral home metal marker inscribed: "Alois Mathis 1926-1973."

MILLER Curtis	1931		Yes
MILLER Elizabeth	1941		Yes
MILLER Melinda	1886 1943		No

Other Info: Grave marked with a funeral home metal marker.

MILLER Thomas	03 Sep. 1972		No

Other Info: Grave marked with a funeral home metal marker.

MORGAN Alex Jr.	07 Sep. 1891 16 Dec. 1913		Yes

Inscription: "Died Tues 2:30 PM...Gone But Not Forgotten."

MORGAN Fannie	1860 1931		Yes
MORGAN Lucyntha	1859 23 July 1954		Yes

Inscription: "Faithful To Her Trust Even Unto Death." Footstone inscribed: "L.M."

MORGAN Mattie			No

Other Info: Grave marked with a funeral home metal marker, mostly unreadable.

MORGAN William J.	28 Mar. 1909 01 Oct. 1972		Yes
MOSBY John	14 Feb. 193_		No

Other Info: Grave is marked with a funeral home metal marker. Difficult to read the date.

MOSELY			Yes

LAST NAME First Name	Date of Birth Date of Death Age at Death	Maiden Name Spouse	Tombstone
	Other Info: Slate marker which is very difficult to read.		
MOSLEY Pearl V.	17 May 1921 26 May 1939		Yes
MOSS Yaren			Yes
	Other Info: Grave is marked with a slate stone. Difficult to read.		
PATTERSON Alex	30 Aug. 1957		No
	Other Info: Grave marked with a funeral home metal marker.		
PATTERSON Ethel	1921 1981		No
	Other Info: Grave marked with a funeral home metal marker.		
PEAKS Claiborne	26 May 1919 27 Dec. 1944		Yes
	Inscription: Claiborne served as inscribed: "Virginia PFC 366 Inf. World War II."		
PEAKS Eva	05 Apr. 1966		No
	Other Info: Grave is marked with a funeral home metal marker.		
PEAKS Howard Lee Sr.	15 June 1934 10 Apr. 1985	Peaks, Dorothy B.	Yes
	Inscription: "In Loving Memory...Father."		
	Other Info: Grave is also marked with a funeral home metal marker inscribed: "Howard Peaks Sr. 1934-1985."		
PEAKS James N.	1916 1962		Yes
PEAKS Joseph			No
	Other Info: Grave is marked with a funeral home metal marker.		
PEAKS Mary	1899 1977		Yes
	Other Info: Grave is also marked with a funeral home metal marker inscribed: "Mary C. Peaks 1898-1975."		
PEAKS Nelson	1893 1961		Yes

LAST NAME First Name	Date of Birth Date of Death Age at Death	Maiden Name Spouse	Tombstone
PEAKS Phyllis E.	15 May 1915 13 Apr. 1968		Yes

Inscription: "Gone, But Not Forgotten."

| PEAKS
Rhoda | 25 Apr. 1925 | | Yes |

Inscription: "At Rest."

| PEAKS
Tyrone | 13 Aug. 1956
28 Sep. 1974 | | Yes |

Inscription: "At Rest."

| PEAKS
Virginia | 04 July 1923
23 Apr. 1948 | | Yes |

Inscription: "At Rest." Footstone inscribed: "Daughter."

| PERKINS
Tom | 1891
1940 | | No |

Other Info: Grave marked with a funeral home metal marker.

| SEAY | 13 Sep. ____ | | Yes |

Other Info: Slate marker which is very difficult to read.

| SEAY
Bill | | | Yes |

Inscription: "At Rest."

| SEAY
James H. | 25 Aug. 1955 | | Yes |

Inscription: James served as inscribed: "New York PVT 857 Co. Trans Corps World War I."

| SEAY
Jess | | | Yes |

Other Info: Grave is marked with a slate stone. Difficult to read.

| SEAY
John J. | 1920
1969 | | Yes |

Inscription: "Husband...We Miss You."

| SEAY
L. E. | | | Yes |

Other Info: Grave is marked with a slate stone. Difficult to read.

LAST NAME First Name	Date of Birth Date of Death Age at Death	Maiden Name Spouse	Tombstone
SEAY Susie	13 Sep. 1897 04 Dec. 1925	Seay, Thearon	Yes

Inscription: "At Rest."

Other Info: Shares a headstone with her husband.

SEAY Thearon	27 Sep. 1894 04 Mar. 1974	Seay, Susie	Yes

Inscription: "At Rest."

Other Info: Shares a headstone with his wife.

SEAY William E.	1925 1985		No

Other Info: Grave is marked with a funeral home metal marker.

SEAY Willie	17 Aug. 1866 14 July 1922		Yes

SMITH Arthur	20 Jan. 1913 15 July 1963		Yes

Inscription: Arthur served as inscribed: "Virginia CPL CO C 91 Engineer Regt World War II."

Other Info: Grave also marked with a funeral home metal marker inscribed: "Arthur Smith 1913-1963."

SMITH John			No

Other Info: Grave is marked with a funeral home metal marker. Difficult to read.

SMITH John Frank	1900 1943		No

Other Info: Grave is marked with a funeral home metal marker.

SMITH Millie Ann	1873 1943		Yes

Other Info: Grave also marked with a funeral home metal marker inscribed: "Millie Ann Smith 1873-1943."

SMITH Virginia T.	25 Sep. 1924 16 Dec. 1976		Yes

Inscription: "Mother."

Other Info: Grave is also marked with a funeral home metal marker inscribed: "Virginia Smith 1924-1976."

LAST NAME First Name	Date of Birth Date of Death Age at Death	Maiden Name Spouse	Tombstone
SPRADLEY Alex	26 Feb. 1966		No

Other Info: Grave is marked with a funeral home metal marker.

SPRADLEY Alexandria	1921 1946		No

Other Info: Grave marked with a funeral home metal marker.

SPRADLEY Clarence R.	1932 1976		No

Other Info: Grave is marked with a funeral home metal marker.

SPRADLEY Flossie Mae	1925 1975		Yes

Other Info: Grave marked with a funeral home metal marker.

SPRADLEY Fred	31 May 1892 30 May 1964		Yes

Inscription: Fred served as inscribed: "West Virginia PVT US Army World War I."

SPRADLEY George A.	1884 1979		Yes

SPRADLEY Joshua II	28 Oct. 1908 28 Apr. 1964		Yes

Inscription: "There Is No Grief Where Love Blooms In Memory's Garden."

SPRADLEY Lela Virginia	1904 1969		No

Other Info: Grave is marked with a funeral home metal marker.

(Unknown) Fannie I.			Yes

Other Info: Grave is marked with a slate stone. Difficult to read.

(Unknown) Mattie			Yes

Other Info: Grave is marked with a slate stone. Difficult to read.

(Unknown) Thomas	1860 1927		Yes

Other Info: Difficult to read this marker.

LAST NAME First Name	Date of Birth Date of Death Age at Death	Maiden Name Spouse	Tombstone
(Unknown) Walter	June 1948		No

Other Info: Grave is marked with a funeral home metal marker that is mostly unreadable.

WATKINS Agnes	1872 1956		No

Other Info: Grave marked with a funeral home metal marker.

WORD Elsie Lila	05 Sep. 1917 03 Nov. 1975		Yes

WORD Mamie	1935		Yes

Inscription: "Mother."

WORD Mary	1899 1980		No

Other Info: Grave is marked with a funeral home metal marker.

WORD Richard Shelton	21 Jan. 1941 06 Oct. 1984		Yes

Inscription: "Shirley Boy"

Sharon Baptist Church Cemetery - Hwy 622

AGEE Elezea	15 Jan. 1913 12 Dec. 1984	Baber Agee, Tyree	Yes

Other Info: Shares a headstone with her husband. Daughter of Lawson Tyler Baber and Elezea Steger Baber.

AGEE John Bushrod	07 July 1865 22 Aug. 1957	Agee, Mary Lou Steger	Yes

Other Info: Shares a headstone with his wife.

AGEE Martha Ann	1849 1932		Yes

Inscription: "At Rest."

AGEE Mary Lou	29 Jan. 1875 09 Dec. 1948	Steger Agee, John Bushrod	Yes

Other Info: Shares a headstone with her husband.

LAST NAME First Name	Date of Birth Date of Death Age at Death	Maiden Name Spouse	Tombstone
AGEE Tyree	16 May 1914 11 June 1964	Agee, Elezea Baber	Yes

Other Info: Shares a headstone with his wife. Irvin Tyree Agee was married to Mabel Elezea Baber Agee; neither used their given first name.

AGEE Willie Ford	01 Oct. 1924 11 June 1968	Agee, Virginia Smith	Yes
AYRES McKenna	28 Mar. 1905 10 June 1964	Ayres, Lena Self	Yes

Inscription: "Rest In Peace."

BABER Clinton T.	1884 1936	Baber, Lily Norvell	Yes

Other Info: Shares a headstone with his wife.

BABER Florrie A.	15 July 1892 04 Feb. 1976	Baber, Luther L.	Yes

Other Info: Shares a headstone with her husband.

BABER George Agee	1880 1949	Baber, Julia T.	Yes

Inscription: "Asleep In Jesus."

Other Info: Shares a headstone with his wife.

BABER Julia T.	1882 1978	Baber, George Agee	Yes

Inscription: "Asleep In Jesus."

Other Info: Shares a headstone with her husband.

BABER Lily	1886 1972	Norvell Baber, Clinton T.	Yes

Other Info: Shares a headstone with her husband.

BABER Luther L.	05 Apr. 1882 30 Sep. 1968	Baber, Florrie A.	Yes

Other Info: Shares a headstone with his wife.

BANTON Bernard W.	25 Sep. 1891 29 June 1963	Banton, Elizabeth C.	Yes

Other Info: Shares a headstone with his wife.

BANTON Charles Wesley	18 Aug. 1934 17 Sep. 1965		Yes

LAST NAME First Name	Date of Birth Date of Death Age at Death	Maiden Name Spouse	Tombstone
BANTON Edmond			Yes

Inscription: He served as inscribed: "CSA Co E 21 VA Inf CSA."

BANTON Elizabeth C.	18 June 1888 13 Nov. 1967	Banton, Bernard W.	Yes

Other Info: Shares a headstone with her husband.

BANTON Elsie Mae	1909 1962		Yes
BANTON Ida A.	1863 1933	Banton, Watson C.	Yes

Inscription: "Mother."

BANTON John Wesley	31 Mar. 1886 31 Jan. 1955	Banton, Maude Scott	Yes

Inscription: Footstone inscribed the same as the headstone.

Other Info: Shares a headstone with his wife.

BANTON Julia A.	05 Apr. 1847 04 Apr. 1927		Yes
BANTON Lee	1908 1975	Banton, Ruby May	Yes
BANTON Lee Whitfield	1884 1944		Yes
BANTON Lizzie Maxey	1880 1970		Yes
BANTON Maude Scott	28 Nov. 1893 08 Apr. 1981	Banton, John Wesley	Yes

Other Info: Shares a headstone with her husband.

BANTON Watson C.	1865 1944	Banton, Ida A.	Yes

Inscription: "Father."

BRYANT Bertha	23 Apr. 1902 09 July 1981	Farrish Bryant, Frank Walker	Yes

Inscription: "In God We Trust."

Other Info: Shares a headstone with her husband.

LAST NAME First Name	Date of Birth Date of Death Age at Death	Maiden Name Spouse	Tombstone
BRYANT Frank Walker	26 Mar. 1889 12 Mar. 1960	Bryant, Bertha Farrish	Yes

Inscription: "In God We Trust."

Other Info: Shares a headstone with his wife.

| BRYANT
James A. | 01 Oct. 1907
25 Apr. 1932 | | Yes |

Inscription: "Son." "On That Happy Golden Shore, Where the Faithful Part No More, Meet Me There."

Other Info: Shares a headstone with his mother, Susie J. Bryant.

| BRYANT
Susie A. | 20 Apr. 1873
26 Dec. 1957 | | Yes |

Inscription: "Mother." "On That Happy Golden Shore, Where the Faithful Part No More, Meet Me There."

Other Info: Shares a headstone with her son, James A. Bryant.

| CAUL
James W. | 05 June 1885
18 Nov. 1971 | Caul, Mollie B. | Yes |

Other Info: Shares a headstone with his wife.

| CAUL
Mollie B. | 12 Mar. 1876
12 June 1937 | Caul, James W. | Yes |

Other Info: Shares a headstone with her husband.

| DAVIS
Charles | 31 July 1856
24 July 1939 | | Yes |

| DAVIS
Lawrence A. | 19 Sep. 1906
12 Sep. 1966 | | Yes |

Inscription: He served as inscribed: "Virginia SGT 469 Service SQ AAF World War II."

| DAVIS
Lelia May | 31 May 1864
16 Mar. 1939 | | Yes |

| DAVIS
Mary Indie | 06 July 1901
04 Sep. 1944 | | Yes |

| FARRISH
Clyde R. | 1878
1965 | Farrish, Rosa B. | Yes |

Inscription: "In God We Trust."

Other Info: Shares a headstone with his wife.

LAST NAME First Name	Date of Birth Date of Death Age at Death	Maiden Name Spouse	Tombstone
FARRISH Joan Mildred	09 May 1962 03 Oct. 1979		Yes

Inscription: "To Know Her Was To Love Her."

Other Info: Daughter of John Corbett Farrish and Lois Parcell Farrish.

| FARRISH
John C. | 18 Nov. 1921
08 Sep. 1985 | Farrish, Lois Parcell | Yes |

Inscription: He served as inscribed: "TEC 5 US Army World War II."

Other Info: Son of Clyde R. and Rosa Staton Farrish.

| FARRISH
Rosa B. | 1883
1969 | Farrish, Clyde R. | Yes |

Inscription: "In God We Trust."

Other Info: Shares a headstone with her husband.

| FORD
(Baby) | 1970
1970 | | Yes |

| HALL
Eliza Ann | 06 Mar. 1819
Apr. 1881 | Hall, Rev. Wm. C. | Yes |

Inscription: "Wife of Rev. Wm. C. Hall...Married June 7, 1838...She was an obedient daughter, a faithful and affectionate wife: A devoted mother; a kind neighbor; a true friend; and a sincere christian." "Her children rise up and call her blessed; her husband also, and he praiseth her."

Other Info: The tombstone has been broken and patched back together on the death date line, and it is very difficult to read.

| HAYES
Earnest Glenn | 19 Apr. 1923
19 Nov. 1979 | | Yes |

Inscription: Footstone shows he served as inscribed: "Earnest Glenn Hayes SSgt US Army World War II."

| IRELAND
George Bennett | 01 Jan. 1911
26 Oct. 1979 | Ireland, Hazel Rush | Yes |

Inscription: "Father."

| JONES
Mary | 10 Apr. 1892
01 June 1975 | Miller
Jones, Vie Ethridge | Yes |

Other Info: Shares a headstone with her husband.

| JONES
Richard L. Rev. | 30 June 1903
11 Mar. 1967 | Jones, Rosa Mullins | Yes |

LAST NAME	Date of Birth	Maiden Name	Tombstone
First Name	Date of Death	Spouse	
	Age at Death		

Inscription: "Father." "I Have Fought A Good Fight."

Other Info: Shares a headstone with his wife.

| JONES | 25 July 1889 | | Yes |
| Vie Ethridge | 24 Sep. 1960 | Jones, Mary Miller | |

Other Info: Shares a headstone with his wife.

| LIGHTFOOT | 03 Apr. 1943 | | Yes |
| Alvin Wallace | 05 Mar. 1975 | | |

Inscription: "In Loving Memory."

| LINDSAY | 17 May 1882 | | Yes |
| Lucy B. | Oct. 1944 | | |

| LOWMAN | 08 May 1903 | | Yes |
| Charles W. | 02 July 1975 | Lowman, Mary M. | |

Other Info: Shares a headstone with his wife.

| LOWMAN | 29 July 1907 | | Yes |
| Mary M. | 04 Nov. 1975 | Lowman, Charles W. | |

Other Info: Shares a headstone with her husband.

| MAXEY | 09 Feb. 1921 | | Yes |
| Allen Franklin | 19 June 1969 | Maxey, Ethel Duty | |

Inscription: "Together Forever." Footstone shows he served as inscribed: "Allen F. Maxey Virginia CPL Army Air Forces World War II Feb. 9, 1921-June 19, 1969."

Other Info: Shares a headstone with his wife.

| MAXEY | 12 Feb. 1901 | Baber | Yes |
| Annie | 18 Dec. 1980 | Maxey, Samuel Allen | |

Other Info: Shares a headstone with her husband.

| MAXEY | 16 Mar. 1900 | | Yes |
| Bennie W. | 25 June 1971 | Maxey, Ruby S. | |

| MAXEY | 08 Aug. 1898 | | Yes |
| C. Lewis | 31 Dec. 1983 | Maxey, Lola S. | |

Inscription: "In God's Hands."

| MAXEY | 14 May 1869 | | Yes |
| Clara Gentry | 07 Aug. 1962 | | |

Inscription: Footstone inscribed: "C.G.M."

LAST NAME First Name	Date of Birth Date of Death Age at Death	Maiden Name Spouse	Tombstone
MAXEY Ethel	07 June 1929 16 Dec. 1984	Duty Maxey, Allen Franklin	Yes

Inscription: "Together Forever."

Other Info: Shares a headstone with her husband.

MAXEY Etta	09 July 1900 28 Dec. 1978	Self Maxey, Leonard F.	Yes

Other Info: Shares a headstone with her husband.

MAXEY Floyd Thomas	21 Apr. 1934 27 Dec. 1976		Yes
MAXEY George Albert	05 May 1868 30 Nov. 1947	Maxey, Laura Agre	Yes

Other Info: Shares a headstone with his wife.

MAXEY Laura	01 June 1858 01 Mar. 1942	Agee Maxey, George Albert	Yes

Other Info: Shares a headstone with her husband.

MAXEY Laura Ellen	30 Sep. 1887 29 Sep. 1958		Yes
MAXEY Leonard F.	01 May 1890 10 Oct. 1983	Maxey, Etta Self	Yes

Other Info: Shares a headstone with his wife.

MAXEY Oscar Blackwell	30 July 1892 28 Aug. 1921	Maxey, Ella Banton	Yes
MAXEY Samuel Allen	27 July 1893 21 May 1972	Maxey, Annie Baber	Yes

Inscription: Footstone shows he served as inscribed: "Samuel Allen Maxey Virginia PVT Co I 164 Infantry World War I July 27, 1894 - May 23, 1972." (Ed's note: There are some discrepencies between the dates on the footstone and the dates on the headstone.)

Other Info: Shares a headstone with his wife.

MAXEY Thomas Aubra	14 Sep. 1884 11 Jan. 1975		Yes
MOORE Kemper	1964		No

Other Info: Grave marked with a Funeral Home metal marker.

LAST NAME First Name	Date of Birth Date of Death Age at Death	Maiden Name Spouse	Tombstone
MOSELEY Ira A.	23 May 1881 12 Aug. 1967		Yes

Inscription: (Masonic Symbol)

NORVELL Hay Booth	05 Jan. 1880 06 Aug. 1952	Norvell, Emma B.	Yes
NUCKOLS Gertrude	1878 1952		Yes
NUCKOLS James Thomas	1881 1950		Yes
PATTESON Annette	1893 1967	Holman Patteson, Thomas Earl	Yes

Other Info: Shares a headstone with her husband.

PATTESON Buford B.	1897 1985	Patteson, Lily M.	Yes

Other Info: Shares a headstone with his wife. Buford Bingham Patteson was born on November 28, 1897, the son of Hamilton Cosby Patteson and Ella Bingham Patteson.

PATTESON Ella L.	20 Mar. 1875 17 July 1958	Bingham Patteson, H. C.	Yes

Inscription: "At Rest...Wife of H. C. Patteson..Be Strong In the Lord."

PATTESON H. C.	23 Apr. 1869 30 Aug. 1942	Patteson, Ella L. Bingham	Yes

Inscription: "Be Strong In the Lord."

PATTESON H. Cosby	14 July 1904 17 Oct. 1978	Patteson, Ruby Lee	Yes

Inscription: "In Loving Memory."

Other Info: Shares a headstone with his wife and infant son.

PATTESON (Infant son)	23 Oct. 1930 23 Oct. 1930		Yes

Inscription: "In Loving Memory."

Other Info: Shares a headstone with his father and mother, H.C. and R. L. Patteson.

PATTESON Lily M.	1894 1974	Patteson, Buford B.	Yes

Other Info: Shares a headstone with her husband.

LAST NAME First Name	Date of Birth Date of Death Age at Death	Maiden Name Spouse	Tombstone
PATTESON Luther Wesley	27 July 1893 10 Sep. 1974	Patteson, Ethleen Maxey	Yes

Inscription: Footstone shows he served as inscribed: "Luther W. Patteson CPL US Army Jul 17, 1893 - Sep 10, 1974."

Other Info: Shares a headstone with his wife.

| PATTESON
Ruby Lee | 12 July 1906
12 Oct. 1972 | Patteson, H. Cosby | Yes |

Inscription: "In Loving Memory."

Other Info: Shares a headstone with her husband and infant son.

| PATTESON
Thomas Earl | 1882
1964 | Patteson, Annette Holman | Yes |

Inscription: "M.D." Footstone inscribed: "At Rest."

Other Info: Shares a headstone with his wife.

| PIERCE
Ben Archer | 1870
1941 | Pierce, Martha Ellen | Yes |

Inscription: "Father...They Are Gone But Not Forgotten."

Other Info: Shares a headstone with his wife.

| PIERCE
Martha Ellen | 1886
1935 | Pierce, Ben Archer | Yes |

Inscription: "Mother...They Are Gone But Not Forgotten."

Other Info: Shares a headstone with her husband.

| RANSON
John James | 27 Jan. 1916
25 May 1973 | | Yes |

| RANSON
Nora | 21 Aug. 1887
27 Sep. 1969 | Spencer
Ranson, Virgil Whitcomb | Yes |

Inscription: "Married June 3, 1908."

Other Info: Shares a headstone with her husband.

| RANSON
Virgil Whitcomb | 17 Mar. 1885
07 Nov. 1964 | Ranson, Nora Spencer | Yes |

Inscription: "Married June 3, 1908."

Other Info: Shares a headstone with his wife.

| RUSH
Betty P. | 28 July 1872
19 Oct. 1965 | Rush, James A. | Yes |

LAST NAME First Name	Date of Birth Date of Death Age at Death	Maiden Name Spouse	Tombstone

Other Info: Shares a headstone with her husband.

| RUSH
Bruce N. | 19 Oct. 1903
03 Sep. 1984 | Rush, Edith T. | Yes |

Inscription: "Father."

| RUSH
James A. | 28 Aug. 1870
24 Jan. 1924 | Rush, Betty P. | Yes |

Other Info: Shares a headstone with his wife.

| RUSH
Rolfe L. Sr. | 05 Oct. 1894
03 Apr. 1961 | Rush, Lillian R. | Yes |

| SELF
A. Bessie | 08 Sep. 1895
28 Nov. 1975 | Winfrey
Self, John Holman | Yes |

Inscription: "Mother."

Other Info: Shares a headstone with her husband.

| SELF
Helen W. | 16 Jan. 1904
18 Jan. 1969 | Self, Julius E. | Yes |

Other Info: Shares a headstone with her husband.

| SELF
John Holman "J" | 06 Apr. 1892
18 May 1974 | Self, A. Bessie Winfrey | Yes |

Inscription: "Father." Footstone shows he served as inscribed: "John H. Self AS US Navy Apr. 6, 1892 - May 18, 1974."

| SELF
John Walter | 07 Aug. 1931
17 Sep. 1983 | Self, Elizabeth Moss | Yes |

Inscription: Footstone shows he served as inscribed: "John Walter Self Sgt US Army Korea."

| SELF
Julius E. | 27 Aug. 1899
25 Oct. 1982 | Self, Helen W. | Yes |

Other Info: Shares a headstone with his wife.

| SELF
Maude E. | 21 Apr. 1885
05 Sep. 1951 | Bransford
Self, William Thompson | Yes |

Other Info: Shares a headstone with her husband.

| SELF
William Thompson | 19 Sep. 1880
26 Apr. 1961 | Self, Maude E. Bransford | Yes |

Other Info: Shares a headstone with her husband.

LAST NAME First Name	Date of Birth Date of Death Age at Death	Maiden Name Spouse	Tombstone
SMITH Dabney Andy	20 Sep. 1871 10 Mar. 1950		Yes
SMITH Rosa C.	05 May 1896 26 Apr. 1952	Smith, Thomas C.	Yes

Other Info: Shares a headstone with her husband.

SMITH Thomas C.	27 Feb. 1875 10 Mar. 1950	Smith, Rosa C.	Yes

Other Info: Shares a headstone with his wife.

SNODDY William A.	26 May 1941 26 Aug. 1949		Yes

Inscription: "Asleep In Jesus."

SOUTHWARDS Minnie W.	1911 1971	Southwards, Theodore R.	Yes

Other Info: Shares a headstone with her husband.

SOUTHWARDS Theodore R.	1895 1960	Southwards, Minnie W.	Yes

Other Info: Shares a headstone with his wife.

STEGER Abe J.	18 July 1875 11 Apr. 1962	Steger, Nannie S.	Yes

Other Info: Shares a headstone with his wife.

STEGER Alice Josephine	1885 1974	Steger, Frank Walker	Yes

Other Info: Shares a headstone with her husband.

STEGER Elizabeth F.	27 Apr. 1884 27 Sep. 1959		Yes
STEGER Frank Walker	1877 1941	Steger, Alice Josephine	Yes

Other Info: Shares a headstone with his wife.

STEGER Maryanne	25 Apr. 1918 17 Mar. 1962	Baber	Yes

Inscription: "To Know Her Was To Love Her."

STEGER Nannie S.	08 Mar. 1877 19 May 1960	Steger, Abe J.	Yes

Other Info: Shares a headstone with her husband.

LAST NAME First Name	Date of Birth Date of Death Age at Death	Maiden Name Spouse	Tombstone
STEGER Sallie Hill	06 July 1879 30 Oct. 1968		Yes

Inscription: "Pray for one another, that you may be saved."

TAPSCOTT Allen Walker	19 Oct. 1879 10 June 1971	Tapscott, Annie Adkins	Yes

Inscription: (Masonic Symbol)

Other Info: Shares a headstone with his wife.

TAPSCOTT Annie	02 June 1886 07 Jan. 1968	Adkins Tapscott, Allen Walker	Yes

Other Info: Shares a headstone with her husband.

TAPSCOTT Clifford T.	1907 1942		Yes

Inscription: ""Tho Lost To Sight To Memory Dear." Footstone inscribed: "C.T.T."

TAPSCOTT Joseph R.	06 Feb. 1905 03 Nov. 1980		Yes

Inscription: (Masonic Symbol)

TAPSCOTT Lizzie Ayres	15 June 1880 07 June 1976		Yes
TAPSCOTT Mamie	1887 1888		Yes

Inscription: "Daughter."

Other Info: Shares a headstone with her mother, Mary Baber Tapscott, and brother, Tucker.

TAPSCOTT Mary	1858 1888	Baber	Yes

Inscription: "Our Mother."

Other Info: Shares a headstone with her son, Tucker, and daughter, Mamie.

TAPSCOTT Tucker	1884 1899		Yes

Inscription: "Son."

Other Info: Shares a headstone with his mother, Mary Baber Tapscott, and sister, Mamie.

LAST NAME First Name	Date of Birth Date of Death Age at Death	Maiden Name Spouse	Tombstone
TAPSCOTT Vincent	23 Mar. 1908 01 Oct. 1979	Tapscott, Marjorie B.	Yes
WEBSTER Field O.	23 Oct. 1883 05 Aug. 1969	Webster, Mary S.	Yes
WILKINSON Ashby S.	1865 1949	Wilkinson, Nannie S.	Yes

Other Info: Shares a headstone with his wife.

WILKINSON Nannie S.	1858 1949	Wilkinson, Ashby S.	Yes

Other Info: Shares a headstone with her husband.

WINFREY Annie E. T.	1877 1972	Winfrey, Harvey E.	Yes
WINFREY Egbert B.	21 Nov. 1892 02 June 1984	Winfrey, Lottie S.	Yes

Inscription: He served as inscribed: "PVT US Army World War I."

Other Info: Shares a headstone with his wife.

WINFREY Harvey E.	1874 1955	Winfrey, Annie E. T.	Yes
WINFREY Lottie S.	30 July 1895 20 June 1984	Winfrey, Egbert B.	Yes

Other Info: Shares a headstone with her husband.

WOODFIN Cora	10 Aug. 1897 05 Jan. 1976	Banton Woodfin, Wiley Haskins	Yes

Inscription: "In Loving Memory."

Shelton - F. and D. Shelton Family - Black - Hwy 663

MILLER Harriet	Apr. 1845 19 Jan. 1909	Miller, Chesley	Yes

Inscription: " ... Wife of C. Miller ... A Tender Mother And A Faithful Friend." Footstone inscribed: "H.M."

SHELTON (child)			No

Other Info: Known to be buried here, but grave marked by fieldstones only. The child of Flemming I. Shelton.

LAST NAME First Name	Date of Birth Date of Death Age at Death	Maiden Name Spouse	Tombstone
SHELTON Dicie	27 Jan. 1912 76 yr.	Shelton, Flemming	Yes
SHELTON (female)			No

Other Info: Known to be buried here, but grave marked by fieldstones only. This person was the sister of Carrie Shelton Eldridge.

Shumaker - B. F. Shumaker Family - Hwy 631

SHUMAKER Benjamin F.	1847 1932	Shumaker, Betty E.	Yes

Other Info: Shares a headstone with his wife.

SHUMAKER Betty C.	12 Sep. 1888 23 Mar. 1977	Catlett Shumaker, Harrison	Yes

Inscription: Footstone inscribed: "Mother."

Other Info: Grave is also marked by a funeral home metal marker inscribed: "Bettie Catlett Shumaker 1888 - 1977." She shares a headstone with her husband. (Ed's note: Her first name is spelled differently on the headstone and the metal marker.)

SHUMAKER Betty E.	1842 1923	Shumaker, Benjamin F.	Yes

Other Info: Shares a headstone with her husband.

SHUMAKER Essie J.	1855 1937		Yes
SHUMAKER Harrison	15 Jan. 1887 01 Sep. 1978	Shumaker, Betty C.	Yes

Inscription: Footstone is inscribed: "Father."

Other Info: Grave is also marked by a funeral home metal marker. He shares a headstone with his wife.

Slave Cemetery at "Col Alto" (Black) - Hwy 601

Other Info: There are several graves marked by fieldstones only in the woods between the homes at Col. Alto and the Johnson family home. It was relayed to me (the editor) from the story told by an aged black lady who lived in the neighborhood. She did not know what family the slaves belonged to, but I believe they were probably the house slaves that belonged to the Bondurant /Langhorne/ etc. families that lived at "Col Alto."

LAST NAME	Date of Birth	Maiden Name	Tombstone
First Name	Date of Death	Spouse	
	Age at Death		

Smyrna Methodist Church Cemetery - Hwy 15

| ADDLEMAN | 13 Sep. 1841 | | Yes |
| Perry | 22 Oct. 1900 | | |

Inscription: "Asleep In Jesus. Peaceful Rest."

| ALLEN | 15 Aug. 1865 | | Yes |
| Ernest G. | 28 Dec. 1929 | | |

Inscription: "In Loving Memory of My Dear Husband...A Place Is Vacant In Our Home Which Never Can Be Filled." Footstone inscribed: "E.G.A."

| ALLEN | 18 Apr. 1871 | | Yes |
| Gilbert | 14 Jan. 1949 | | |

Inscription: "At Rest."

| ALLEN | 21 Nov. 1882 | | Yes |
| Nannie Etta | 04 Feb. 1960 | | |

Inscription: "Loving Memories Never Die, As Years Roll On and Days Pass By, In Our Hearts A Memory Is Kept Of One We Loved and Will Never Forget." Footstone inscribed: "N.E.A."

| ALLEN | 02 Nov. 1838 | Gills | Yes |
| Virginia | 07 Mar. 1907 | Allen, W.W. | |

Inscription: "Our Mother...Wife of W. W. Allen. Rock of Ages Cleft For Me, Let Me Hide Myself In Thee." Footstone inscribed: "V.A."

| ALLEN | | | Yes |
| W. W. | | Allen, Virginia Gills | |

Inscription: He served as inscribed: "CO K 4 VA CAV C.S.A."

| AUSTIN | 1875 | | Yes |
| John Blackwell | 1930 | Austin, Minnie Pollard | |

Other Info: Shares a headstone with his wife.

| AUSTIN | 1906 | | Yes |
| Marvin Blackwell | 1983 | Austin, Katie Kidd | |

| AUSTIN | 1874 | Pollard | Yes |
| Minnie | 1953 | Austin, John Blackwell | |

Other Info: Shares a headstone with her husband.

| AYERS | 1906 | | Yes |
| James E. | 1980 | Ayers, Sarah B. | |

Other Info: Shares a headstone with his wife.

LAST NAME First Name	Date of Birth Date of Death Age at Death	Maiden Name Spouse	Tombstone
AYERS Sarah B.	1909 1981	Ayers, James E.	Yes

Other Info: Shares a headstone with her husband.

| BAILEY
Courtney D. | 25 Oct. 1884
14 Mo. | | Yes |

| BAILEY
F. M. (Mrs.) | 29 Mar. 1839
27 Jan. 1934 | Bailey, S. D. | Yes |

Inscription: "May the Resurrection Find Thee On the Bosom Of Thy God." Footstone inscribed: "F.M.B."

| BAILEY
Grace Hannah | 12 July 1902
30 Apr. 1903 | | Yes |

Inscription: "Suffer Little Children To Come Unto Me."

| BAILEY
Henry Pugh | 1898
1977 | Bailey, Mildred McCorkle | Yes |

Other Info: Shares a headstone with his wife.

| BAILEY
John Blanton | 19 Oct. 1915
21 Oct. 1915 | | Yes |

Inscription: "A Little Bud of Love, To Bloom With God Above."

| BAILEY
Lottie H. | 04 July 1892
10 July 1980 | Bailey, Yancy Elam | Yes |

Inscription: "Thy Kingdom Come." Footstone inscribed: "L.H.B."

Other Info: Shares a headstone with her husband.

| BAILEY
Mattie | 1877
1959 | Pugh
Bailey, William E. | Yes |

Inscription: Footstone inscribed: "M.P.B."

Other Info: Shares a headstone with her husband.

| BAILEY
Mildred | 1901
1979 | McCorkle
Bailey, Henry Pugh | Yes |

Other Info: Shares a headstone with her husband.

| BAILEY
S. D. | 22 Feb. 1837
10 Jan. 1887 | Bailey, F. M. | Yes |

Inscription: "At Rest."

LAST NAME	Date of Birth	Maiden Name	Tombstone
First Name	Date of Death	Spouse	
	Age at Death		

Other Info: A C.S.A. metal marker also is by this tombstone. On the back of the marker is a picture of the Confederate Flag and the letters: C.S.A. On the front of the marker are the words: "Deo Vindice 1861 1865."

| BAILEY | 28 Aug. 1925 | | Yes |
| Thomas Jordan | 05 Nov. 1988 | Bailey, Nancy Agee | |

| BAILEY | 1872 | | Yes |
| William E. | 1954 | Bailey, Mattie Pugh | |

Inscription: Footstone inscribed: "W.E.B."

Other Info: Shares a headstone with his wife.

| BAILEY | 16 June 1896 | | Yes |
| Yancy Elam | 11 June 1975 | Bailey, Lottie H. | |

Inscription: "Thy Kingdom Come." Footstone inscribed: "Y.E.B."

Other Info: Shares a headstone with his wife.

| BAILEY | 05 Aug. 1870 | | Yes |
| Yancy R. | 26 Oct. 1890 | | |

Inscription: "In Heaven ..."

| BALDRIDGE | 1884 | | Yes |
| Hallie B. | 1966 | | |

| BALDWIN | 06 Aug. 1873 | | Yes |
| Betty Allen | 06 Feb. 1948 | | |

Inscription: "At Rest."

| BALDWIN | 1892 | | Yes |
| Cora C. | 1991 | Baldwin, W. H. | |

Other Info: Shares a headstone with her husband.

| BALDWIN | 1857 | | Yes |
| H. O. | 1935 | | |

Other Info: Shares a headstone with three other Baldwin family members, five Spencer family members, and one Hix family member.

| BALDWIN | 1898 | | Yes |
| J. E. | 1928 | | |

Other Info: Shares a headstone with three other Baldwin family members, five Spencer family members, and one Hix family member.

| BALDWIN | 1883 | | Yes |
| S. Helen | 1903 | | |

LAST NAME First Name	Date of Birth Date of Death Age at Death	Maiden Name Spouse	Tombstone
	Other Info: Shares a headstone with three other Baldwin family members, five Spencer family members, and one Hix family member.		
BALDWIN S. Joe	13 Feb. 1882 21 Yr. 9 Mo.		Yes
	Inscription: "Thy Will Be Done. My Darling Child...Sweetly Fell Asleep In Jesus."		
BALDWIN Susan	1858 1931		Yes
	Other Info: Shares a headstone with three other Baldwin family members, five Spencer family members, and one Hix family member.		
BALDWIN W. H.	1893 1936	Baldwin, Cora C.	Yes
	Other Info: Shares a headstone with his wife.		
BATES Alsee	25 Nov. 1911 04 Oct. 1980		Yes
	Inscription: "At Rest." Footstone inscribed: "A.B."		
BATES Charlotte	1910 1988		No
	Other Info: Grave marked with a funeral home metal marker.		
BAUGHAN D. H.	01 Nov. 1932 09 May 1958		Yes
BAUGHAN D. Houston	29 July 1894 17 May 1946		Yes
BAYS Darrell Lee Rev.	27 Oct. 1920 22 Aug. 1990	Bays, Sylvia Mae	Yes
BERSCH James E.	19 June 1887 26 Oct. 1924	Bersch, Lucy Phaup	Yes
	Inscription: "Beloved One, Farewell." Footstone inscribed: "Father."		
BERSCH Lucy	03 Mar. 1893 04 Feb. 1986	Phaup Bersch, James E.	Yes
	Inscription: "Mother."		
BROWN Annie Louise	27 Mar. 1890 28 Dec. 1971	Jones Brown, William Edward	Yes
	Other Info: Shares a headstone with her husband.		

LAST NAME First Name	Date of Birth Date of Death Age at Death	Maiden Name Spouse	Tombstone
BROWN William Edward M.D.	22 Jan. 1885 17 Mar. 1958	Brown, Annie Louise Jones	Yes

Other Info: Shares a headstone with his wife.

CALDWELL Margaret Hamilton	22 Feb. 1880 24 Feb. 1979		Yes
CHICK Margaret Moss	1862 1916		Yes
COX Addison	1866 1948	Cox, Emily Rice	Yes

Other Info: Shares a headstone with his wife.

| COX Cobbs N. | 29 June 1861 11 July 1939 | | Yes |

Inscription: Footstone inscribed: "C.N.C."

| COX Emily Rice | 1877 1968 | Cox, Addison | Yes |

Other Info: Shares a headstone with her husband.

| COX Ida B. | 28 Dec. 1861 24 Apr. 1954 | | Yes |
| COX J. Henry | 1851 1916 | Cox, Molllie Baughan | Yes |

Inscription: "The Morning Cometh."

| COX James B. | 23 Dec. 1935 | | Yes |

Inscription: He served as inscribed: "Virginia PVT. U.S. Army."

| COX Joseph Benjamin | 26 May 1861 11 Oct. 1931 | | Yes |

Inscription: "His Record Is On High."

COX Marie Spencer	23 Dec. 1884 11 Nov. 1949		Yes
COX Mollie	03 Nov. 1855 08 Aug. 1892	Baughan Cox, J. Henry	Yes
COX William Slaughter	27 May 1885 23 July 1968		Yes
CRUTE Hattie	16 July 1856 20 Feb. 1937	Gannaway Crute, John Nicholas	Yes

LAST NAME First Name	Date of Birth Date of Death Age at Death	Maiden Name Spouse	Tombstone
CRUTE Hattie Winefred	01 Aug. 1888 18 Aug. 1910		Yes

Inscription: "Asleep In Jesus. Peaceful Rest." Footstone inscribed: "H.W.C."

CRUTE Henry Nicholas	04 May 1893 30 May 1957		Yes
CRUTE John Nicholas	10 Oct. 1858 27 May 1908	Crute, Hattie Gannaway	Yes
DAVIS Ella R.	1840 1912	Davis, Richard A.	Yes
DAVIS Lucy W.	1838 1908		Yes
DAVIS Nannie B.	28 Sep. 1875 27 Sep. 1960		Yes
DAVIS Richard A.	1832 1908	Davis, Ella R.	Yes
DUNKUM Alice White	1967		Yes

Inscription: Footstone inscribed: "A.W.D."

DUNKUM Alma	26 July 1898 05 Dec. 1989	Duncan Dunkum, Wesley Earl	Yes

Other Info: Shares a headstone with her husband.

DUNKUM John Emmett	1988		Yes

Inscription: Footstone inscribed: "J.E.D."

DUNKUM Mattie Frances	1951		Yes

Inscription: Footstone inscribed: "M.F.D."

DUNKUM Minnie Toler	1936		Yes

Inscription: Footstone inscribed: "M.T.D."

DUNKUM Wesley Earl	22 Sep. 1897 08 Apr. 1972	Dunkum, Alma Duncan	Yes

Other Info: Shares a headstone with his wife.

DUNN Mabel Baughan	15 Mar. 1906 27 June 1983		Yes

LAST NAME First Name	Date of Birth Date of Death Age at Death	Maiden Name Spouse	Tombstone
DUTY John Lenard	20 June 1891 12 June 1950		Yes

Inscription: "Rest In Peace."

| DUTY Martha Jane | 30 Sep. 1906 16 Feb. 1972 | Davis | Yes |

Inscription: "Rest In Peace."

| ELAM Eliza F. | 09 Aug. 1849 22 July 1932 | Elam, George W. | Yes |

Inscription: "Mother. Asleep In Jesus." Footstone inscribed: "E.F.E."

Other Info: Shares a headstone with her husband.

| ELAM George Thomas | 17 Jan. 1876 12 June 1963 | | Yes |

Inscription: Footstone inscribed: "G.T.E."

| ELAM George W. | 09 Sep. 1847 08 Oct. 1930 | Elam, Eliza F. | Yes |

Inscription: "Father. Asleep In Jesus." Footstone inscribed: "G.W.E."

Other Info: Shares a headstone with his wife.

| ELAM John Richard | 1874 1951 | | Yes |

| ELCAN Marcus Cleveland | 20 Apr. 1878 26 Jan. 1969 | Elcan, Marie Jones | Yes |

Other Info: Shares a headstone with his wife.

| ELCAN Marie | 02 Dec. 1892 23 Mar. 1981 | Jones Elcan, Marcus Cleveland | Yes |

Other Info: Shares a headstone with her husband.

| ELLIOTT Horace B. | 1853 1910 | | Yes |

| ELLIOTT Mary | 09 May 1881 02 Mar. 1973 | Cox Elliott, Wyatt Garnett | Yes |

Inscription: Footstone inscribed: "Mother."

Other Info: Shares a headstone with her husband.

| ELLIOTT Wyatt Cook | 27 Nov. 1903 23 Aug. 1987 | | Yes |

LAST NAME First Name	Date of Birth Date of Death Age at Death	Maiden Name Spouse	Tombstone
ELLIOTT Wyatt Garnett	08 June 1879 18 Feb. 1954	 Elliott, Mary Cox	Yes

Inscription: Footstone inscribed: "Father."

Other Info: Shares a headstone with his wife.

| EPPARD
Emma J. | 1876
1954 |
Eppard, John A. | Yes |

Inscription: "When Day Is Done."

Other Info: Shares a headstone with her husband.

| EPPARD
John A. | 1873
1937 |
Eppard, Emma J. | Yes |

Inscription: "When Day Is Done."

Other Info: Shares a headstone with his wife.

| ERICSON
Clinton N. | 04 Dec. 1896
12 Dec. 1972 | | Yes |

Inscription: "Father."

| FINCH
Bessie B. | 1896
1967 | | Yes |

| FLIPPIN
Roberta Allen | 28 May 1876
28 Oct. 1929 | | Yes |

Inscription: "At Rest."

| FORBES
Alice | 19 Jan. 1875
17 Aug. 1958 | Smith
Forbes, Ira Dabney | Yes |

Inscription: Footstone inscribed: "A.S.F."

| FORBES
Ira Dabney | 08 May 1871
09 Apr. 1939 |
Forbes, Alice Smith | Yes |

Inscription: Footstone inscribed: "I.D.F."

| GARNETT
A. C. | 12 Mar. 1823
10 Sep. 1907 |
Garnett, Susan Frances | Yes |

Inscription: "In Memory Of ...His Trust Was In God. He Died In the Faith. He Has Gone From His Loved Ones, His Children, His Wife, Whom He Willingly Toiled For, And Loved As His Life; Though With Sorrowing Hearts, We Laid Him To Rest, We Will Meet Him Again, In the Land Of the Blest." Footstone inscribed: "A.C.C." Back of stone inscribed: "Garnett."

LAST NAME First Name	Date of Birth Date of Death Age at Death	Maiden Name Spouse	Tombstone
GARNETT Annie Spencer	04 Oct. 1887 21 Oct. 1982		Yes
GARNETT Carroll Nelson	17 July 1911 06 Mar. 1945		Yes
GARNETT Edwin Crute	1878 1949		Yes
GARNETT Grace	1880 1973	Elcan Garnett, John Cook	Yes
GARNETT John Cook	1874 1962	Garnett, Grace Elcan	Yes
GARNETT Lucy Davis	1879 1965		Yes
GARNETT Lucy P.	1907 1908 7 Mo.		Yes

Other Info: Shares a headstone with her brother, William C. Garnett.

GARNETT Susan Frances	27 July 1830 11 Mar.	Garnett, A. C.	Yes

Inscription: "In Memory Of Our Precious Mother...In Devotion To Her L
...Simple Christian Faith...ng Give..." Footstone inscribed: "S.F.G."

Other Info: This is a slate headstone, and many of the words are shaled off. Soon it will be impossible to read the engraving.

GARNETT Thomas Sidney	07 Aug. 1873 19 May 1951		Yes
GARNETT William C.	1912 2 Dy		Yes

Other Info: Shares a headstone with his sister, Lucy P. Garnett.

GARNETT Willis Cook	10 Oct. 1913 25 Feb. 1984		Yes

Inscription: He served as inscribed: "U.S. Army WWII."

GARNETT Wm. E.	22 Dec. 1849 29 Apr. 1935		Yes

Inscription: "In Memory Of..." Footstone inscribed: "W.E.G."

GILLS Joseph Wiley	28 Apr. 1875 28 May 1921	Gills, Lorena Bailey	Yes

LAST NAME First Name	Date of Birth Date of Death Age at Death	Maiden Name Spouse	Tombstone

Other Info: Shares a headstone with his wife.

| GILLS
Lorena | 11 Feb. 1877
06 May 1929 | Bailey
Gills, Joseph Wiley | Yes |

Other Info: Shares a headstone with her husband.

| GRIFFITH
Carroll E. | 24 Jan. 1920
06 July 1976 | | Yes |

Inscription: He served as inscribed: "Sgt. U. S. Army World War II."

| GRIFFITH
David A. | 16 Dec. 1891
09 Mar. 1962 | Griffith, Lottie D. | Yes |

Inscription: Footstone inscribed: "Daddy."

Other Info: Shares a headstone with his wife.

| GRIFFITH
Lottie D. | 11 July 1892
23 Apr. 1963 | Griffith, David A. | Yes |

Inscription: Footstone inscribed: "Mama."

Other Info: Shares a headstone with her husband.

| GRIGG
Gordon Glenn | 1901
1945 | Grigg, Pettice Forbes | Yes |

| GRIGG
Pettice | 1902
1980 | Forbes
Grigg, Gordon Glenn | Yes |

| HARVEY
Caleb Cushing | 1876
1948 | Harvey, Mary Baldwin | Yes |

Inscription: Footstone inscribed: "C.C.H."

Other Info: Shares a headstone with his wife.

| HARVEY
Caleb Cushing Jr. | 1924
1969 | | Yes |

| HARVEY
Mary | 1888
1977 | Baldwin
Harvey, Caleb Cushing | Yes |

Inscription: Footstone inscribed: "M.B.H."

Other Info: Shares a headstone with her husband.

| HEARN
Ruth | 07 Aug. 1889
11 Jan. 1971 | Phaup
Hearn, William L. | Yes |

Inscription: "Mother Sweet Sleep."

LAST NAME First Name	Date of Birth Date of Death Age at Death	Maiden Name Spouse	Tombstone
HEARN William L.	25 Dec. 1888 03 May 1960	Hearn, Ruth Phaup	Yes

Inscription: "Sweet Sleep."

| HICKMAN John Carl | 1917 1990 | | No |

Other Info: Grave marked by a funeral home metal marker.

| HIX (Infant) | 24 Jan. 1937 24 Jan. 1937 | | Yes |

Inscription: "Infant Son of Cook and Hilda Hix."

Other Info: Shares a headstone with four Baldwin family membes, and five Spencer family members.

| HOWE Mildred Irving | 07 Feb. 1904 20 Mar. 1987 | | Yes |

| HUBBORD M. M. J. | 06 Apr. 1815 09 Nov. 1899 | | Yes |

Inscription: "In Memory of ... At Rest."

| HUTCHINGS Roland J. | 1902 1973 | Hutchings, Virginia F. | Yes |

Other Info: Shares a headstone with his wife.

| HUTCHINGS Virginia F. | 1900 1982 | Hutchings, Roland J. | Yes |

Other Info: Shares a headstone with her husband.

| JOHNS Reuben S. | 1902 1971 | | Yes |

Inscription: (Masonic Symbol)

| JONES Annette Royall | 09 Aug. 1949 29 Aug. 1964 | | Yes |

| JONES Edna | 09 June 1882 07 Mar. 1967 | Elcan Jones, Joseph Louis | Yes |

Other Info: Shares a headstone with her husband.

| JONES Florence W. | 13 Aug. 1888 01 Nov. 1969 | | Yes |

| JONES (infant) | 04 Nov. 1959 05 Nov. 1959 | | Yes |

LAST NAME First Name	Date of Birth Date of Death Age at Death	Maiden Name Spouse	Tombstone
	Inscription: "Infant Son of M. Clevland and Eliz. Jones."		
JONES (Infant)	16 Jan. 1928 17 Jan. 1928		Yes
	Inscription: "Infant Daughter of P. Monroe and Ruby S. Jones."		
JONES Joseph Louis	01 Jan. 1887 11 June 1971	Jones, Edna Elcan	Yes
	Other Info: Shares a headstone with his wife.		
JONES Mary	13 Oct. 1864 21 May 1942	Crute Jones, Paul Marion	Yes
	Other Info: Shares a headstone with her husband.		
JONES Paul Dibrell	22 Mar. 1919 26 Nov. 1963		Yes
	Inscription: He served as inscribed: "Virginia 1st Lt. 142 INF. 36 INF. Div. World War II SS-BSM-PH."		
JONES Paul Dibrell Jr.	20 Nov. 1951 05 Sep. 1985		Yes
	Inscription: "Tho He Were Dead Yet Shall He Live."		
JONES Paul Marion	15 Dec. 1859 11 Jan. 1919	Jones, Mary Crute	Yes
	Other Info: Shares a headstone with his wife.		
JONES Paul Monroe	21 July 1894 04 Sep. 1954	Jones, Ruby Sledd	Yes
JONES Ruby	07 Apr. 1894 02 Sep. 1991	Sledd Jones, Paul Monroe	Yes
	Other Info: Grave is also marked by a funeral home metal marker inscribed: "Ruby S. Jones 1894-1991."		
KIDD Beulah B.	02 Aug. 1886 10 June 1969	Kidd, Henry C.	Yes
	Inscription: "He Giveth His Beloved Sleep." Footstone inscribed: "Mother."		
	Other Info: Shares a headstone with her husband.		
KIDD Henry C.	07 May 1875 06 June 1952	Kidd, Beulah B.	Yes
	Inscription: "He Giveth His Beloved Sleep." Footstone inscribed: "Father."		
	Other Info: He shares a headstone with his wife.		

LAST NAME First Name	Date of Birth Date of Death Age at Death	Maiden Name Spouse	Tombstone
LAMBERTSON Hattie E.	13 July 1928 25 Aug. 1983	Lambertson, Roy F. Jr.	Yes

Inscription: "In God's Care."

Other Info: Shares a headstone with her husband.

LAMBERTSON Roy F. Jr.	19 Jan. 1927 20 Apr. 1983	Lambertson, Hattie E.	Yes

Inscription: "Footstone inscribed to show that he served: "Roy F. Lambertson Jr. LCDR US NAVY World War II Jan. 19, 1927 Apr. 20, 1983."

Other Info: Shares a headstone with his wife.

LEE Anderson Watkins Jr.	24 June 1896 01 Jan. 1988	Lee, Lelia F. Smith	Yes
LEGRAND Bessie Loula	01 Apr. 1892 27 Nov. 1944	Plunkett Legrand, Wyatt Archer	Yes
LEGRAND Raymond Elliott	01 Apr. 1915 15 Oct. 1988		Yes
LEGRAND Wyatt Archer	03 Nov. 1887 13 Aug. 1952	Legrand, Bessie Loula Plunkett	Yes
LEWIS Herbert B.	25 Aug. 1885 01 Oct. 1937		Yes

Inscription: "He Died As He Lived, A Christian."

MARKS James E.	1882 1962	Marks, Susie R.	Yes

Inscription: Footstone inscribed: "Father."

Other Info: Shares a headstone with his wife.

MARKS Susie R.	1885 1964	Marks, James E.	Yes

Inscription: Footstone inscribed: "Mother."

Other Info: Shares a headstone with her husband.

MARKS William Joseph	13 Oct. 1948 14 Oct. 1948		Yes
MEADOWS Ella Mae	02 July 1883 28 Apr. 1971		Yes
MILLS Virginia Steger	10 July 1890 14 Apr. 1960		Yes

LAST NAME First Name	Date of Birth Date of Death Age at Death	Maiden Name Spouse	Tombstone
MOSS George William	1857 1939		Yes
PAIS Elwood Alexander	09 Feb. 1913 23 Jan. 1978	Pais, Harriett Garnett	Yes

Inscription: Footstone inscribed to show that he served: "Elwood A. Pais Capt U.S. Army World War II Feb. 9, 1913 Jan. 23, 1978."

PATTERSON Lelia M.	12 Mar. 1881 15 Feb. 1908	Patterson, Camm	Yes

Inscription: "Wife of Camm Patterson."

PHAUP Ann Eliza	07 May 1828 06 Mar. 1904	Phaup, John J.	Yes

Inscription: "A Lowly Follower Of Her Lord Above, While Here On Earth Her Soul On Heaven Was Kept; Her Word Was Kindness, Her Deeds Were Love, Her Spirit Humble and Her Life Well Spent; These, These, and Not This Stone Shall Be Her Monument. Erected By Her Sons." Footstone inscribed: "A.E.P."

PHAUP Annie Julia	21 Sep. 1887 10 Aug. 1984		Yes
PHAUP Crosby Samuel	13 Oct. 1915 18 Mar. 1975	Phaup, Helen Moren	Yes

Inscription: "Married Aug. 18, 1953."

PHAUP Earl B.	08 May 1918 12 Mar. 1991		Yes

Inscription: He served as inscribed: "S Sgt US Army World War II."

PHAUP Earl Dwight	04 June 1946 27 Sep. 1990		Yes

Other Info: Grave also marked by a funeral home metal marker inscribed: "E. Dwight Phaup 1946-1990."

PHAUP Edward S.	1958 1991		Yes

Inscription: "Nearer My God To Thee."

PHAUP George Leroy	11 Feb. 1883 18 June 1971	Phaup, Minnie Dunkum	Yes

Inscription: "Father. Married Jan. 20, 1909." Footstone inscribed: "Father."

Other Info: Shares a headstone with his wife.

LAST NAME First Name	Date of Birth Date of Death Age at Death	Maiden Name Spouse	Tombstone
PHAUP Henry	27 Nov. 1854 28 Aug. 1934		Yes

Inscription: "Friends To Their Country and Believers In Christ." Footstone inscribed: "H.P."

Other Info: Shares a headstone with his twin brother, Robert Phaup.

| PHAUP
Henry Reeves | 18 July 1885
22 Feb. 1961 | Phaup, Ruth M. | Yes |

Inscription: Footstone inscribed: "H.R.P."

Other Info: Shares a headstone with his wife.

| PHAUP
Jas. G. | 25 July 1852
24 Sep. 1881 | | Yes |

Inscription: "In Memory of ...Farewell Dear Friend and Be Content, I Was Not Yours, But Only Lent, Dry Up Those Tears and Weep No More, I Am Not Lost But Gone Before." Footstone inscribed: "J.G.P."

| PHAUP
John J. | 09 July 1825
16 Sep. 1893 | Phaup, Ann Eliza | Yes |

Inscription: (Masonic Symbol.) "In Loving Remembrance of ... He Giveth His Beloved Sleep." Footstone inscribed: "J.J.P."

| PHAUP
John J. | 21 Aug. 1879
27 Oct. 1979 | Phaup, Marrietta L. | Yes |

Inscription: "Father."

| PHAUP
Lucy | 1858
1942 | Carter
Phaup, Wm. J. | Yes |

Inscription: "Mother. Wife of W. J. Phaup. At Rest." Footstone inscribed: "L.C.P."

| PHAUP
Marrietta L. | 21 Sep. 1881
21 June 1951 | Phaup, John J. | Yes |

Inscription: "Mother."

| PHAUP
Marvin M. | 27 June 1920
15 Feb. 1986 | | Yes |

| PHAUP
Minnie | 30 July 1886
29 Nov. 1968 | Dunkum
Phaup, George Leroy | Yes |

Inscription: "Mother." Footstone inscribed: "Mother."

Other Info: Shares a headstone with her husband.

LAST NAME First Name	Date of Birth Date of Death Age at Death	Maiden Name Spouse	Tombstone
PHAUP Robert	27 Nov. 1854 02 Jan. 1934		Yes

Inscription: "Friends To Their Country and Believers In Christ."

Other Info: Shares a headstone with his twin brother, Henry Phaup."

| PHAUP
Ruth M. | 01 June 1893
18 Aug. 1982 | Phaup, Henry Reeves | Yes |

Other Info: Shares a headstone with her husband.

| PHAUP
Susanna Lee | 18 Oct. 1866
24 Mar. 1936 | | Yes |

Inscription: "Our Sister. Dau. of J.H. & S.E. Phaup." Footstone inscribed: "S.L.P."

| PHAUP
W. Vaden | 31 Jan. 1881
29 Aug. 1903 | | Yes |

Inscription: "None Knew Thee But Loved Thee." Footstone inscribed: "W.V.P."

| PHAUP
Walter R. | 14 mo. | | Yes |

Inscription: "Infant Son of W.J. & L.V. Phaup. Safe in the Arms of Jesus." Footstone inscribed: "W.R.P."

| PHAUP
Wm. J. | 06 June 1850
04 Aug. 1894 | Phaup, Lucy Carter | Yes |

Inscription: "In Loving Remembrance Of ... He Being Dead Yet Speaketh." Footstone inscribed: "W.J.P."

| PHAUP
Wm. R. | 20 Dec. 1820
22 Sep. 1911 | | Yes |

Inscription: "In Loving Memory of Our Uncle ... To Know Him Was To Love Him." Footstone inscribed: "W.R.P."

| PHAUPP
Willie Moses | 18 June 1908
24 Nov. 1910 | | Yes |

Inscription: "Darling We Miss Thee." Footstone inscribed: "W.M.P."

Other Info: The surname is spelled with three "P's" on this headstone.

| POLLARD
D. E. | | Pollard, Sarah Jane | Yes |

Inscription: He served as inscribed: "Sgt. Co. K 4 VA CAV C.S.A." Footstone inscribed: "D.E.P."

LAST NAME First Name	Date of Birth Date of Death Age at Death	Maiden Name Spouse	Tombstone
POLLARD Edward Ernest	1892 1973	Pollard, Lois Dillon	Yes

Other Info: Shares a headstone with his wife.

POLLARD Leon	1875 1944		Yes
POLLARD Lois	1900 1972	Dillon Pollard, Edward Ernest	Yes

Other Info: Shares a headstone with her husband.

POLLARD Sarah Jane	1838 1928	Pollard, D. E.	Yes
PUGH Erma H.	07 Dec. 1886 11 May 1967		Yes
RAINEY Dallas Homer	1891 1975	Rainey, Louise Morris	Yes
RAINEY Isaac Wallace	1919 1988		Yes
RAINEY Louise	1894 1959	Morris Rainey, Dallas Homer	Yes
RIDER Warren E.	05 June 1919 29 Aug. 1977	Rider, Dorothy L.	Yes

Inscription: He served as inscribed: "TEC4 US Army World War II."

SCOTT James E.	1882 1973	Scott, Flossie S.	Yes
SEAMSTER Walter W.	03 June 1904 08 Jan. 1952		Yes

Inscription: Footstone inscribed: "W.W.S."

SILBY Joe Baxter	1901 1969		No

Other Info: Grave is marked by a funeral home metal marker.

SLOAN Maxie Lee D.	28 Aug. 1937 27 Feb. 1974		Yes

Inscription: "Rest In Peace."

SLOAN Vernon Lee	23 Jan. 1954 01 Sep. 1973		Yes

Inscription: "Rest In Peace."

LAST NAME First Name	Date of Birth Date of Death Age at Death	Maiden Name Spouse	Tombstone
SLOAN Willie S. Sr.	1928 1984		No

Other Info: Grave marked by a funeral home metal marker.

SMITH Alvin Lee	08 Nov. 1869 25 May 1933		Yes
SMITH Bernard Clay	1918 1973	Smith, Ruby M.	Yes

Inscription: He served as inscribed on the footstone: "Bernard Clay Smith Virginia TEC3 US Army World War II Nov. 22, 1918 June 28, 1973."

SMITH Elizabeth Spencer	23 May 1912 03 Mar. 1962		Yes
SMITH Fannie Cox	16 Dec. 1890 18 Feb. 1963		Yes
SMITH Frankie A.	02 Mar. 1877 10 June 1910		Yes

Inscription: Footstone inscribed: "F.B.S." [sic]

SMITH Hubert M.	1872 1955		Yes
SMITH Manie Cox	28 Feb. 1887 09 Dec. 1976		Yes
SMITH Martha V.	04 July 1838 11 Jan. 1919		Yes

Inscription: "Our Mother. With Christ In Heaven." Footstone inscribed: "M.V.S."

SPENCER Eliz. B.	1881 1939		Yes

Other Info: Shares a headstone with four other Spencer family members, four Baldwin family members, and one Hix family member.

SPENCER Ellen M.	1914 1921		Yes

Other Info: Shares a headstone with four other Spencer family members, four Baldwin family members, and one Hix family member.

SPENCER J. B.	1925 1932		Yes

Other Info: Shares a headstone with four other Spencer family members, four Baldwin family members, and one Hix family member.

LAST NAME First Name	Date of Birth Date of Death Age at Death	Maiden Name Spouse	Tombstone
SPENCER W. B.	1917 1922		Yes

Other Info: Shares a headstone with four other Spencer family members, four Baldwin family members, and one Hix family member.

| SPENCER W. Bocock | 1882 1937 | | Yes |

Other Info: Shares a headstone with four other Spencer family members, four Baldwin family members, and one Hix family member.

| SPENCER William Herbert Sr. | 07 Aug. 1909 13 Feb. 1980 | | Yes |

Inscription: "A Loving Father."

| SPENCER Willis Thomas | 19 Sep. 1923 15 Jan. 1991 | Spencer, Helen Shepard | Yes |

Other Info: Grave is also marked with a funeral home metal marker.

STEGER Herbert D.	02 May 1879 03 Feb. 1941		Yes
STEGER Herbert D. Jr.	20 Dec. 1913 18 Nov. 1984	Steger, Mary Spencer	Yes
STEGER Susie M.	25 Jan. 1877 20 May 1957		Yes

Inscription: "Aunt."

VANDERWAAL Frances	1924 1979	Kidd Vanderwaal, James D.	Yes
WEAVER Ada Ann	04 Apr. 1879 15 Apr. 1950		Yes
WEAVER Betsey Ann	02 June 1851 16 Jan. 1938		Yes
WEAVER Charles Ray	20 Sep. 1921 05 June 1957		Yes

Inscription: Footstone inscribed: "C.R.W."

| WEAVER Cora E. | 20 Aug. 1901 01 May 1987 | Weaver, Oscar F. | Yes |

Other Info: Shares a headstone with her husband.

| WEAVER Emma D. | 23 Mar. 1900 21 Apr. 1975 | | Yes |

LAST NAME / First Name	Date of Birth / Date of Death / Age at Death	Maiden Name / Spouse	Tombstone
WEAVER Floyd W.	07 Dec. 1899 15 Nov. 1938		Yes
WEAVER Oscar F.	27 Apr. 1885 09 Jan. 1966	Weaver, Cora E.	Yes

Other Info: Shares a headstone with his wife.

WEAVER Robert M.	21 May 1934 17 Aug. 1989		Yes
WEAVER Saul	11 Nov. 1921		Yes
WHITLOW Minnie	09 Aug. 1880 03 Sep. 1969	Dowdy Whitlow, Wiley Hubbard	Yes

Inscription: "At Rest."

WHITLOW Wiley Hubbard	25 May 1883 17 Oct. 1958	Whitlow, Minnie Dowdy	Yes

Inscription: "At Rest."

WISE Charles R.	29 Feb. 1864 02 Aug. 1942		Yes

Inscription: "At Rest."

WISE Charles Richard Jr.	09 Apr. 1901 19 oct. 1959		Yes
WISE Corbin Steger	25 Aug. 1902 27 Feb. 1972		Yes
WISE Gracie Lillian	16 Apr. 1926 07 July 1988	Stables Wise, Harry Edward Sr.	Yes
WISE Harry G.	08 Feb. 1897 24 Jan. 1918		Yes

Inscription: He served as inscribed: "Co. G. 116 U.S. Inf."

WISE Jennie B.	26 Oct. 1878 25 Feb. 1919		Yes

Inscription: "At Rest." Footstone inscribed: "J.B.W."

YOUNG Lorraine A.	03 Jan. 1924 31 Mar. 1991	Young, Garvis C.	Yes

Inscription: "Mother."

LAST NAME First Name	Date of Birth Date of Death Age at Death	Maiden Name Spouse	Tombstone

Stanton Family Cemetery (Black) - Hwy 677

CLARK Ella	1923	Stanton Clark, James	Yes
CLARK James	1933	Clark, Ella Stanton	No

Other Info: Grave marked by a funeral home metal marker.

CLARK Unice Lee	1940		No

Other Info: Grave marked by a funeral home metal marker.

EANS Thomas	1934	Eans, Znada F.S.	Yes

Other Info: He was the second husband of Znada (Fleming) (Stanton) Eans (Inge).

JACKSON John	1938	Jackson, Hallie Clark	Yes
RANDOLPH Ada		Stanton Randolph, Willie C.	No
RANDOLPH Ariannah	1923	Stanton Randolph, James	No
RANDOLPH James	1921	Randolph, Ariannah Stanton	No
RANDOLPH Willie C.	1936	Randolph, Ada S.	Yes

Other Info: He has a World War I military tombstone.

SCOTT Harriet "Hattie"	1941	Stanton	No

Other Info: Grave is marked by a funeral home metal marker.

STANTON Bertha	1918		No
STANTON Daniel	1790 (after 1853)	Stanton, Nancy	No

Other Info: This cemetery was put on the National Register of Historic Places and also on the Virginia Landmarks Register in 1992. Consequently, a lengthy report of the history of this cemetery is on file. There are 36 +/- grave sites, with three graves marked by government tombstones for World War I soldiers, and some

LAST NAME First Name	Date of Birth Date of Death Age at Death	Maiden Name Spouse	Tombstone

marked by funeral home metal markers; the rest being marked by unengraved slate markers and fieldstones.

STANTON Mary	1865		No

Other Info: Died at age 11 yrs.

STANTON Nancy	1801 1853	Stanton, Daniel	No

STANTON Nancy	1890	Trent Stanton, Sidney	No

Other Info: Daughter of Thomas Trent, shoemaker.

STANTON Schuyler	1882		No

STANTON Sidney Trent	circa 1910		No

STANTON Sidney "Trent" Jr.	1929		No

STANTON William	1899		No

Other Info: He died before his first birthday.

WHEELER Judith Ann		Stanton Wheeler, William	No

WHEELER William	1874	Wheeler, Judith A. S.	No

WHITE Sophronia		Stanton White, John	No

Other Info: She was the daughter of Daniel and Nancy Stanton.

Thomas Family/Thomas Farm Cemetery - Hwy 669

BARKER Daisy Walker	23 Feb. 1913 25 Sep. 1916		Yes

Inscription: "Dau. of W. L. & Edna Barker ... This Fair Flower In Paradise Shall Bloom." Footstone inscribed: "D.W.B."

BARKER Robert James	05 Nov. 1880 05 June 1937		Yes

Inscription: "Father." Footstone inscribed: "R.J.B."

LAST NAME	Date of Birth	Maiden Name	Tombstone
First Name	Date of Death	Spouse	
	Age at Death		

Other Info: Robert's Mother was a Thomas; he died in West Virginia and was brought back here to the family homeplace for burial.

| FLIPPEN | 15 Oct. 1905 | | Yes |
| Lacy C. | 24 Sep. 1908 | | |

Inscription: "Gone But Not Forgotten." Footstone inscribed: "L.C.F."

Other Info: Daughter of Hattie Thomas Flippen.

| THOMAS | | | Yes |
| | 02 Apr. 1885 | | |

Inscription: Grave marked with fieldstones with handcarved inscriptions that are difficult to read.

| THOMAS | 11 Sep. 1893 | Martin | Yes |
| Annie | 15 Feb. 1919 | Thomas, Stewart | |

Other Info: Annie was the first wife of Stewart Thomas. She and their son, Thomas J., died in the Flu Epidemic.

| THOMAS | 01 Mar. 1921 | | Yes |
| Ben L. | 23 July 1936 | | |

Other Info: He is the brother of Henry Thomas.

| THOMAS | | | Yes |
| C. | 03 Oct. 1883 | | |

Inscription: Grave marked with fieldstones with handcarved inscriptions that are difficult to read.

| THOMAS | 1818 (circa) | | No |
| Elizabeth | | Thomas, Robert W. | |

Other Info: Grave marked by fieldstones only, but known to be buried here beside her son, Thomas. Wife of Robert W. Thomas and Mother of : George W., James E., David "Davy" B., Thomas H., Robert, Norvell, Augusta and Mary.

| THOMAS | 18 Nov. 1887 | | Yes |
| Elwood Campbell | 18 Jan. 1940 | | |

Inscription: "Father. His Toils Are Past His Work Is Done He Fought the Fight The Victory Won." Footstone inscribed: "E.C.T."

| THOMAS | | | Yes |
| J. E. | 27 Sep. __47 | | |

Inscription: Grave marked with fieldstones with handcarved inscriptions that are difficult to read. The year of death might be " 49 ".

| THOMAS | | | Yes |
| J. F. | 25 Feb. 1880 | | |

LAST NAME First Name	Date of Birth Date of Death Age at Death	Maiden Name Spouse	Tombstone

Inscription: Grave marked with fieldstones with handcarved inscriptions that are difficult to read.

| THOMAS
J. H. | 1851
20 Jun. 188_ | | Yes |

Inscription: Grave marked with fieldstones with handcarved inscriptions that are difficult to read.

| THOMAS
Mary H. | 18 Oct. 1868
14 Dec. 1931 | Thomas, Thomas H. | Yes |

Inscription: "In My Fathers House Are Many Mansions." Footstone inscribed: "M.H.T."

Other Info: Wife of Thomas H. Thomas, and Mother of: Elwood, Beecher, Letcher, Stewart, Hattie and Clayton Thomas.

| THOMAS
Robert W. | 1818 (circa) | Thomas, Elizabeth | Yes |

Inscription: Robert W. served as inscribed: "22 BN VA Inf. C.S.A."

| THOMAS
Thomas H. | 1851
1923 | Thomas, Mary H. | Yes |

Inscription: "Out Of Shadows Into Reality." Footstone inscribed: "T.H.T."

| THOMAS
Thomas J. | 23 Aug. 1918
19 Jan. 1919 | | Yes |

Other Info: Son of Stewart and Annie Martin Thomas. He and his Mother died in the Flu Epidemic.

Tolbert - Sallie Tolbert Family - Hwy 640

| DURIE
Teresa | | | No |

Other Info: Known to be buried here. Graves marked by fieldstones.

| MORRIS
Mary | 1842 (circa) | | No |

Other Info: Known to be buried here. Graves marked by fieldstones only.

| TOLBERT
(infant son) | | | No |

Other Info: Infant son of Andrew "Jack" Tolbert and his wife, Susie Bryant Tolbert. There are also two Tolbert infant girls buried here. All graves marked by fieldstones only.

LAST NAME	Date of Birth	Maiden Name	Tombstone
First Name	Date of Death	Spouse	
	Age at Death		

| TOLBERT | 1840 (circa) | | No |
| Sallie | | | |

Other Info: All graves marked by fieldstones only. Sallie is the mother of Thomas Henry Tolbert. He and his wife are buried at Chestnut Grove Church.

Toney Family - Hwy 15 (Near Int. with Hwy 631)

| TONEY | 25 Jan. 1901 | | Yes |
| Angus L. | 08 Nov. 1957 | | |

Inscription: Footstone inscribed: "A.L.T."

| TONEY | 23 Nov. 1873 | | Yes |
| Anna F. | 23 Feb. 1957 | Toney, Lemuel F. | |

Inscription: "Mother. Rest In Peace."

| TONEY | | | Yes |
| Arthur Burnett | 28 Oct. 1918 | | |

Inscription: Arthur served as inscribed: "Virginia Seaman 2 CL USNRF." (Died while on duty during the War.) Footstone inscribed: "A.B.T."

| TONEY | 07 Nov. 1898 | | Yes |
| Bessie A. | 16 Apr. 1989 | | |

Inscription: "Rest In Peace."

Other Info: Grave is also marked by a funeral home metal marker.

| TONEY | 23 Apr. 1893 | | Yes |
| Harold M. | 20 Dec. 1954 | | |

Inscription: Harold served as inscribed: "Virginia PVT CO B 329 MG Bn World War I." Footstone inscribed: "H.M.T."

| TONEY | 1928 | | Yes |
| Herman V. | 1928 | | |

| TONEY | 21 Mar. 1871 | | Yes |
| Lemuel F. | 31 Oct. 1963 | Toney, Anna F. | |

Inscription: "Father. Rest In Peace."

Other Info: Grave is also marked by a funeral home metal marker inscribed: "Lemuel Franklin Toney 1871 - 1963."

| TONEY | 20 Dec. 1913 | | Yes |
| Leslie F. | 12 Nov. 1993 | | |

Inscription: Leslie served as inscribed: "PFC US Army World War II."

LAST NAME	Date of Birth	Maiden Name	Tombstone
First Name	Date of Death	Spouse	
	Age at Death		

Other Info: His grave is also marked by a funeral home metal marker.

| TONEY | 16 June 1926 | | Yes |
| Melvin Milton | 14 Mar. 1992 | | |

Inscription: Melvin served as inscribed: "US Army World War II." Footstone inscribed: "M.M.T."

| TONEY | 06 Aug. 1927 | | Yes |
| Percy Arthur | 04 Aug. 1991 | | |

Inscription: Percy served as inscribed: "PFC US Air Force." Footstone inscribed: "P.A.T."

| TONEY | 18 Apr. 1903 | | Yes |
| Russell L. | 17 Nov. 1963 | | |

Other Info: Grave is also marked with a funeral home metal marker inscribed: "Lemuel Russell Toney 1903 - 1963."

| TONEY | 17 June 1906 | | Yes |
| Thelma L. | 19 June 1994 | | |

| TONEY | 20 Oct. 1908 | | Yes |
| Wrennie J. "Teddy" | 19 Aug. 1985 | | |

Inscription: "At Rest."

"Town Cemetery" - Hwy 664

| AMOS | | | No |

Other Info: At least ten children of Ida Amos, all under the age of five years when they died, are known to be buried here. Graves marked by fieldstones only.

| BURNLEY | | Bryant | No |
| Angie | | | |

Other Info: A Burnley child, son of Angie B. Burnley who died between 1906 - 1907 is also buried here. Graves are marked by fieldstones only.

| BURNLEY | | | No |
| Ella | | | |

Other Info: Daughter of Eliza (Burnley) Taylor. Grave marked by fieldstones only.

| RAGLAND | | | No |
| Elizabeth | | Ragland, Thomas | |

Other Info: Grave marked by fieldstones only, but known to be buried here beside her husband.

LAST NAME	Date of Birth	Maiden Name	Tombstone
First Name	Date of Death	Spouse	
	Age at Death		

RAGLAND　　　　　　　　　　　　　　　　　　　　　　　　　　　　No
Thomas　　　　　　　　　　　　　Ragland, Elizabeth

Other Info: Many people buried in this cemetery with their graves marked by fieldstones only. Only the general location of the cemetery is known. It could not be found at this time.

TAYLOR　　　　　　　　　　　　　　　　　　　　　　　　　　　　　No
Eliza

Other Info: Eliza Taylor was the mother-in-law of Angie B. Burnley. Grave marked by fieldstones only.

Trinity Presbyterian Church Cemetery - Hwy 670

ADAMS　　　　08 Aug. 1873　　　　Hanes　　　　　　　　　　Yes
Dantie　　　　03 July 1967　　Adams, William Wallace

Other Info: Shares a headstone with her husband.

ADAMS　　　　　　09 Sep. 1880　　　　　　　　　　　　　　　　Yes
William Wallace　19 Nov. 1969　　Adams Dantie Hanes

Other Info: Shares a headstone with his wife.

ALLEN　　　　　　1907　　　　　　　　　　　　　　　　　　　　Yes
Leona S.　　　　1949

BALTIMORE　　　　　　　　　　　　　　　　　　　　　　　　　　Yes
Sallie Ann　　　29 Dec. 1912　　Baltimore, James
　　　　　　　　85 yr.

Inscription: "Wife of James Baltimore. Sleep Dear Mother and Take Thy Rest, God Called Thee Home, He Thought It Best." Footstone inscribed: "S.A.B."

BARRY　　　　　　1892　　　　　　　Holman　　　　　　　　　Yes
Anna　　　　　　　　　　　　　　Barry, Fred R.

Inscription: "Wife of Fred R. Barry."

Other Info: No date of death inscribed on headstone.

BROOKS　　　　08 Feb. 1891　　　　　　　　　　　　　　　　　Yes
Harold C.　　　03 Aug. 1963　　Brooks, Mary E.

BROOKS　　　　　1922　　　　　　　　　　　　　　　　　　　　Yes
Margaret Lee　　1986

BROOKS　　　　　1892　　　　　　　　　　　　　　　　　　　　Yes
Mary E.　　　　　1958　　　　　Brooks, Harold C.

LAST NAME First Name	Date of Birth Date of Death Age at Death	Maiden Name Spouse	Tombstone
BROWN Ballard A.	JUNE 1878 May 1899		Yes
BROWN Ida F.	14 Nov. 1849 26 Mar. 1887	Brown, John J.	Yes

Inscription: "In Memory Of ... Wife Of J. J. Brown. Let Me Die the Death Of the Righteous and Let My Last End Be Like His."

BROWN John Bentley	01 July 1885 07 Dec. 1975		Yes
BROWN John J.	Feb. 1849 Feb. 1903	Brown, Ida F.	Yes
BROWN Margaret N.	Mar. 1852 Mar. 1932		Yes
BUMPAS Evans George	20 Nov. 1813 15 Aug. 1892	Bumpas, Juliet Mary Hill	Yes

Inscription: "The Morning Cometh." Footstone inscribed: "E.G.B."

Other Info: Shares a headstone with his wife.

BUMPAS Juliet Mary	01 Oct. 1825 01 Jan. 1900	Hill Bumpas, Evans George	Yes

Inscription: "The Morning Cometh."

Other Info: Shares a headstone with her husband.

BUMPAS Sarah Frances	14 Mar. 1848 05 July 1855		Yes

Inscription: "Dau. of E.G. & J.M. Bumpas ... On That Bright Immortal Shore We Shall Meet To Part No More." Footstone inscribed: "S.F.B."

CATLETT Caroline D.	20 Feb. 1939 24 Oct. 1974		Yes

Inscription: "In Memory of ..."

DAVIS C. Louis	1912 1982	Davis, Mary I.	Yes

Other Info: Shares a headstone with his wife.

DAVIS Carrie A.	1866 1922		Yes

Inscription: "My Sister. There Is No Death! The Stars Go Down To Rise Upon Some Fairer Shore; and Bright In Heaven's Jewelled Crown They Shine Forever More."

LAST NAME First Name	Date of Birth Date of Death Age at Death	Maiden Name Spouse	Tombstone
DAVIS John	1832 1900		Yes

Inscription: He served as inscribed: "Lieut. Co. C 44 Va. Regt. Confederate States Army."

DAVIS Mary I.	1908 1967	Davis, C. Louis	Yes

Other Info: Shares a headstone with her husband.

DAVIS Matthew Moyle	04 Nov. 1857 11 Feb. 1914		Yes

Inscription: "Asleep In Jesus."

DAVIS Phineas A. (Col.)	28 Jan. 1834 22 Aug. 1872		Yes

Inscription: (Masonic Symbol) "In Memory of ... His Memory To Our Hearts His Spirit To His God." Footstone inscribed: "P.A.D.:

DUPUY Mollie N.	05 Dec. 1891 55 yr.	Dupuy, J. T. Dr.	Yes

Inscription: "Asleep In Jesus. Wife of Dr. J. T. Dupuy. The World Is Better For Her Having Lived In It."

EDWARDS Carrie T.	01 Oct. 1849 03 Oct. 1876	Edwards, John W.	Yes

Inscription: "In Memory Of ... Beloved Wife Of ... " Footstone inscribed: "Carrie T."

Other Info: Shares a headstone with her two infant children.

EDWARDS Carrie T.	13 Aug. 1876 03 Apr. 1877		Yes

Inscription: "Beloved child of John W. Edwards." Footstone inscribed: "Baby Carrie T."

Other Info: Shares a headstone with her mother and an infant brother.

EDWARDS John T.	25 Aug. 1871 20 Oct. 1871		Yes

Inscription: "Beloved child of John W. Edwards." Footstone inscribed: "John T."

Other Info: Shares a headstone with his mother, and his infant sister.

EDWARDS John W.	22 Jan. 1825 19 Feb. 1901	Edwards, Carrie T.	Yes

LAST NAME First Name	Date of Birth Date of Death Age at Death	Maiden Name Spouse	Tombstone
	Inscription: (Masonic Symbol) "Sacred To the Memory Of ... Born ... At Llamberis. N. Wales. Died ... At Arvonia. Va."		
EVANS Cora Saunders	1884 1964		Yes
FICKLEN Frances	03 May 1839 09 Jan. 1888	Pannill Ficklen, James Burwell	Yes
	Inscription: "Blessed Are the Dead Which Die In the Lord."		
	Other Info: Shares a headstone with her husband.		
FICKLEN James Burwell	01 Oct. 1830 31 Jan. 1883	Ficklen, Frances Pannill	Yes
	Inscription: "Blessed Are the Dead Which Died In the Lord."		
	Other Info: Shares a headstone with his wife.		
FONTAINE Abram W.	21 Mar. 1832 05 Aug. 1883		Yes
	Inscription: "Sacred To the Memory of ... Well Done, Thou Good and Faithful Servant: Enter Thou Into the Joy Of the Lord." Footstone inscribed: "A.W.F."		
FONTAINE Clement Overton	11 Dec. 1875 16 Mar. 1907		Yes
	Inscription: "They Rest From Their Labours."		
FUQUA Albert Terrell	25 Dec. 1883 07 Apr. 1960		Yes
FUQUA Fern Pritts	18 Jan. 1900 06 Jan. 1972		Yes
FUQUA Lucille Stevens	18 Aug. 1914 14 May 1984		Yes
FUQUA Richard Wilson	27 July 1885 19 Sep. 1965		Yes
FUQUA Robert Hill	13 Sep. 1878 25 Sep. 1915		Yes
FUQUA Samuel	03 Sep. 1841 29 May 1912		Yes
FUQUA Samuel Fountain	17 Mar. 1881 24 May 1952		Yes
GALT Mary			Yes

LAST NAME First Name	Date of Birth Date of Death Age at Death	Maiden Name Spouse	Tombstone

Inscription: "Sister of Anna Galt Holman."

Other Info: No dates inscribed on this headstone.

| GILLESPIE
James L. H. | 07 Nov. 1828
16 July 1862 | | Yes |

Inscription: He served as inscribed: "Carrol Rifles, Co. K. 11th Regt. Miss. Vols., C.S.A." (Masonic Symbol) "In the Full Hope Of the Gospel."

Other Info: The headstone is signed at the bottom: "Rogers & Miller"

| GOLDEN
Mattie J. | 01 Apr. 1990
88 yr. | | No |

Other Info: Grave is marked by a funeral home metal marker.

| GORMOURS
John R. | 1889
1958 | Gormours, Lou M. | Yes |

| GORMOURS
Julia Moss | 1876
1955 | | Yes |

Inscription: "God's Greatest Gift Returned To God - Our Mother." Footstone inscribed: "Mother."

| GORMOURS
Lou M. | 1894
1967 | Gormours, John R. | Yes |

| GORMOURS
William Rolph | 1884
1934 | | Yes |

Inscription: "Gone, But Not Forgotten." Footstone inscribed: "Father."

| GORMUS
Roger G. | 1918
1988
70 yr. | | No |

Other Info: Grave marked by a funeral home metal marker.

| HALL
James S. | 1852
1903 | | Yes |

| HANES
Mattie D. | 19 June 1841
11 Mar. 1923 | | Yes |

| HANES
Walter T. | 1839
1921 | | Yes |

| HERNDON
Virginia | 1851
1903 | Oslin | Yes |

| HOLMAN
Anna | 29 Sept. 1849
10 Mar. 1935 | Galt
Holman, William Henry | Yes |

LAST NAME First Name	Date of Birth Date of Death Age at Death	Maiden Name Spouse	Tombstone

Inscription: "Mother."

Other Info: Shares a headstone with her husband.

| HOLMAN
George Payne | June 1874
12 May 1904 | | Yes |
| HOLMAN
George Payne | | | Yes |

Inscription: "Father Of William Henry Holman."

Other Info: No dates inscribed on this headstone.

HOLMAN Henry Taylor	1922 1957		Yes
HOLMAN James Winn	22 Aug. 1879 04 July 1906		Yes
HOLMAN Martha Myers	14 May 1884 26 Feb. 1955		Yes
HOLMAN Mary Galt	12 Feb. 1878 08 Dec. 1964		Yes
HOLMAN Randolph Bryan	28 Jan. 1886 30 Nov. 1962		Yes
HOLMAN Robert Malcolm	30 Jan. 1888 28 June 1957		Yes
HOLMAN Thomas Ellis	19 Mar. 1881 11 Dec. 1885		Yes

Inscription: "Son of W. H. & A.H. (sic) Holman. Safe In the Arms Of Jesus."

| HOLMAN
William Galt | Jan. 1876
Aug. 1954 | | Yes |
| HOLMAN
William Henry | 06 Apr. 1841
20 Mar. 1898 | Holman, Anna Galt | Yes |

Inscription: "Father."

Other Info: Shares a headstone with his wife.

| JEFFERIES
George M. | 23 Apr. 1871
16 Mar. 1966 | Jefferies, Jennie H. | Yes |

Inscription: Footstone inscribed: "Father."

Other Info: Shares a headstone with his wife.

Last Name First Name	Date of Birth Date of Death Age at Death	Maiden Name Spouse	Tombstone
JEFFERIES George McKendree	12 May 1912 02 Oct. 1989 77 yr.	Jefferies, Sarah Edna Wood	Yes

Other Info: Grave also marked by a funeral home metal marker.

JEFFERIES Jennie H.	26 Mar. 1869 31 Dec. 1957	Jefferies, George M.	Yes

Inscription: Footstone inscribed: "Mother."

Other Info: Shares a headstone with her husband.

JONES Anne	08 Dec. 1870 30 yr.	Jones, J. E.	Yes

Inscription: "Mother."

Other Info: At bottom of headstone it is signed: "M. R. Jones Arvonia."

JONES Harriett Elizabeth	27 Oct. 1908 08 July 1985		Yes

Inscription: "Hattie. To Know Her Was To Love Her."

JONES Lottie Pitts	13 May 1889 27 Nov. 1976		Yes

JONES Louis Dibrell	11 July 1916 26 Apr. 1935		Yes

JONES Plummer Flippen	29 Aug. 1875 23 Feb. 1968		Yes

KEEL Charles Whittington M.D.	1871 1914		Yes

Inscription: Back of headstone inscribed: "Keel."

LeSUEUR Caroline	03 Jan. 1902 21 Sep. 1983	Patteson LeSueur, Frank Irving	Yes

Other Info: Shares a headstone with her husband.

LeSUEUR Charles Fontaine Jr.	1903 1904		No

LeSUEUR Frank Irving	02 Aug. 1882 29 June 1964	LeSueur, Caroline Patteson	Yes

Inscription: (Masonic Symbol)

Other Info: Shares a headstone with his wife.

LAST NAME First Name	Date of Birth Date of Death Age at Death	Maiden Name Spouse	Tombstone
LeSUEUR Henrietta	1841 1909	Lightfoot LeSueur, L. B.	Yes

Inscription: Footstone inscribed: "H.L.L."

Other Info: Shares a headstone with her husband.

LeSUEUR L. B.	1843 1914	LeSueur, Henrietta Lightfoot	Yes

Inscription: Footstone inscribed: "L.B.L."

Other Info: Shares a headstone with his wife.

LeSUEUR L. B. Jr.	04 June 1874 12 Nov. 1920		Yes
LeSUEUR Susan	28 Apr. 1929		Yes
NICHOLAS Alexander Duval	08 Dec. 1899 29 Jan. 1970		Yes

Inscription: As inscribed on the footstone, he served as follows: "Alexander D. Nicholas PVT BTRY E 11 Field ARTY World War I Dec. 8, 1899 Jan. 29, 1970." (Masonic Symbol)

NICHOLAS George B.	1870 1949	Nicholas, Lucy C.	Yes

Other Info: Shares a headstone with his wife.

NICHOLAS Lucy C.	1884 1955	Nicholas, George B.	Yes

Other Info: Shares a headstone with her husband.

NICHOLAS Reuben O.	24 Nov. 1873 13 Oct. 1961		Yes

Inscription: "In Loving Memory."

NORVELL David R.	11 May 1844 12 Oct. 1907		Yes

Inscription: "Blessed Are the Dead Who Die In the Lord." Footstone inscribed: "D.R.N."

NORVELL Florence S.	04 Oct. 1885 11 Oct. 1960		Yes
NORVELL Mary E.	06 Dec. 1858 24 Mar. 1927		Yes

Inscription: Footstone inscribed: "M.E.N."

LAST NAME First Name	Date of Birth Date of Death Age at Death	Maiden Name Spouse	Tombstone
OSLIN Hugh P.	1918 1957		Yes
OSLIN Virginia	1831 1910	Lesueur	Yes

Inscription: On back of headstone is inscribed: "OSLIN."

OSLIN W. H.	22 Sep. 1859 24 Sep. 1922		Yes

Other Info: Engraving of a mill with a waterwheel at top of headstone.

OSLIN W. Hugh Jr.	22 Oct. 1890 01 Sep. 1951		Yes

Inscription: "Our Loved One."

PAINTER Janet	29 Jan. 1938 04 Nov. 1990	Nicholas	Yes
PATTESON Nettie	1875 1964	Davis Patteson, Peter Broaddus	Yes

Other Info: Shares a headstone with her husband.

PATTESON Peter Broaddus	1867 1959	Patteson, Nettie Davis	Yes

Other Info: Shares a headstone with his wife.

PENDLETON Alexander Russell	1897 1946		Yes

Inscription: "An Honest Man's the Noblest Work Of God."

PENDLETON James Alexander	08 Apr. 1935 25 Nov. 1952		Yes

Inscription: "Jimmy. To Know Him Was To Love Him."

ROBERTS Charles E.	1884 1967	Roberts, Mary S.	Yes

Other Info: Shares a headstone with his wife.

ROBERTS Mary S.	1892 1952	Roberts, Charles E.	Yes

Other Info: Shares a headstone with her husband.

SATTERFIELD George Whitney	11 Oct. 1880 23 Sep. 1948	Satterfield, Lillian Proffitt	Yes

Inscription: (Masonic Symbol) "Dying Is But Going Home."

LAST NAME First Name	Date of Birth Date of Death Age at Death	Maiden Name Spouse	Tombstone
SATTERFIELD Lillian	31 May 1884 20 Jan. 1955	Proffitt Satterfield, George Whitney	Yes
SAUNDERS J. Holman	1885 1927		Yes
SAUNDERS John H.	21 Feb. 1934 82 yr. 5 mo. 22 dy.		No

Other Info: Grave marked by a funeral home metal marker.

SMITH Susan C.	20 Jan. 1836 07 Oct. 1887	Smith, G. W.	Yes

Inscription: "In Memory Of Our Mother ... Wife Of ..." Footstone inscribed: "S.C.S."

SNODDY Annie Myrtie	1886 1889		Yes
SNODDY Luther R.	1852 1909	Snoddy, Nannie G.	Yes

Inscription: Footstone inscribed: "L.R.S."

Other Info: Shares a headstone with his wife.

SNODDY Mellville F.	1878 1879		Yes
SNODDY Nannie G.	1851 1931	Snoddy, Luther R.	Yes

Other Info: Shares a headstone with her husband.

SNODDY Thomas P.	1889 1949		Yes

Inscription: Footstone inscribed: "T.P.S."

STAPLES George B.	20 Sept. 1858 10 Aug. 1902		Yes

Inscription: "Come Ye Blessed. Gone But Not Forgotten." Footstone inscribed: "G.B.S."

STAPLES J. J.	08 Oct. 187_		Yes

Other Info: This is a slate headstone with the inscriptions scratched on by hand - very difficult to read.

STAPLES Maggie M.	18 Sep. 1860 28 Mar. 1898	Staples, James R.	Yes

LAST NAME First Name	Date of Birth Date of Death Age at Death	Maiden Name Spouse	Tombstone

Inscription: "Wife of James R. Staples."

| STAPLES
Margaret Anne | 07 Feb. 1897
13 Oct. 1899 | | Yes |

Inscription: "In Memoriam Our Baby ... Dau. of P. W. & V.D. Staples. Budded On Earth To Bloom In Heaven."

| STAPLES
Mary A. | 05 May 1855
27 Feb. 1907 | Staples, Mathew S. | Yes |

Inscription: "Wife of M. S. Staples." Footstone inscribed: "Mother."

| STAPLES
Mathew S. | 1853
1937 | Staples, Mary A. | Yes |

Inscription: "Father."

| STAPLES
Walter Capt. | 11 May 1825
26 Jan. 1913 | | Yes |

Inscription: "May He Rest In Peace." Footstone inscribed: "W.S."

| TAYLOR
Acey W. | 17 May 1937
03 May 1980 | Taylor, Mary Davis | Yes |

Inscription: "Nearer My God To Thee."

| TAYLOR
Elizabeth S. | 1855
1940 | | Yes |

| TAYLOR
John L. | 1856
1933 | | Yes |

| TAYLOR
S. Elizabeth | 14 Feb. 1848
21 June 1904 | Taylor, Zachary | Yes |

Inscription: "To The Memory of ... Beloved Wife of Zachary Taylor. Safe In the Arms of Jesus. Taylor."

| TAYLOR
Zachary | 1850
1934 | Taylor, S. Elizabeth | Yes |

Inscription: "Lead Kindly Light."

| THOMPSON
Ann | 15 Mar. 1824
11 Nov. 1882 | Scott
Thompson, Rev. Wm. S. | Yes |

Inscription: "Wife of Rev. W.S. Thompson...Sorrow & Sighing Shall Flee Away."

| THOMPSON
Clemmie F. | 1861
1936 | | Yes |

Other Info: This grave also marked by a funeral home metal marker.

LAST NAME First Name	Date of Birth Date of Death Age at Death	Maiden Name Spouse	Tombstone
THOMPSON John W.	1865 1941		Yes

Other Info: This grave is also marked by a funeral home metal marker.

| THOMPSON
William S. Rev. | 12 Oct. 1812
07 Oct. 1889 | Thompson, Ann Scott | Yes |

Inscription: "In Memory of ... Well Done Thou Good & Faithful Servant."

Other Info: This grave was moved here from Seven Islands Farm family cemetery. The footstone inscribed: "W.S.T." is still at the Seven Islands family cemetery.

| TOMS
Jonathan | 10 Feb. 1861
30 yr. | | Yes |

Inscription: "Sacred To the Memory Of ... Native of Cornwal (sic) England."

| TREYNOR
Nannie J. | 1921
1929 | | Yes |

Inscription: "Gone To Be An Angel." Footstone inscribed: "N.J.T."

| (Unknown) | | | Yes |

Other Info: There is a large slate/stone crypt behind the chapel. No one seems to know who is buried in it. It has been said that it was an unidentified clown who was performing at a circus set up nearby when he died. I have also been told that this unidentified clown was buried in the field to the North of the chapel; his grave never having been marked by anything other than a fieldstone.

| WHEELER
Ella | 1863
1935 | Barger
Wheeler, John D. | Yes |

Inscription: "Mother."

Other Info: Shares a headstone with her husband.

| WHEELER
John D. | 1860
1948 | Wheeler, Ella Barger | Yes |

Inscription: "Father."

Other Info: Shares a headstone with his wife.

| WOOLDRIDGE
Josephine | 01 Aug. 1891
19 Dec. 1979 | Oslin | Yes |

Inscription: "Mother."

LAST NAME	Date of Birth	Maiden Name	Tombstone
First Name	Date of Death	Spouse	
	Age at Death		

Unknown - Hwy 740

Other Info: From the int. of Hwy 655 and Hwy 740, go NW on Hwy 740 approx. 2.4 miles. The cemetery is located just beside the road on the left. There are 6 graves, and one had a funeral home metal marker at its head, that was unreadable. (1987) Others were marked with fieldstones only. Does anyone know what family burying ground this is?

Unknown at "Tall House" property - Hwy 631

Other Info: This cemetery has been obliterated, but it used to be on the left of the driveway going to the house. It was located about 100 ft. down the driveway on the left, in front of a small shed that is still there (1986). There were 6-8 graves, but never any tombstones. Does anyone known what family belonged to this burying ground?

Unknown on Shumaker family property - Hwy 631

Other Info: This cemetery was located on the Shumaker property to the North of Hwy 631, at the sharp curve in the road. It was at the right of the house towards two sheds. There were never any tombstones, but the depressions showed that there were 4-6 graves here. Does anyone know what family burying ground this was?

Warminster Baptist Church Cemetery (Black) - Hwy 664

| BROWN | 02 Jan. 1923 | Yes |
| Delaware Henry | 09 July 1970 | |

Inscription: "Flood." He served as inscribed: "PVT. U.S. ARMY WORLD WAR II."

Other Info: Son of Pauline L. Brown and brother of Joe Brown.

| BROWN | 1916 | Yes |
| Joe | 1937 | |

Inscription: "Brother."

Other Info: Son of Pauline L. Brown and brother of Delaware Henry Brown.

| BROWN | 15 Nov. 1882 | Yes |
| Pauline L. | 28 Dec. 1970 | |

Inscription: "Mother."

Other Info: Mother of Joe and Delaware "Flood" Brown.

LAST NAME First Name	Date of Birth Date of Death Age at Death	Maiden Name Spouse	Tombstone
COLEMAN Alex	1886 1976		No

Other Info: Grave marked by a funeral home metal marker.

| DIBBLE
Neal L. | 1917
1974 | | No |

Other Info: Grave marked by a funeral home metal marker.

| JOHNSON
Florence | 1918
1980 | Moss | Yes |

Other Info: Mrs. David Johnson, she was the mother of eight sons: Samuel, Robert, John, Willie, James, David Jr., Isaiah and Jackie Johnson. Also, the sister of Eva Moss Vaughters.

| JONES
Elsie K. | 1936
1980 | Johnson
Jones, Frazier Mays | No |

Other Info: Grave is marked by a funeral home metal marker.

| JONES
Frazier Mays | 1935
1985 | Jones, Elsie K. | Yes |

Other Info: Son of Wyatt N. & Nellie Mays Jones.

| LEE
Clarence | 1920
1983 | | No |

Other Info: Grave marked by a funeral home metal marker.

| NICHOLAS
Annie M. | 09 June 1903
12 July 1970 | | Yes |

Inscription: "In Loving Memory."

| PATTERSON
Elnora W. | 1919
1970 | | Yes |

Inscription: "Gone But Not Forgotten."

| PATTERSON
Samuel R. | 10 Aug. 1904
05 Feb. 1982 | | Yes |

Inscription: He served as inscribed: "PVT. U.S. ARMY WORLD WAR II."

| PERKINS
Lena D. | 1895
1972 | | No |

Other Info: Grave is marked by a funeral home metal marker.

| ROSE
Ella P. | 16 Aug. 1900
06 Mar. 1966 | | Yes |

LAST NAME First Name	Date of Birth Date of Death Age at Death	Maiden Name Spouse	Tombstone

Inscription: "Asleep In Jesus."

| TWYMAN
John J. | 14 Sep. 1900
06 Apr. 1983 | Twyman, Willie E. | Yes |

Other Info: Shares a headstone with his wife. His grave is also marked by a funeral home metal marker inscribed: "John J. Twyman 1901 (sic) - 1983."

| TWYMAN
Willie E. | 01 Apr. 1900
14 Jan. 1980 | Twyman, John J. | Yes |

Other Info: Shares a headstone with her husband.

| VAUGHTERS
Eva | 1921
1974 | Moss | No |

Other Info: Grave marked by a funeral home metal marker.

| WAYNE
Nora A. | 15 Sep. 1911
09 Sep. 1967 | | Yes |

Inscription: "The Lord Is My Shepherd, I Shall Not Want."

Other Info: Nora A. Wayne is the wife of Samuel P. Wayne.

| WAYNE
Samuel P. | 1908
1982 | Wayne, Nora A. | No |

Other Info: Grave is marked by a funeral home metal marker.

Welcome Wesleyan Methodist Church - Hwy 15

| AMOS
Hubbard L. | 25 Feb. 1931
20 June 1984 | | Yes |

Other Info: Grave is also marked by a funeral home metal marker inscribed: "Hubbard Lewis Amos 1931-1984."

| CHILDRESS
Jimmy Dale | 16 June 1959
12 Jan. 1980 | | Yes |

| DOWDY
Beulah | 03 Mar. 1897
06 Dec. 1966 | | Yes |

| DOWDY
Marshall L. | 05 May 1914
24 Dec. 1964 | | Yes |

Inscription: He served as inscribed: "Virginia SGT. US Army World War II."

| DUNKUM
Benjamin S. | 1877
1967 | Dunkum, Ella Dowdy | Yes |

LAST NAME First Name	Date of Birth Date of Death Age at Death	Maiden Name Spouse	Tombstone

Other Info: Shares a headstone with his wife.

| DUNKUM
Ella | 1880
1946 | Dowdy
Dunkum, Benjamin S. | Yes |

Other Info: Shares a headstone with her husband.

| DUNKUM
Myrtle B. | 1901
1973 | Dunkum, Willie H. | Yes |

Inscription: Footstone inscribed: "Mother."

| EMERT
Sandra Jo | 15 Oct. 1963
19 Oct. 1963 | | Yes |

| GARY
Elijah Hanes | 18 May 1894
26 Sep. 1976 | Gary, Lizzie Self | Yes |

| GRANDSTAFF
Evelyn Morrison | 04 Oct. 1916
27 Feb. 1962 | Grandstaff, James M. | Yes |

| HILL
Edna Mae | 1891
1974 | Hill, Joseph Felix | Yes |

Inscription: "Mother."

Other Info: Shares a headstone with her husband.

| HILL
Joseph Felix | 1887
1975 | Hill, Edna Mae | Yes |

Inscription: "Father."

Other Info: Shares a headstone with his wife.

| LIGHTFOOT
Clyde A. | 1910
1983 | Lightfoot, Alice H. | Yes |

Other Info: Grave is also marked by a funeral home metal marker inscribed: "Clyde Aubrey Lightfoot."

| MARION
Johnny L. | 19 Aug. 1929
24 Sep. 1984 | Marion, Susie M. | Yes |

Inscription: "Wed Apr. 20, 1951."

Other Info: Grave is also marked by a funeral home metal marker.

| NAGLE
Charles F. | 1914
1970 | | No |

Other Info: Grave is marked by a funeral home metal marker.

| SAYLOR
Paul K. | 23 June 1907
21 Sep. 1974 | Saylor, Mildred M. | Yes |

LAST NAME First Name	Date of Birth Date of Death Age at Death	Maiden Name Spouse	Tombstone
SHERRILL Norris R.	13 Oct. 1901 16 Apr. 1967	Sherrill, Ivey M.	Yes
SMITH Patricia A.	22 Feb. 1961 19 Apr. 1961		Yes
SNODDY Gordon Lee	04 Aug. 1889 23 May 1966	Snoddy, Gracie Self	Yes

Other Info: Shares a headstone with her husband.

SNODDY Gracie	12 May 1889 06 Dec. 1962	Self Snoddy, Gordon Lee	Yes

Other Info: Shares a headstone with her husband.

SNODDY Thomas Elwood	04 Oct. 1916 21 June 1978	Snoddy, Jean Emert	Yes

Inscription: "Father." He served as inscribed on the footstone: "Thomas Elwood Snoddy TEC5 US Army World War II."

TONEY Carrie Etta	03 Nov. 1906 15 Apr. 1983		Yes

"Wheatland" Homeplace - Hwy 633

Other Info: Indian Mound located on Bishop Creek. The local residents have always known where these Indian burial mounds are located, and they should always be preserved.

Wootten - Clifford Wootten Family - Hwy 640 (Slate River Forest Road)

WOOTTEN Clifford		Wootten, Hallie S.	No

Other Info: Known to be buried here beside his wife and mother. All graves marked by fieldstones only.

WOOTTEN Hallie		Stanley Wootten, Clifford	No

Other Info: Known to be buried here beside her husband. All graves marked by fieldstones only.

LAST NAME First Name	Date of Birth Date of Death Age at Death	Maiden Name Spouse	Tombstone

Wright

WRIGHT Charlie	1840 - 1850s		Yes

Inscription: Charlie served as inscribed: "Co C 3rd VA Reg. C.S.A."

Other Info: There are possibly 16 + or - graves in this cemetery. Many are Toney and Wright family members. Only one tombstone was found.

Index

A

Abraham
  Carrie Jones, 1
  Samuel E., 1
Absher
  Albert Lee, 18
  Belle Wood, 18, 19
  Betty Compton, 18, 19
  Charles C., 18, 19
  Daniel Lee, 19
  Edith G., 19
  Elizabeth, 18
  Ellen Carbaugh, 19, 20
  Fanny A., 19, 20
  Harriette Agnes, 19
  Lane Edward, 19
  Lee B., 18, 19
  Millie Herndon, 19, 20
  Minnie E., 18, 19
  Oscar Watson, 18, 19
  Walter Paris, 19, 20
  William Bee, 19, 20
  William E., 19, 20
Adams
  Dantie Hanes, 254
  Lelia A., 32, 33
  T. Chambers, 33
  William Wallace, 254
Adcock
  Bessie Charlotte Hardiman, 33
  Carrie P., 33
  David Walker, 33
  Mary Miss, 65
  Wesley, 65
  Wesley T., 33
Addleman
  Perry, 228
Aderhold
  Dewey Hubbard, 167
Agee
  Agnes Wright S. Wright, 95
  Cornelius Hamilton, 20, 21
  Elezea Baber, 214, 215
  Francis Lee, 108
  Frank Garland, 20
  Garland Price, 20
  Georgie Ellen, 106
  Irene Dunkum, 108
  Iris M., 1
  Jacob, 20
  Joe Gilbert, 95
  John Bushrod, 214
  L. R., 108
  Martha Ann, 214
  Mary Catherine, 21
  Mary Lou Steger, 214
  Mary Nuckols, 20
  Mary Price, 20
  Nannie Maxey, 107
  Robert, 107
  Rosa K. C., 20
  Rosa Kate Claiborne, 21
  Ruby Moss, 1
  Susie Putney Dunkum, 108
  Tommy T., 1
  Tyree, 214, 215
  Virginia Hooper, 21
  Virginia Smith, 215
  Willie Anderson, 1
  Willie Ford, 215
  Wm. C., 21
Allen
  Billy W.S., 33
  Carrie S., 33
  Charlie B., 33
  Doris T., 167
  Emma Raikes, 167
  Ernest G., 228
  Frank Acie, 33
  Frank R., 167
  George Thomas, 167
  Gilbert, 228
  Gladys D., 33
  Henry F., 167
  J. Lenard, 33
  James C., 167
  Jamie Franklin, 167
  Leona S., 254
  Mary Barton, 167
  Mary Harris, 33, 34
  Mary Lesueur, 33
  Nannie Etta, 228
  Nicholaus Reed, 167
  Ronald Lee, 34
  Virginia Gills, 228
  W. W., 228
  Willie Samuel, 34
Allison
  I.D. Mrs., 4
Almond
  Davis, 65
  Janie M., 65
Amiss
  Eva Moss, 65
  John Calvin, 65
  Phillip W., 65
Amos, 253
  Hubbard L., 268
  Samuel, 166
  Tinker, 166
Anderson
  Alexander Marshall, 65
  Andrew W., 108
  Anne Follkes, 6
  Bessie, 109
  Brenda P., 109
  Cammie R., 5
  Charlie Edward, 179
  Claude Wood, 5
  Earl, 2
  Edward Pratt, 5
  Edward Van, 5, 6
  Elizabeth Flood, 3
  Ella Boatwright, 109, 110
  Esta, 3
  Estelle Vaughn, 5
  Etta Sinclair, 5
  Evelyn Meade, 5
  Fannie D., 109
  Fleeta, 3
  Florence Virginia, 3
  Grover Morten, 3
  Hazel Martin, 109
  Herbert B., 109
  Herbert M., 109
  Herman Shield, 5
  Irma B., 110
  Irma Bickford, 109
  James, 6
  James M., 3
  James Meade, 5, 6
  Jennie Goodman, 109, 110
  John P., 109
  John Penick, 109, 110
  John W., 109, 110
  Joseph W., 5
  Juan A., 6
  Juan R., 6
  Juan Raymond, 6
  Lillie I., 6
  Lucy Wootten, 109, 110
  Luther A., 110
  Maitland Hilston, 110
  Martha Flood, 3
  Martha M. Flood, 6
  Mary Ellen, 110
  Mattie, 18
  Mildred W., 6
  Nannie Louise, 110
  Nannie Steger, 5, 6
  O. W., 110
  Oly Louis, 109, 110
  Pattie Coleman, 5, 6
  Reese Moses, 3
  Robert B., 109, 110
  Sallie Harris, 110
  Samuel Knight Polk, 3

273

Index

Shelva Jean Christian, 110
Stuart Granville, 110
T. B., 109
Thomas Bernice, 110, 111
Vera Preston, 111, 115, 133
Virginia, 109
Virginia Davis, 110, 111
William B., 6
William Bennett, 3
William Bryant, 109
William Robert, 3
Andrews
  Fred, 151
Apperson
  Ada Anderson, 111
  B. L., 112
  Braxton Lee, 111
  Dorothy Whitlow, 111
  Edward, 111
  Infant Boy, 111
  James L., 168
  John P., 65
  John Werna, 111
  Lemuel W., 111
  Lemuel Wertley, 111
  Margaret F., 168
  Mary G., 66
  Paul L., 168
  Ruby A., 111
  Ruby Apperson, 111
  S. Frances, 168
  Samuel Wertley, 111
  Thomas J., 168
  Virginia T., 112
  Winnie H., 112
Atkinson
  John W., 34
  Willie W., 34
Atwater
  William Bulluck sic, 180
Austin
  A. A., 3
  Harrison, 203
  James E., 203
  John Blackwell, 228
  Katie Kidd, 228
  Margaret, 204
  Marvin Blackwell, 228
  Mary A., 4
  Minnie Pollard, 228
  Samuel, 204
  Thomas T., 164
Ayers
  Annie, 204
  James E., 228, 229
  James Nathan, 168
  Margarett L., 168
  Nannie Sue, 34
  Sarah B., 228, 229
  Virginia T., 168
Ayres
  Aileen Harris, 168
  Dora, 34
  John James, 168
  John McGuire, 168, 169
  John R., 34
  Kate, 34
  Lena Self, 215
  McKenna, 215
  Sarah, 34
  Sarah Allen, 168, 169
  Willie, 35

B

Baber
  Agness, 112
  Clinton T., 215
  Florrie A., 215
  George Agee, 215
  Granville R., 66
  Julia T., 215
  Lily Norvell, 215
  Luther L., 215
  Mary Hardiman, 66
  Mary Jane, 112
  W. H., 112
  William H., 112
Bagby
  Callie P., 112
  Charles, 204
  Charles W., 204
  Elizabeth, 204
  Floyd, 204
  Infant Twins, 204
  James, 204
  John, 204
  Josephine, 204
  Katie, 204
  Loniel sic B., 112
  Matilda, 204
  Mattie, 204
  Phyllis, 205
  Verna M., 105
  Wiley, 205
Bailey
  Courtney D., 229
  Edward M., 112
  Elizabeth E., 112
  F. M., 229
  F. M. Mrs., 229
  Grace Hannah, 229
  Henry Pugh, 229

Infants, 180
John Blanton, 229
Lottie H., 229, 230
Mattie Pugh, 229, 230
Mildred McCorkle, 229
Nancy Agee, 230
Nancy H., 180
S. D., 229
Thomas Jordan, 230
William A., 180
William E., 229, 230
Yancy Elam, 229, 230
Yancy R., 230
Baird
  Bill Daniel, 4
  Clarke, 4
  Hubert, 4
  James, 4
  John Robert, 181
  Mattie Belle, 4
  Minnie, 4
Baldridge
  Hallie B., 230
Baldwin
  Betty Allen, 230
  Cora C., 230, 231
  H. O., 230
  J. E., 230
  S. Helen, 230
  S. Joe, 231
  Susan, 231
  W. H., 230, 231
Ballowe
  Alice K., 151
  Charles R., 151
  Charles S., 151
Baltimore
  James, 254
  Sallie Ann, 254
Banton
  Ada B., 181
  Albert Glover, 35
  Alex, 35
  Alex Sizer Wilson, 31
  Alexander, 35, 36
  Bernard W., 215, 216
  Carrie Lee Huddleston, 35
  Charles H., 35
  Charles M., 31
  Charles Mitchell, 31
  Charles Wesley, 215
  David A., 181
  Decker, 181
  Dottie N. L. P., 31
  Edmond, 216
  Elizabeth C., 215, 216

Index

Ella B., 35, 36
Elsie Mae, 216
Emmett Mitchell, 35
Eugene K., 35
Eugene Kenneth, 35
Francis Mitchell, 31
George W., 181
Henry G., 35, 36
Hick, 66
Ida A., 216
Ida Virginia, 181
Jessie Pendleton, 66
John A., 66
John Wesley, 216
Julia A., 216
L. E., 36
Lee, 216
Lee Whitfield, 216
Lena C., 96
Letcher L., 181
Lillian C., 35, 36
Lizzie Maxey, 216
Lucy Walker, 36
Male, 181
Mary L., 36
Maude Scott, 216
"Murray ""Shortie""", 181
"Narcissus Lee ""Dottie"" Peters", 31
Percy J., 181
Robert Allen, 1
Robert Lee, 36
Ruby May, 216
Samuel, 66
Shirley Mae, 181
Sidney A., 66
Tandy H., 96
Wallace Woodrow, 181
Walter, 36
Watson C., 216
William A., 181
arker
Baby, 36
Daisy Walker, 249
Edna W., 21
Evie, 36
Frank, 36
Frank Mrs., 37
Frank R., 37
John A., 37
Lucy, 37
Robert J., 21
Robert James, 249
Sidney Allen, 37
Wiley, 37
Wm. Lee, 21

Barksdale
  Mollie, 37
Barrett
  Lucy, 205
Barry
  Anna Holman, 254
  Fred R., 254
Bates
  Alsee, 231
  Charlotte, 231
Baughan
  D. H., 231
  D. Houston, 231
Bays
  Darrell Lee, 231
  Sylvia Mae, 231
Beasley
  Nannie Poe, 166
Beatty
  Clarence C., 66
  Lucille B., 66
Belcher
  Jimper B., 112
Benninghove
  Irvin, 66
Berry
  J. Ivanhoe, 66
  Josephine, 66
  W.S., 67
Bersch
  James E., 231
  John Christian, 112, 113
  Lucy Phaup, 231
  Virginia Dunkum, 112, 113
Besendorfer
  Erich Whitman, 21
Bickford
  Bobby, 113
  Debbie T., 113
  Dovie C., 113
  James Oral, 113
  Louise Davidson, 113
  Vernon E., 113
Bixler
  Alexander, 15
  Frank, 15
  Irene C., 15
  Irene Crews, 15
Blackwell
  Douglas Wayne, 37
  Emmett Lee, 113
  Joseph W., 37
  Mattie Rogers, 37
  Robert L., 37
  Roy Franklin, 38
Bland

Emily L., 17
Blanks
  Terrell, 67
Boatwright
  Annie Elizabeth Sibley, 113
  Benjamin S., 113
  Carlton F., 113
  Edna Marion, 113
  Ellen J. H., 114
  Ellen J. Hudgins, 114
  Eva Anderson, 114
  George Carlton, 114
  Grace Leolene, 114
  James Franklin, 114
  Norma Putney, 114
  P. P., 114
  Reuben Curtis, 114
  Wm. G., 113
Boggs
  Clarence W., 114
  Kathleen Taylor, 114
Bolden
  John, 205
Bolding
  Lorena Smith, 205
Bollinger
  Male, 182
Bondurant
  Virginia Baker, 102
Booker
  Anderson W., 151
  Annie Rosen, 151
  Ernest R., 205
  John C., 205
  John Randolph, 205
  Leake B., 151
  Mattie V., 205
  Myrtle, 151
  Virginia Pearl, 205
Bosley
  Glenn, 169
  Margaret H., 169
Bostain
  Edward J., 182
  Ruth Baird, 182
Bowling
  Ernest H., 151, 152
  Sarah Johns, 151, 152
Boyd
  Wade Glenwood, 182
Branch
  Baby, 15
  Glen Edward, 1
  Richard Arlen, 1
Bransford
  Glenna, 21

Index

John, 38
Walter P., 21
Bray
  Charles C., 96
  Crawford, 97
  Joan E., 97
Breed
  George Frederick, 114
  Jeanne Riddle, 114
Brickey
  Ronald C., 67
Brock
  Deems B., 38
  Flora E., 38
Brooks
  Ethel, 152
  Florence Boatwright, 114
  Harold C., 254
  Lucy, 152
  Margaret Lee, 254
  Mary E., 254
  Richard, 152
  T. S., 152
Brown
  Amanda M., 114
  Amy Queen, 205
  Annie Louise Jones, 231, 232
  Ballard A., 255
  Delaware Henry, 266
  Fred, 206
  Gabriel, 31
  Gabriel Willis, 18
  Harrie, 16
  Ida A., 206
  Ida F., 255
  Jennette, 206
  Joe, 266
  John Bentley, 255
  John J., 255
  Margaret N., 255
  Martha A. B., 31
  Martha A. Baird, 31
  Pauline L., 266
  Sally Daisy, 206
  William, 231, 232
  Willie, 18
  Wilson, 206
Bryant
  Andrew J., 114, 115
  Belle, 38
  Bertha Farrish, 216
  Bertha Farrish, 217
  Bettie G., 114, 115
  Ethel B., 164
  Frank Walker, 216, 217
  James A., 217
  Johnnie J., 164
  Nannie S., 67
  Pelham, 115
  Richard L., 115
  Sallie R., 6, 7
  Susie A., 217
  Thomas William, 115
  Verna Stinson, 115
  Warren A., 6, 7
Bullard
  Lula Yates Anderson, 7
  Wm. E., 7
Bumpas
  Evans George, 255
  Juliet Mary Hill, 255
  Sarah Frances, 255
Burnley
  Angie Bryant, 253
  Ella, 253
Butler
  Elias Athol, 115

C

Caldwell
  Margaret Hamilton, 232
Call, 94
  Addie M., 67
  Alfred, 67, 68
  Charles E., 67
  Cosby, 67
  Edna G., 67
  George W., 67
  George Washington, 68
  James Daniel, 169
  Josephine, 67, 68
  Mable Call, 68
  Mattie F., 68
  Patti Jane, 68
  Richard, 169
  Robert J., 68
  Rosa Lee, 68
  Willie Wooton, 169
Cann
  Mary Anderson, 115
Carey
  Ida P., 161
Carrington
  Estelle Mahon, 115
  Robert Bernard, 115
Carruthers
  Emma Carter, 182
  John Aden, 182
Carter
  Alice W., 115
  Eva M. Young, 152
  Gay Bradley, 115
  George W., 152, 182
  James H., 115, 116
  James N., 152, 153
  Lee Roy, 22
  M. Eddie, 116
  Mary B., 115, 116
  Merrie V. Word, 152, 153
  Nannie Oliver, 22
Carwile
  Arthur P., 153
  Beulah Garrett, 153
Case
  Ann D., 116
  Tatum, 116
Catlett
  Alfred N., 68
  Caroline D., 255
  Florence M., 68
  Garnett E., 68
  John Edward, 68
  Margaret M., 68
  Phillip B., 38
  Rosa Swann, 38
  William E., 68
Caul
  James W., 217
  Mollie B., 217
Cave
  Bessie Hurt, 116
  Bessie Hurt, 116
  Charles Wesley, 116
Chambers
  John Russell, 64
  Peter, 64
Chance
  Terry Lynn, 182
Chappell
  Graham T., 153
  Graham Trent, 153
  William H., 153
Charlton
  Edgar Anderson, 68, 69
  J. Spottswood, 69
  John J., 69
  John R., 69
  S. L., 69
  Theresa Johnson, 68, 69
Chick
  Margaret Moss, 232
Chidester
  Clyde L., 97
  Mary J., 97
Childress
  Albert K., 116
  children, 64
  Dennis Elvin, 69

Index

Elizabeth V., 97
Frank A., 97
Hallie B., 164
Helen, 22
James, 97
Jimmy Dale, 268
Maree, 116
Mayme N., 116
Princess, 116
Robert C., 164
Robert L., 22
Sarah B., 22
Walter F., 116
Wealthia Davis, 117
William Harrison, 117
William Thomas, 117
Chinn
  Dee L., 182
Christian
  Andrew M., 69
  Anna Sharp, 182
  Annie, 38
  "Bernard Lee Jr. ""Bernie""", 69
  Bernice D., 169
  C. Viola, 117
  Charles L., 38
  Clarice H., 117
  Elsie D., 169, 170
  Ernest T., 7
  Fitz Lee, 38
  G. Norman, 117
  H. Leslie, 169
  James Donald, 69
  James Oscar, 117, 118
  James Wiley, 169
  John Henry, 39
  John M., 117
  Laura C., 117, 118
  Leonard, 169, 170
  Lillian Hudgins, 118
  Lucy Jane, 39
  Martha B., 7
  Nancy V., 170
  Nellie Davis, 117, 118
  Robert, 39
  Shirley Worley, 169
  Thomas Ashby, 118
  Thomas L., 117, 118
  Thomas Reeves, 182
Claiborne
  Aubra Price, 69
  Laura Garnett, 22
  Marshall P., 69
  Martha E., 22
  Martha Elizabeth, 22
  Temple Irving, 22

  Temple Irving Sgt., 22
  Thomas O., 22
Clark
  Ella Stanton, 248
  James, 248
  Unice Lee, 248
Clayton
  John Stuart, 118
Cobbs
  Sue, 108
  Sultania, 206
Cole
  A. P., 118
  Andrew Howard, 118
  Cornelia B., 118
  Cornelia Boatwright, 118
  Edward Sidney, 118
  Estelle Mahon, 118
  Ferd W., 7
  Grace West, 118
  Grace West, 118
  Juan B., 7
  Lucy Roberts, 7
  May, 7
  Milton W., 7
  Minnie C., 7
  Thomas William, 118
Coleman
  Alex, 267
  Carrie, 206
  Evelyn A., 8
  John, 202
  John E., 206
  Julius A., 8
  Mack, 69
  Minnie Morgan, 8
  Ollie, 69
Collins
  Harry R., 15
  John, 39
Conner
  Beulah, 69
  Janie Cobb, 70
  William Rolfe, 70
Cook
  Arminta M., 70
  Silas M., 70
Cooper
  Edward Mercer, 70
  Virginia Phaup, 70
Cottman
  Clarissa G., 206
Cowan
  Margaret Morgan, 8
  Stephen Green, 8
Cox

Addison, 232
Annie Jones, 153
Cobbs N., 232
Emily Rice, 232
Geneva Oakley, 153
George Henry, 153
Ida B., 232
J. Henry, 232
James B., 232
Joseph Benjamin, 232
Marie Spencer, 232
Mollie Baughan, 232
Molllie Baughan, 232
William Slaughter, 232
Craft
  David Arnold, 70
Creasey
  Betty S., 70
  Robert L., 70
Crews
  Albert, 16
  Dora Elder, 16
  Fannie Davis, 16
  Jesse, 16
  "John Whitcomb Pratt ""Pratt""", 16
  Lou, 16
  Sarah Eliza, 16
  William A., 16
  "William ""Bill""", 16
  "William ""Billy""", 16
Crow
  C. F., 183
  Charles Ferdinand, 182, 183
  Infant, 182
  Infants, 183
  James C., 183
  Julia Stokes, 183
  Maude Shepard, 183
  Myrtle A., 182
  Myrtle Anderson, 183
  R. J. H., 183
  Robert J. H., 183
  Sue Harrison, 183
Crute
  Hattie Gannaway, 232, 233
  Hattie Winefred, 233
  Henry Nicholas, 233
  John Nicholas, 232, 233
Culbreth
  Dolly Hooper, 70
  Harry Clay, 70
  Mary Truitt, 70
Currier
  Ardella Peters, 31
  Richard Ernest, 31

Index

D

Dameron
  John, 64
  Lucy Eliza Harris, 64
  Margaret, 64
  Mary, 64
  Nancy, 64
Daniel
  John William, 119
  Willis Alice, 119
Davidson, 65
  Annie R., 8
  Deliah White, 39
  Hallie G., 8
  John I., 119
  Mary J., 8
  Richard T., 8
  Sarah B., 119
  Thomas E., 8
  William H., 119
Davies
  Carl Wm., 119
Davis
  Annie E., 119
  C. Louis, 255, 256
  Carrie A., 255
  Charles, 217
  Charles Eugene, 70
  Edna Christian, 119, 120
  Edward Melvin, 120
  Ella R., 233
  Florence T., 22, 23
  Frank Lee, 120
  George F., 120, 122
  Grafton Gates, 120
  Hettie, 126
  Hettie Painter, 120
  Janie M., 122
  Janie M. Mrs., 120
  Jefferson, 120, 126
  Jerry Leroy, 120
  John, 256
  John Thomas, 120
  John W., 22, 23
  Josephine S., 183
  Katie F., 120, 121
  Kenneth E., 23
  Lawrence A., 217
  Lelia May, 217
  Leslie L., 120, 121
  Louise Hardiman, 39
  Lucy Clarke, 70
  Lucy W., 233
  Mae Snoddy, 120
  Martha K., 71
  Mary F., 121
  Mary I., 255, 256
  Mary Indie, 217
  Mathew M., 183
  Matthew Moyle, 256
  Mattie D., 120, 121
  Melvin L., 121
  Merrill K., 120, 121
  Nancy C., 121, 122
  Nannie B., 233
  Ora Newton, 121
  Patty, 206
  Pearl H., 71
  Percy G., 71
  Phineas A. Col., 256
  Richard A., 233
  Rosa S., 71
  Roy M., 39
  Roy Mahlon, 121
  Russell L., 121
  S. F., 126
  Samuel Rufus, 121
  Wesley Thompson, 121, 122
  William A., 120, 122
  William J., 121, 122
  Willie A., 120, 122
  Willie Oscar, 23
Dawson
  Virgil Wayne, 71
Dean
  Carrie Alma, 39
  Etta Barker, 39, 40
  George W., 71
  John William, 39, 40
  L. Ernest, 39, 40
  Louis R., 40
  Margaret C., 71
  Martha Harris, 39, 40
  Mary Sharpe, 40
  Robert Lee, 40
  William R., 104
Deane
  Edythe Mae, 122
  Joseph T., 122
  Lillian Johnson, 122
  Myrtle Emmett, 122
Denicourt
  Agnes Shepard, 184
  Gerald M., 184
Denison
  Barbara C., 184
  Raymond, 184
Dennis
  Edmund Smith, 23
  Edna England, 23
Dibble
  Neal L., 267
Dolan
  Rachel A., 23
Dorrier
  Alice Forbes, 153
  Goldie, 153
  John William, 153
  Walter, 153
Dowdy
  Annie Wooten, 154
  Beulah, 268
  Floyd G., 154
  Herman L., 154
  Kate C., 184
  Marshall L., 268
  Shirley Preston, 154
  Thomas H., 184
Drake
  Francis Anderson, 170
Duncan
  Carlos A., 170
  Church Hill, 170
  George W., 40
  Harve Curtis, 184
  Jeanette, 170
  Josie Lee, 170
  Lonnie Mitchell, 170
  Pearl D., 40, 41
  Robert, 40
  Robert James, 41
  Robert L., 41
  Ruby Jamerson, 170
  W. Church, 40, 41
  Willie C., 41
  Willie J., 41
Dunkum
  Alice White, 233
  Alma Duncan, 233
  Annie Newton, 171
  Baby, 41
  Benjamin S., 268, 269
  Brad Sterling, 170
  Charles Acy, 41
  Claude L., 170, 171
  Ella Dowdy, 268, 269
  Emma T., 41
  Eugene E., 41
  George Lumsden, 171
  Isia Frances, 8
  Janie Wood, 71
  John Emmett, 233
  John J., 171
  Joshua Elijah, 171
  Julian Clyde, 71
  Katie A., 171
  Lennon J., 171
  Lenwood, 42

Index

Leslie Bersch, 71
Mattie Frances, 233
Minnie Toler, 233
Myrtle B., 269
Nannie L., 170, 171
Paul Beattie, 42
Robert Henry, 8
Rosa L., 23
S. Willie, 122
Stephen W., 42
W. Elijah, 23
Wesley Earl, 233
Willie H., 269
Dunn
   Joyce Ann, 71
   Mabel Baughan, 233
Dunnevant
   Horace E., 164, 165
   Mildred W., 164, 165
Dunsford
   Amaranda, 42
   Willie, 42
Dupuy
   J. T. Dr., 256
   Mollie N., 256
Durie
   Teresa, 251
Duty
   David Lemuel, 95
   Eugena, 9
   John Lenard, 234
   Martha Jane Davis, 234
Dyches
   Garland Dr., 71
   Mary N., 71

E

Eans
   Thomas, 248
   Znada F.S., 248
Eaton, 154
Edmonds
   George, 206
   Louis, 207
   Phil More, 207
   Susan, 207
   Thyra, 71
Edmunds
   James, 207
Edwards
   Carrie T., 256
   John T., 256
   John W., 256
   Ruth Gleaner, 72
Elam
   Eliza F., 234
   George Thomas, 234
   George W., 234
   Irma C., 184
   John Richard, 234
   Mattie Guthrie, 184, 185
   William Archer, 184, 185
Elcan
   Marcus Cleveland, 234
   Marie Jones, 234
   Marie Jones, 234
Eldridge
   Carrie, 227
Elgin
   Frances H., 42
   John D., 42
Elliott
   Horace, 96
   Horace B., 234
   Mary Cox, 234, 235
   Nannie Garnett, 96
   Wyatt Cook, 234
   Wyatt Garnett, 234, 235
Emerson
   Lelia Bailey, 185
Emert
   Myra Sutton, 72
   Samuel Rufus, 72
   Sandra Jo, 269
England
   Anna Palmore, 23
   W. I., 23
Eppard
   Emma J., 235
   John A., 235
Ericson
   Clinton N., 235
"Evans,"
   Louisa W., 72
Evans
   Cora Saunders, 257
   John, 72
   Louisa W., 72

F

Falls
   Frances Wade, 171
   Francis W., 171
Fariss
   Oakley Taylor, 72
Farrar
   Eva Louise, 42
   John Spencer, 42
   Kenneth Wayne, 42
   Lewis Edgar, 42, 43
   Minnie Jamerson, 72
   Pocahontas J., 43
   Richard Mayo, 72
Farris
   Mary, 43
   Mary Elizabeth Huddleston Wright, 185
Farrish
   Burney C., 154
   Clyde R., 217, 218
   Joan Mildred, 218
   John C., 218
   Lois Parcell, 218
   Rosa B., 217, 218
Ferguson
   Female Banton, 185
   Male, 185
Ficklen
   Frances Pannill, 257
   James Burwell, 257
Fielding
   Dianna Pearson, 72
Fields
   Harold W., 185
   Zanie T., 185
   Zanie Trent, 185
Finch
   Bessie B., 235
Fisher
   Ella T., 122
Fittz
   Sally O., 9
Fitzgerald
   Elizabeth A., 72
   Emmett W., 72
Flippen
   Edward Wesley, 122, 123
   Lacy C., 250
   Mariah C., 123
   Nettie F., 123
Flippin
   Roberta Allen, 235
Flood
   Howell Luther, 9
   J. M., 177
   James, 178
   William Irving, 9
Flurry
   Blanch L., 123
   John H., 123
Fones
   Joseph William, 185
   Mary Virginia, 95
   Solon Boston, 95
   William A., 96
   William S., 185
Fontaine
   Abram W., 257

Index

Clement Overton, 257
Forbes
  Alexander, 154
  Alice Smith, 235
  Charles Wm., 154
  Cleveland, 185, 186
  Cleveland Owen III, 186
  Dorothy, 186
  Elizabeth Gilliam, 154
  Elizabeth H. Hall, 186
  Elizabeth Hall, 186
  Elizabeth Venable, 154, 155
  Ira Dabney, 235
  James Henry, 154, 155
  Julia Gilliam, 154, 155
  Ruth Shepard, 185, 186
Ford
  Baby, 218
Foster
  A. Courtney, 186
  Catherine Hobson, 72
  Martha O., 186
Francisco
  Peter, 202
Fuqua
  Albert Terrell, 257
  Fern Pritts, 257
  Lucille Stevens, 257
  Richard Wilson, 257
  Robert Hill, 257
  Samuel, 257
  Samuel Fountain, 257

G

Galt
  Mary, 257
Gannaway
  Eula Gary, 186
  Richard W., 186
  Richard Winston, 186
Garland
  Dr. G. P., 187
  Frances W., 186, 187
  G. P., 186
  Joseph L., 186, 187
  Mary R., 186, 187
Garnett
  A. C., 235, 236
  Annie Spencer, 236
  Carroll Nelson, 236
  Edwin Crute, 236
  Grace Elcan, 236
  John Cook, 236
  Lucy Davis, 236
  Lucy P., 236
  Susan Frances, 235, 236

  Thomas Sidney, 236
  William C., 236
  Willis Cook, 236
  Wm. E., 236
Garrett
  Annie O., 171
  Edward B., 171
  Herbert N., 171
  John E., 72
  John Henry, 161
  Viola Louise, 161
  Virginia O., 171
  Whitchomb sic P., 171
  William Pratt, 171
Garton
  John, 73
  Lily, 73
Gary
  Elijah Hanes, 269
  Lizzie Self, 269
Gentry
  A. Estelle Mrs., 123
  Mary Sue, 9
Gilbert
  Martha Stinson, 187
Giles
  Emma Word, 207
  Emma Word, 207
  Joshua A., 207
Gillespie
  James L. H., 258
Gilliam
  Annie, 9
  Edward Cook, 9
  Lelia Fitttz, 9
  Luther P., 73
  Mary Lillian, 9
  Robert Van, 9
  Spencer, 9
  Susie Shepherd, 73
  William Edward, 101
Gills
  Joseph Wiley, 236, 237
  Lorena Bailey, 236, 237
Glover
  Ashland B., 9
  Edward Lee, 9
  Eva Davidson, 10
  John W., 10
  Lewis T., 10
  Lucy A., 10
  Marvin Agee, 10
  Paul L., 10
  Rena Roberts, 10
  Roma Miss, 10
  Wilbur W., 10

Godsey
  Ernest L., 73
  "Johnny M. ""Snake""", 73
Goin
  Bobby, 73
  Emily Frances, 73
  Leslie Thomas, 73
  Robert L., 73
  Sarah S., 73
Goins
  Floyd Lacy, 73
Golden
  Mattie J., 258
Goode
  Martha J., 123
  Wm. J. C., 123
Goodman
  Ada Toler, 123, 124
  Ava G., 123
  Edward A., 123, 124
  Georgia Putney, 187
  Hubert Coleman, 187
  L. Layton, 124
  M. W., 124
  Nannie F., 124
  Pocahontas Coleman, 187
  William Ivey, 187
Gordon, 73
  Elizabeth, 207
  Henry W., 207
  Josh, 207
  Lila, 207
Gormours
  John R., 258
  Julia Moss, 258
  Lou M., 258
  William Rolph, 258
Gormus
  Alfred T., 24
  Bert H., 24
  Douglas Forrest, 171
  Frances T., 171, 172
  Georgia Lee G., 172
  John Junior, 73
  John Willie, 73
  Lawrence B., 24
  Lillian E., 24
  Robert W., 171, 172
  Roger G., 258
  Rosen Herman, 172
Grandstaff
  Evelyn Morrison, 269
  James M., 269
Gregory
  Florence I., 150
  Maria, 150

Index

Obadiah, 150
Griffin
  Gerald L., 74
Griffith
  Carroll E., 237
  David A., 237
  Lottie D., 237
Grigg
  Elijah H., 187
  Gordon Glenn, 237
  Inez H., 187, 188
  Infant, 187
  Julia Inez, 187
  Minnie G. Wise, 187
  Pettice Forbes, 237
  Philip Edward, 187, 188
Gunter
  Elizabeth, 101
  "Paul M. Jr. ""Jasper""", 165
  Robert C., 101
Guthrie
  Annie H., 188, 189
  Blythe Samuel, 188
  Charles Roy, 188, 189
  Elizabeth G., 188
  Elizabeth Guthrie, 188
  Forrest, 188, 189
  James Rappe, 188
  Leonard, 188
  Margaret Kent, 188, 189
  Mary F. S., 188
  Mary Frances Spencer, 189
  Paula Ann Butrem, 189
  Thomas G., 188, 189
  Thomas Wills, 189

H

Hackett
  L., 74
  Milly, 108
Hall
  Eliza Ann, 218
  Gerald Ray, 24
  James S., 258
  Wm. C., 218
Hamby
  Graham G., 74
  Graham Graniel, 74
  Jasper D., 74
  Retha Rebecca A., 74
Hammond
  Betty Shepard, 189
Hammonds
  Mattie Baird, 189
Hanes
  Ada C., 74, 75

Garland Brown, 74
  J. B., 74, 75
  J. Blackwell Jr., 75
  Mattie D., 258
  Meade Carter, 75
  Nancy Lee Trible, 75
  Samuel H., 75
  Walter T., 258
Hanrahan
  Charles Patrick, 124
Hardiman
  Charles D., 43
  Elizabeth L., 43
  Emma Sharpe, 43
  Howard Sherman, 43
  Leonard Reeves, 43
  Luther Wilfred, 43, 44
  Mary Lillian, 43
  Mollie S., 75
  Susie W., 43, 44
  Wesley Earl, 44
  Wilfred Curtis, 44
  William, 75
  William E., 75
Harding
  Bessie Garrett, 124
  Comma C., 124
  John W., 124
  Lawrence W., 124
Harris
  Alma M., 44, 45
  Bernard Elijah, 44
  Beulah Stephens, 44, 45
  Charlie T., 44
  Clyde, 75
  Edna Bell, 44
  Eunice Pittiet, 44
  Infant, 44
  J. Edgar, 172
  James D., 44, 45
  James Dabney, 44, 45
  James Walter, 45
  Jessie Murray, 75
  John, 45
  John E., 44, 45
  Joseph D., 45
  Joseph Isaiah, 172
  Judith A., 44, 45
  Julian Newton, 125
  Katherine D., 172
  Lucy Jane Mrs., 107
  Mary E., 45, 46
  Mary Ellen Maxey, 107
  Mary Frances, 45
  Mary Lillian Wade, 172
  Mary Lula, 107

Mattie LeSueur, 46
  Millard Fillmore, 10
  Nannie E., 45
  Paula Elizabeth, 46
  R. W., 125
  Raymond B., 172
  Robert H., 46
  Ruth Virginia, 46
  Therie N., 46
  Thomas Alfred, 46
  William E., 46
  Willie E., 45, 46
  Willliam R., 104
Harrison
  Janie Thompson, 125
Hart
  Mary Thomas, 172
Harvey
  Caleb Cushing, 237
  Carrie Cheatham, 75
  Carrie Cheatham, 76
  Catherine Beatty, 75
  Jesse Buford, 75
  Jesse L., 75, 76
  Julia, 207
  Mary Baldwin, 237
  Myrtie R., 172
  Sandy E., 172
Hayden
  Edna H., 125
  John W., 125
Hayes
  Earnest Glenn, 218
Hearn
  Ruth Phaup, 237, 238
  William L., 237, 238
Heath
  Sam, 76
Hebditch
  J. W., 155
  Joseph B., 155
  Kate, 155
  William A., 155
Hedrick
  Frank, 10
Hembree
  Henry C., 97
  Maggie J., 97
Herndon
  Henry W., 125
  Joan Hawkins, 125
  Rosa L., 125
  T. Douglas, 125
  Virginia Oslin, 258
Hickman
  John Carl, 238

Index

Hill
  Edna Mae, 269
  Joseph Felix, 269
  Mary C., 46
  Samuel J., 47
Hix
  Infant, 238
Hocker
  Ned Edward, 179
Hodges
  Jesse J., 125
  Vearnie S., 125
Holland
  Willie, 161
Holman
  Anna Galt, 258, 259
  George Payne, 259
  Hartwell J., 102
  Henry Taylor, 259
  James S., 102
  James Winn, 259
  Jane Elizabeth, 102
  Judith H. S., 103
  Judith Hales Spencer, 102
  "Martha Ellen ""Barley""", 102
  Martha Myers, 259
  Mary Galt, 259
  Randolph Bryan, 259
  Robert Malcolm, 259
  Tandy, 102, 103
  Thomas Ellis, 259
  William Galt, 259
  William Henry, 258, 259
Holmes
  Estelle, 161
Hooe
  Winnie Davis, 125
Hooper
  John, 155
  Lucy, 155
Horne
  Margaret A., 10
Horsley
  Bluefield, 103
  Charles, 103
  Jean, 103
  "John ""Goat""", 104
  Trig, 104
Howe
  Mildred Irving, 238
Hubbard
  Ann R. Stinson, 11
  J. W., 11
Hubbord
  M. M. J., 238
Huddleston

A. Lee, 189
Albert G., 47
Annie Pearl, 189, 191
Charles, 191
Chas. A., 189
Child, 189
Churchill Jackson, 76
Daisy, 190
Drewey W., 190
Forest, 190
Gladys, 190
Infant, 47, 190
James A., 47
John, 190
John Morton III, 190
Josephine G., 47
Mary C., 47
Mary Elizabeth Wright, 190
Mary Sue, 190
Mrs., 191
Peter, 190, 191, 192
Rees Jeff, 189
Rees sic Jeff, 191
Reese Jeff, 191
Robert, 190, 191
Robert Wesley, 191
Samuel Allen, 191
Sarah Farris, 191
Thomas, 191
Thomas C., 191
Thomas H., 192
Thomas J., 76
Tom, 192
Virginia Catlett, 192
Virginia Farris, 192
Walter L., 192
William Robert, 192
Willie Addie, 76
Hudgins
  A. S., 126, 127
  Abner Lee, 126, 127
  Alma Martin, 126, 128
  Ashby H., 126
  Bessie L. P., 128
  Bessie Lee Patteson, 126
  Blanche S., 126, 127
  Burley, 126
  Cassie L., 126
  Edna Lee, 126
  Edner Putney, 126
  Eliza B., 126
  Elizabeth B., 127
  Emma C., 126, 127
  Flossie B., 127
  George R., 127
  Howard A., 126, 127

L. Allison, 127
Lucille Stinson, 127, 129
Lucy J. Wren, 127, 128
Mary A., 126, 127
Mary Davis, 127, 129
Mattie Gormus, 24
Milton F., 128
Nola Davis, 128
Olive E., 128
R. B. Mr., 128
Reuben, 128
Reuben B., 126, 128
Robert F., 128, 129
Robert Henry, 127, 128
Sarah S., 128
Thomas Harold, 128
Thomas Lee, 126, 128
Tom Henry, 127, 129
Willie O., 128, 129
Willy Martain sic, 129
Woodrow, 127, 129
Hudnall
  Gracie B., 47
  Harry Lee, 47
Hughes
  D. E., 192
  John Cabble, 192
  Louise G. R., 192
  Louise Gates Richardson, 192
Hurt
  infant, 32
  infant son, 32
  Minnie G., 129
  Mitchell H., 129
Huskey
  Loyd Hudson, 47
  Mary Etta Dunn, 47
  Raymond Frank, 47
Huston
  Conway, 76
Hutchings
  Roland J., 238
  Virginia F., 238

I

Ireland
  George Bennett, 218
  Hazel Rush, 218

J

Jackson
  Archer Deacon, 179
  Bessie T., 129
  Bessie Thompson, 129, 144
  Hallie Clark, 248
  James F., 129

Index

John, 248
W. Ethel Harris, 179
Willie H., 179
amerson
   Alfred Coghill, 76
   Alice I., 97
   Andrew David, 49
   Andrew Lawrence, 129, 130
   Annie L., 97, 100
   Baby, 97
   Baby Girls, 97
   Berta Amos, 98, 100
   Bertha Banton, 47
   Bettie V., 98
   Billy Lee, 47, 48
   Bossieux J., 48, 49
   Carrie Sharp, 98, 99
   Carrington Morel, 48
   Charlie M., 98
   Clarence Keith, 76
   Clayton Allen, 98
   David Ray, 98
   Dolly A., 98, 99
   Dora Banton, 48
   Dorothy Beatrice, 48
   Dorothy S., 48
   Earl Leroy, 48
   Earl W., 48, 49
   Earnest F., 76
   Ellie Irene, 192
   Elven O., 98
   Estelle Virginia, 98
   Flora Brock, 48, 49
   Floyd M., 98
   Frank, 98, 100
   Henry L., 192
   Herman Gordon, 98
   Infant, 48
   Infant Son, 99
   James E., 76
   James Myrtle, 76
   Jessie M., 48
   John D., 99
   John Henry, 77
   John Walter, 98, 99
   Joseph C., 77
   Joseph W., 48
   Josiah T., 98, 99
   Juanita H., 99
   Judson H., 99
   Julius Harding, 99
   Kimbow, 48
   Leonard Lee, 99
   Lewis Daniel, 99
   Lillie Farrar, 77
   Lois Amiss, 77
   Mable, 99
   Margaret V., 48
   Margaret V. Herndon, 49
   Marvin R., 100
   Marvin Ragland, 99
   Mary, 48
   Mary A., 49
   Mary E., 99
   Mary W., 100
   Mattie E., 49
   Mattie R., 98, 100
   Michael Elton, 49
   Millie L., 48
   Millie L. Kozuhowski, 49
   Nellie G., 165
   Phillis Ann, 100
   Phyllis Adams, 49
   R. Claude, 97, 100
   Raymond W., 165
   Reggie L., 100
   Robert Carroll, 49
   Robert D., 49
   Robert Kary, 100
   Robert Mitchell, 98, 100
   Ruby Harris, 129, 130
   Russell M., 49
   Sam Lee, 99, 100
   "Samuel N. ""Sammy""", 77
   Silvey W., 49
   T. Ashby, 100
   Thomas E., 49
   Thomas Wilbur, 100
   Wanda Butler, 77
   Whitcomb, 77
   William Henry, 77
   Zanie May, 100
James
   Floyd, 172
Jameson
   Joshua O., 50
   "Thomas E. ""Pete""", 48
   Werta E., 50
Jamison
   William J., 104
Jefferies
   George M., 259, 260
   George McKendree, 260
   Jennie H., 259, 260
   Sarah Edna Wood, 260
Jenks, 193
Jiles
   Ivanhoe Anderson, 207
   Sam Edward, 208
Johns
   Reuben S., 238
Johnson
   Abram, 162
   Emma Mrs., 208
   Florence Moss, 267
   Goode W., 130
   James W., 130
   Janette Glenn, 130
   Joseph R., 130
   Louise M., 130
   Lula, 162
   Mary, 17
   Maynard Kenneth, 130
   Nannie Griffith, 130
   Robert H., 130
   Ruth Mitchell, 11
   Yem Gill, 11
Jones
   Anne, 260
   Annette Royall, 238
   Annie Davis, 130
   Annie Lee, 208
   Betty H., 130, 131
   C. Robert, 11
   Clifford Avington, 130
   Dorothy Douglas, 11
   Edna Elcan, 238, 239
   Edward Avington, 130
   Elizabeth, 239
   Elsie K., 267
   Elsie K. Johnson, 267
   Fannie Courtney Lee, 179
   Florence W., 238
   Frazier Mays, 267
   Harriett Elizabeth, 260
   infant, 238
   Infant, 239
   J. E., 260
   James L., 179
   "James Wiley ""Jimmy""", 103
   John P., 208
   John Robert, 130
   Joseph Louis, 238, 239
   Katherine A., 130
   Lottie Pitts, 260
   Louis Dibrell, 260
   Lucile, 162
   M. Clevland, 239
   M. Tandy, 11
   Mary Crute, 239
   Mary Eliza, 11
   Mary Harding, 131
   Mary L. H., 103
   Mary Miller, 218, 219
   Matilda C., 103
   Matilda Caroline, 103
   Myrtle Edwin, 131
   Nettie Johnson, 131

Index

Paul Dibrell, 239
Paul Marion, 239
Paul Monroe, 239
Plummer Flippen, 260
Richard, 218
Rives Jefferson, 77
Rosa Mullins, 218
Roy Berkley, 131
Ruby Sledd, 239
Ruth Amos, 180
Ruth D., 173
Samuel L., 130, 131
Tazwell, 103
Vie Ethridge, 218, 219
Virginia Maxey, 77
Wiley T., 103
William Edward, 173
"William H. Jr. ""Shag""", 180
Justus
  David Hubert, 165

K

Keating
  Carrie B. Woodfin, 131
Keel
  Charles Whittington, 260
Kendall
  Nancy J., 131
  Raleigh T., 131
  Thomas O., 131
Kenney
  Mary Smith, 180
Kern
  Charles, 100, 101
  Christine H., 101
  Christine H. J., 100
Key
  Annie W., 173
  Robert B., 173
Kidd
  Annie B., 155, 156
  Beulah B., 239
  Floyd L., 155
  Henry C., 239
  Martha M., 156
  William J., 155, 156
King
  Doris Eleanor Newton, 131
Knott
  Franklin F., 77
Koenig
  Louis, 131
Kozuhowski
  Chester P., 50
  Millie L. J., 50
Kyle

Annie P., 77
George L., 77
M. M., 105
Mildred Perkins, 104
William P., 105

L

Lambertson
  Hattie E., 240
  Roy F., 240
Langhorne
  Bettie, 208
  Floyd, 208
  Laura, 208
  Willie, 208
Lassenbarry
  E., 208
Laury
  Dora, 105
Lawton
  Mary Frances, 193
  Robert Phillip, 193
Leagus
  Mary, 11
Lee
  Anderson Watkins, 240
  Clarence, 179, 267
  Lelia F. Smith, 240
  Virginia, 179
Legrand
  Bessie Loula Plunkett, 240
  Raymond Elliott, 240
  Wyatt Archer, 240
LeSueur
  Andrew Moses, 50
  Anna Guy, 50
  Annie H., 51
  Baby, 50
  Beulah T., 50, 51
  Billie D., 50
  Blanch D., 52
  Blanch Dunsford, 50
  Caroline Patteson, 260
  Caroline Yancey, 131
  Carrie Frances, 51
  Charles Fontaine, 260
  Clarence Overton, 131
  Clarence W., 51
  Edgar O., 51, 52
  Ethel A., 173
  Floyd Bernard, 51
  Frank Evans, 24
  Frank H., 51
  Frank Irving, 260
  Henrietta Lightfoot, 261
  J. J., 51

J. Leonard, 51
Jack, 77
John C., 52
John Cleveland, 51
John D., 50, 51
John Randolph, 51
Joseph W., 51, 52
Joshua James, 51, 53
Joshua Lee, 50, 52
Kathleen Vestal, 51
L. B., 261
Martha B., 51, 52
Mary Lee, 52
Mary Stone, 52
Mattie G., 52, 53
Mattie S. O., 51
Mattie S. Oliver, 52
Mattie S. T., 53
Mattie Sue Thomas, 52
Pauline Dunkum, 24
Robert M., 52
Robert Moses, 52
Sallie J., 51
Sallie Jamerson, 52
Sarah J., 53
Susan, 261
Travis Conrad, 52, 53
Travis Lee, 53
Viola Taylor, 51, 53
W. J., 53
Wilbur Randolph, 53
Willie A., 53
Willie Archer, 53
Willie D., 52, 53
Willie Dunsford, 53
Lewis
  A. B., 208
  Eliza, 180
  Herbert B., 240
Lightfoot
  Alice H., 269
  Alvin Wallace, 219
  Clyde A., 269
  DeLores A., 24
  James C., 24
Ligon
  Bessie Booker, 156
  David Greenhill, 156
Lindsay
  Lucy B., 219
Lipscomb
  Elizabeth Duncan, 173
Lodge
  S. D., 11
Loudon
  Elvira, 17

Index

Lowe
  Charles A., 53, 54
  Lottie C., 53, 54
Lowman
  Charles W., 219
  Mary M., 219
Lyle
  Claude O., 24

M

Mahon
  Alexander Lee, 132
  Ashby Turner, 132
  Blanche P., 132
  Everett B., 132
  Everett Brown, 132
Maki
  Elmer Leimo, 193
  Mary E. G., 193
  Mary Eliza Guthrie, 193
Mann
  A. W., 105, 106
  J. T., 105
  Lewis D., 105, 106
  Lucy, 104
  Massie Watson, 105
  Mildred T. C., 105
  Mildred T. Coleman, 106
  Robert E., 106
  S. E., 106
  Susan Ellen, 105
March
  Marian Anderson Riddle, 132
Marion
  Johnny L., 269
  Richard D., 132
  Susie M., 269
Marks
  Charles L., 77, 78
  James E., 240
  Margaret A., 24
  Sallie Wood, 77, 78
  Susie R., 240
  William Joseph, 240
Martin
  A. Hamilton, 132
  Alexander H., 132
  Carson Jeff, 54
  Connie Davis, 132, 133
  Florine D., 54
  Julien D., 132
  Lillie D., 132
  Olivia Goode, 133
  Orson Watts, 133
  Russell Algie, 132, 133
  Shirley Jean, 54

  Wilber C., 54
Mathis
  Alois Bagby, 209
Maxey
  Alfred G., 78
  Allen Franklin, 219, 220
  Annie Baber, 219, 220
  Bennie W., 219
  C. Lewis, 219
  Clara Gentry, 219
  Elizabeth M., 78
  Ella Banton, 220
  Ella Thomas, 78
  Ella Thomas, 78
  Ethel Duty, 219, 220
  Etta Self, 220
  Floyd Thomas, 220
  George Albert, 220
  George William, 107
  Horasha Elijah, 78
  "James Ballard ""Ball""", 107
  Laura Agee, 220
  Laura Agre, 220
  Laura Ellen, 220
  Leonard F., 220
  Lola S., 219
  Mary Bryant, 78
  Mary E., 78
  Mary Jane F., 107
  Mary Jane Ferguson, 107
  Mary Lula, 178
  Oscar Blackwell, 220
  Ruby S., 219
  Samuel Allen, 219, 220
  Thomas Aubra, 220
  Thomas E., 78
  W. Lawrence, 78
  Waldo A., 78
McCraw
  Anna C., 54
  Guy, 54
  infant, 156
  Pearl H., 54
  Thomas E., 54
Meador
  Alice G., 25
  Elizabeth Walker, 25
  Frank W., 25
  Hubert L., 55
  James L., 25
  Mary E. S., 55
  Mary E. Sharpe, 55
  Mary W., 25
  Thomas B., 25
  William B., 25
Meadows

  Ella Mae, 240
  Florence Kyle, 79
Medlin
  Harry Milton, 79
  Lee Harden, 79
Mertz
  Carl Fredrick, 133
Messenger
  Alpha E., 133
  Belle P., 133
Miles
  Alma Clayton, 79
  Bernard N., 79
  Bessie S., 79
  Eddie, 79
  John Cosby, 79
  "John M. ""Jack""", 79
  Kate Shumaker, 79
  Mary V., 80
  Thomas Henry, 80
  William H., 80
Miller
  Anna Marie D., 25
  Catharine, 108
  Chesley, 226
  Curtis, 209
  Elizabeth, 209
  Harriet, 226
  Melinda, 209
  R. H., 133
  Thomas, 209
  Villa Allison, 25
  William Thomas, 108
Millikin
  James E., 133
  Mary Jane, 133
Mills
  "Lamartine Paul ""Buck""", 11
  Louise Phelps, 11
  Virginia Steger, 240
Mitchell
  Birdie M., 133
  Doris E., 11
  John Mason, 133
  John W., 133
  Joseph H., 11
  Julia E., 11
  Pearl Newton, 134
  Thomas G., 134
  Walter Herman, 134
Moore
  Annie Harden, 80
  Kemper, 220
  William Wirt, 80
Morgan
  Alex, 209

Index

Billie, 12
C. B., 12
Charles B., 12
Ernest Agee, 12
Fannie, 209
Grace A., 12
Hattie R., 12
Inez A., 12
John C., 12
John P., 12
Judith Chambers, 12
Lollie Inez, 12
Lucyntha, 209
Martha J., 12
Mary E. Coleman, 12, 13
Mary Louise, 13
"Mary ""Sid"" Swartz", 13
Mattie, 209
R. Lewis, 13
Reece A., 13
Richard M., 13
Richard T., 13
Richie I., 13
Robert A., 12, 13
Virgie C., 13
William J., 209
Moring
　LeRoy D., 193
　Vesta G., 193
Morris
　Dorothy S., 156
　Lacy E., 156
　Lacy Earl, 156
　Mary, 251
Morrison
　Grace Godsey, 80
Mosby
　John, 209
Moseley
　Ira A., 221
Mosley, 209
　Pearl V., 210
Moss
　Charlie D., 80
　Clannie L., 80
　Daisy Newton, 55
　Elizabeth T., 2
　Eva, 80
　Evie Sharp, 80
　Frank L., 81
　George William, 241
　Jeff, 2
　Jissie C., 81
　John E., 80
　John Robert, 81
　Joseph H., 81

Laura Toney, 81
Marshall J., 81
Marshall Lee, 2
Phillip S., 81
Robert Andrew, 81
Russell, 81
Russell Sr., 81
Virginia W., 81
W. E., 82
Yaren, 210
Murphy
　Alfred N., 82
　Charlie L., 82
　Charlie W., 82
　Clara C., 82
　Emmett N., 82
　Garland Terry, 82
　George W., 82
　Harry Lynn, 82
　Hillie L., 82
　John Rolf, 82
　Leo, 82
　Richard Donald, 83
　Sandra Kay, 193
　Sarah L. Goins, 83
　W. Hubert, 83
　Wilbur, 83
　William G., 83
Murray
　Mattie A., 193
Myers
　Marjorie Putney, 134

N

Nagle
　Charles F., 269
Newsome
　Mabel Hebditch, 157
Newton
　Ada Dunkum, 173
　Ada Dunkum, 173
　Annie A., 173
　Bobby E., 173
　Charles L., 160
　Eleanora D., 134
　Emmett Leake, 134
　Emmett T., 134
　Frank L., 134
　J. Hypes, 173
　Katie Newton, 134
　Kizzie C. Guthrie, 160
　Nancy C. Guthrie, 160
　Nancy C.G., 160
　R. E., 160
　Robbie W., 160
　Robert W., 160

W. W., 160
Wade Lumsden, 173
Willis Wade, 160
Nicholas
　Alexander Duval, 261
　Annie M., 267
　Dainy L., 55
　George B., 261
　Lucy C., 261
　Reuben O., 261
Nichols
　Isabelle V., 101
　Robert L., 101
Nixon
　Ann Page, 134
　Miles Archie, 134
Noble
　Bertice Jones, 134
　John Weldon, 134
　Weldon Bruce, 134
Norvell
　Charlie S., 83
　David R., 261
　Emma B., 221
　Florence S., 261
　Hay Booth, 221
　Mary E., 261
　Mary J., 83
Novell
　Mary J., 83
Nuckols
　Gertrude, 221
　James Thomas, 221

O

O'Brien
　Amanda F., 160
　Charles H., 160, 161
　Hallie Clarke, 161
　John H., 161
　Mary C., 161
　Percy H., 161
O'Bryant
　Evelyn Walker, 173
　Ida Gertrude, 174
　Joseph Benjamin, 174
　Mary Seay, 174
Old
　Beulah D., 25
Oliver
　Alice J., 25
　Annie J., 55, 56
　Baxter C., 135
　Bettie Miller, 135, 136
　Carrie Whitlow, 25, 26
　Charles Keel, 135

Index

Claude Irvin, 135
Edgar, 25
Florence D., 135
Florence T., 56
Florence Thomas, 55
Grace F., 135
Henry Carol, 26
Herman L., 135
Horace Gordon, 135
Infant, 55
James L., 26
James Lewis, 26
Jane Claudette, 135
John C., 135
John H., 135
John Perkins, 135
Joseph Roy, 55
Louise Wingfield, 136
Lucille T., 26
Mamie Toney, 55
Mary Brock, 55, 56
Murray L., 26
Percy L., 55, 56
Robbie Franklin, 136
Robert Aubrey, 55, 56
Rufus Aubrey, 56
Spencer Lewis, 25, 26
Virginia G., 136
Walter S., 55, 56
William Edgar, 135, 136
William Fitzhugh, 136
William Spencer, 56
William W., 26
)slin
  Hugh P., 262
  Virginia Lesueur, 262
  W. H., 262
  W. Hugh, 262
)wnby
  Grace McCraw, 56
  Newel, 56
  Terry Teresa, 96

P

age
  Maggie, 83
  Teresa Lynn, 83
ainter
  Janet Nicholas, 262
ais
  Elwood Alexander, 241
  Harriett Garnett, 241
arker
  Annie V., 136
  Jessie C., 136
  Luther W., 136

Mary V., 136
Maude W., 136
Oscar W., 136
Rufus I., 136
William, 136
Parsons
  "Elizabeth ""Annie"" Booker", 157
  "Elizabeth ""Annie"" Booker", 157
  Jean Curtis, 157
Patterson
  Alex, 210
  Ann C., 137
  Camm, 241
  Elnora W., 267
  Elwood G., 193
  Ethel, 210
  Irene E., 137
  J. Edgar, 137
  John Dabney, 193
  Kate Miss, 137
  Kemper Withers, 194
  Lelia M., 241
  Louise A., 137
  Robert S., 137
  Sally P., 137
  Samuel R., 267
  Sarah E., 137
  Thomas W., 137
  William Henry, 194
  Willie M., 137
  Wm. Eldon, 137
Patteson
  Annette Holman, 221, 222
  Buford B., 221
  Ella L. Bingham, 221
  Ethleen Maxey, 222
  Frank T., 194
  H. C., 221
  H. Cosby, 221, 222
  Infant son, 221
  Leonard F., 83
  Lily M., 221
  Luther Wesley, 222
  Nettie Davis, 262
  Peter Broaddus, 262
  Rosa L., 194
  Ruby Lee, 221, 222
  Thomas Earl, 221, 222
Payne
  Ossie Irene, 13
  Richard H., 13
Peaks
  Claiborne, 210
  Dorothy B., 210
  Eva, 210
  Howard Lee, 210

James N., 210
Joseph, 210
Mary, 210
Nelson, 210
Phyllis E., 211
Rhoda, 211
Tyrone, 211
Virginia, 211
Pearson
  Annie Charlton, 84
  Annie Charlton, 84
  C. E., 84
  Mary Edna Hardiman, 84
  S. B., 84
  S.B., 84
Pendleton
  Alexander Russell, 262
  Benjamin H., 84
  Charles, 84
  Cora, 84
  Daniel R., 84
  Donald K., 137
  James Alexander, 262
  John Jacob, 84
  Mac P., 84
  Mack, 84
  Ruby D., 137
Perkins
  Albert, 162
  Anna L., 174
  Baby Girl, 162
  Billie, 162
  Charles, 162
  Charles E., 174
  Charles L., 162
  Charles L. Mrs., 162
  Estelle J., 174
  Esther C., 56
  Lena D., 267
  Lester Peyton, 162
  Minerva, 180
  Mollie, 162
  Pete T. D., 174
  Robert, 180
  Sarah P., 105
  Theodore D., 174
  Tom, 211
  Willie Edmund, 162
Perrin
  Charles Nelson, 138
Perrow
  C. Fitzhugh, 165
Perry
  Jimmy Frank, 56
Peters
  Emily, 32

Index

infant, 32
Jefferson A., 32
Parkie E. B., 32
Parkie E. Brown, 32
Pettie
  James U., 106
  Mary O., 106
  Minnie M., 106
Phaup
  Ann Eliza, 241, 242
  Annie Julia, 241
  Crosby Samuel, 241
  Earl B., 241
  Earl Dwight, 241
  Edward S., 241
  George Leroy, 241, 242
  Helen Moren, 241
  Henry, 242
  Henry Reeves, 242, 243
  Jas. G., 242
  John J., 241, 242
  Lucy Carter, 242, 243
  Marrietta L., 242
  Marvin M., 242
  Minnie Dunkum, 241, 242
  Robert, 243
  Ruth M., 242, 243
  Susanna Lee, 243
  W. Vaden, 243
  Walter R., 243
  Wm. J., 242, 243
  Wm. R., 243
Phaupp
  Willie Moses, 243
Phelps
  J. C., 13
Phillips
  Andrew J., 138
  Bernice B., 138
  Durward B., 138
  John R., 138
  Richard Randolph, 138
  Thomas M., 138
  VA. Bagby, 138
  Willie B., 138
Pierce
  Ben Archer, 222
  Martha Ellen, 222
Piercy
  Ellis Walter, 138
  Nancy C., 138
  Walter R., 138
Pippin
  H. Cecil, 138
  Otis S., 139
Pitts

Infant Girl, 139
Mattie Winston, 139
Poe
  Aubrey Jack, 26
  Etta H., 56, 57
  Florence Childress, 26
  Irvin N., 57
  J. Elmo, 56, 57
  James P., 26
  Jane, 166
  John Robert, 57
  John W., 26, 57
  Lee, 166
  Liza V., 27
  Maomi Maxey, 27
  Martha Frances, 27
  Mary Absher, 27
  Mary Amos, 166
  Ruth, 27
  Virginia Worley, 57
  William, 27
  William E., 27
  William Ernest, 27
  Willie Sue Dean, 57
Pollard
  D. E., 243, 244
  Edward Ernest, 244
  Leon, 244
  Lois Dillon, 244
  Sarah Jane, 243, 244
Powers
  C. Burns, 57
  Nell Lowe, 57
Price
  Annie Butler, 84
  Emma Foster, 84
  James Herman, 84
  John, 13
  Robert Henry, 84
  Robert I., 85
  Sallie, 13
Proffitt
  Mattie E., 157
Province
  James S., 13
  Margaret Slater Mrs., 13
  Mary Morgan, 14
  Mary Morgan, 14
  William P., 14
Pugh
  Erma H., 244
Purvis
  Charles Jefferson, 194
  Mary Shepard, 194
Putney
  Baby, 139

Daisy Ruth, 194
Edna Phillips, 139, 140
Elizabeth Hyde, 139
Etta Stinson, 139
James Norman, 139
Julian E., 139
Maude Goode, 139
Richard, 139
S. C., 139
Va. Elizabeth, 139
Wm. Thornton, 139, 140

Q

Quessenberry
  Nancy Wright, 96

R

Ragland
  Charlie E., 101
  Elizabeth, 253, 254
  James T., 194
  Mary V. Jamerson, 194
  Maude Phillips, 140
  Nathaniel E., 194
  Richard B., 174
  Sallie F., 174
  Sally, 167
  Thomas, 253, 254
Rainey
  Anne Trent, 57
  Dallas Homer, 244
  Isaac Wallace, 244
  Louise Morris, 244
  Louise Morris, 244
  Nancy J., 85
  Rufus P., 85
Rakes
  Ada B. Wootton, 174
  Forrest Daniel, 85
  Mabel Ayres, 85
  Thomas G., 174
Randolph
  Ada S., 248
  Ada Stanton, 248
  Ariannah Stanton, 248
  James, 248
  Willie C., 248
Ranson, 84
  Buford N., 85
  Estelle F., 85
  Evelina Binford, 157
  Griffith T., 85
  John James, 222
  Nora Spencer, 222
  Patty, 85
  R. Bennett, 85

Index

Radford B., 85
Tommy, 85
Virgil Whitcomb, 222
W. Malcolm G., 157
Reese
  Charles Edward, 194, 195
  child, 195
  Nealie Thacker, 195
  Nealie Thacker, 194
Rice
  Thomas Edward, 32
Richardson
  Earnest, 157
  James R., 195
  Raymond Allen, 195
  Roland McKenny, 195
  Vivian Allen, 195
Riddle
  Kate Evlyn, 140
Riddleburger
  Mark S., 85
Rider
  Dorothy L., 244
  Warren E., 244
Roberts
  Charles E., 262
  Claude S., 140
  Doris C., 140
  Eveline, 14
  Mary S., 262
  Robert S., 140
  Ruby S., 140
  Troy, 14
Robertson
  Liza Jane, 85
  Matt A., 86
Rose
  Ella P., 267
Rozell
  Ida S., 195
  Joseph J., 195
Rush
  Alma Bryant, 178
  Alma Bryant, 179
  Ann E., 178
  Ben E., 178
  Betty P., 222, 223
  Bruce N., 223
  Clem F., 14
  Eddie S., 178
  Edith T., 223
  Eliza S., 178
  Ella, 179
  Ella G., 14
  G. V., 178
  James A., 222, 223

John, 179
John S., 14, 178
Lillian R., 223
Lou Taylor, 86
Mary F., 178
Mary S., 178
Peter S., 178
Peter Walker, 178, 179
Rolfe L., 86, 223
Sallie J., 179
Vincent, 179
Vincent P., 14

S

Salmon
  Elsie Catlett, 86
Satterfield
  George Whitney, 262, 263
  Lillian Proffitt, 263
  Lillian Proffitt, 262
Saunders
  J. Holman, 263
  John H., 263
Saylor
  Mildred M., 269
  Paul K., 269
Schumaker [sic]
  Charlie E., 86
Scott
  Aubrey Coinard, 86
  Flossie S., 244
  "Harriet ""Hattie"" Stanton", 248
  James E., 244
  James L., 86
  Sarah E., 86
  William Aubrey, 86
Scruggs
  Charles M., 86
  Eliz., 203
  George Edward, 203
  John, 14
  John T., 203
  Lucy R., 203
  Mary Elizabeth, 86
  Mary L., 86
  Mrs., 14
  Nannie A., 203
  William M., 203
Seamster
  Walter W., 244
Seay
  Bill, 211
  Branch Abner, 87
  James H., 211
  Jess, 211
  John J., 211

L. E., 211
Myrtle Steele, 87
Myrtle Steele, 87
Richard, 57
Susie, 212
Thearon, 212
Thelma Elizabeth, 87
William E., 212
Willie, 212
Selden
  Anna W., 17
  Caroline E., 17
  Emma B., 17
  Esther W., 17
  John R., 17
  Samuel M., 17
Self
  A. Bessie Winfrey, 223
  Annie Lightfoot, 87
  Elizabeth Moss, 223
  Frank Hill, 87
  George Luther, 87
  Helen W., 223
  John Holman, 223
  "John Holman ""J""", 223
  John Walter, 223
  Julius E., 223
  Maude E. Bransford, 223
  William Thompson, 223
Senger
  Annie B., 157
  Bessie Shull, 157
  Bessie Shull, 158
  Daniel M., 157, 158
  Edward Roy, 157, 158
  H. Paul, 158
  Jessie W., 158
  Lula M., 158
  Mary K., 158
  T. Massey, 158
Sharp
  Agnes P., 57
  Daniel, 195
  J. Wiley, 87
  Jannie P., 57
  John Littleton, 87
  Mattie V., 87
  Nannie Stinson, 195
  Nannie T., 87
  S. E., 101
  Warren D., 57
  William T., 58
Sharpe
  Alex, 58
  Anne Jannie, 58
  James Daniel, 58

Index

John W., 195
Mary Ann, 58
William Howard, 58
Shelton
  child, 226
  Dicie, 227
  female, 227
  Flemming, 226, 227
Shepard
  Alice Burwell, 195
  E. A., 196
  Edith Loveline, 196
  Edward Bossieux, 196, 197
  Edward Miller, 196
  Edward P., 196
  Edward Poindexter, 196
  Everette Edward, 196, 197
  Georgia J., 196
  Infants, 196
  James Wilson, 196
  Janice S., 196
  John W., 197
  Lula Agnes, 197
  Lula F. H., 196
  Lula F. Harper, 197
  Lula L., 197
  Martha A., 197
  Martha J. G., 198
  Martha J. Guthrie, 197
  Mattie Purvis, 197
  Mattie Purvis, 196
  Miller Jones, 197, 198
  Otis A., 198
  Pearl G., 198
  Rebecca R., 198
  Sarah J. G., 197
  Sarah Jane Gannaway, 198
  W. B., 197
  William B., 198
  William R., 198
Sherrill
  Ivey M., 270
  Norris R., 270
Shields
  Gayle Denison, 198
Shumaker
  Acie C., 87
  Annie Taylor, 88
  B. Frank, 88
  Benjamin F., 227
  Betty C., 227
  Betty C. Catlett, 227
  Betty E., 227
  Carrie G., 88
  Charlie E., 88
  Charlie H., 88

Eddie P., 2
Emma D., 88
Essie J., 227
Fannie S., 88, 90
Garnet Gray, 88
George Pratt, 88
Gladys S., 140
Glenn David, 2
Harrison, 227
Hattie Taylor, 88, 89
Henry T., 89
Jacie Moss, 89
Joe F., 89
John Hill, 88, 89
John J., 27
John W., 89
Louise S., 89
Margaret W., 87
Marshall R., 89
Mazie G., 89
Minnie E., 89, 90
Myrtis L., 89
Nellie T., 89
Norvell E., 89
Percy Mack, 89, 90
Richard H., 140
Russell A., 90
Sidney H., 88, 89
William Hill, 90
Silby
  Joe Baxter, 244
Silvey
  Agnes Beryl, 198
  Dorothy Filer, 198
  Eubelya Richardson, 198
  W. Russell, 198
  William R., 198
Simanske
  Fred M., 140
  Mamie Yancey, 140
Simon
  Evelyn Harris, 14
Simpson
  Carrie Mann, 106
Sloan
  Mattie Lou, 199
  Maxie Lee D., 244
  Spencer L., 199
  Vernon Lee, 244
  Willie S., 245
Slough
  Annette A., 27
  Carlton M., 27
Smith
  Alvin Lee, 245
  Ann Reese, 90

Arthur, 212
Bernard Clay, 245
Carrie Shepard, 90
Dabney Andy, 224
Elizabeth Spencer, 245
Fannie Cox, 245
Frankie A., 245
G. W., 263
Hubert M., 245
Jackson, 199
John, 212
John Frank, 212
Larry, 206
Luther L., 140
Mabel Denton, 90, 91
Manie Cox, 245
Martha V., 245
Mary Bailey, 199
Millie Ann, 212
Patricia A., 270
Robert Garnett, 90
Rosa C., 224
Ruby M., 245
Susan C., 263
Thomas C., 224
Virginia T., 212
William Arnold, 90
William Moses, 90, 91
Snoddy
  Albert Flemming, 140, 141
  Albert Wilford, 140
  Annie Myrtie, 263
  Ashby W., 27, 28
  Aubrey Fleming, 141
  Baby R., 164
  Blanche Wootten, 140, 141
  Gordon Lee, 270
  Gracie Self, 270
  Gracie Self, 270
  Harriet Thornhill, 164
  J. R., 164
  James C., 141
  Jean Emert, 270
  John Robert, 91, 164
  Luther R., 263
  Mellville F., 263
  Nannie C., 263
  Okie S., 27, 28
  Patty Miss, 164
  Reubie Nicholas, 91
  Robert Marion, 141
  Sammie P., 141
  Sydney Hudgins, 141
  Thomas Elwood, 270
  Thomas P., 263
  William A., 224

Index

"William W. ""Oolie""", 91
Snyder
  Mattie O., 28
Sorrentino
  Ella C., 91
  Joseph, 91
Southall
  Albert P., 158
  Edgar B., 158
  Edgar Blair, 158
  Henry A., 158
  L. Page, 158
  Ora Duffy, 158
  Sallie V., 158
  "Wm. D. ""Billy""", 159
Southwards
  Minnie W., 224
  Theodore R., 224
Spencer
  A. Sidney, 199
  Albert Sidney, 199, 200
  Bettie Kish, 199
  Carolyn Ann, 91
  Eliz. B., 245
  Ellen M., 245
  Fannie Charlton, 91
  Gelia S., 199, 200
  Gilbert C., 163
  H. Willard, 199, 200
  Hattie Abner, 199, 200
  Helen Shepard, 246
  Henrietta Virginia, 200
  J. B., 245
  Jennie Corson, 200
  Jennie Mae, 163
  John Y., 200
  Joseph, 163
  Judith Hales, 103
  Katherine Fraser, 200
  Nannie Smothers, 163
  Otell ... iston, 200
  Robert Bruce, 91
  Ruth E., 200
  Thomas, 163
  Virginia B., 199, 200
  W. B., 246
  W. Bocock, 246
  William E., 163
  William Herbert, 246
  William Shepherd, 91
  Willis Thomas, 246
  Wm. Abner, 199, 200
Spradley
  Alex, 213
  Alexandria, 213
  Clarence R., 213

Flossie Mae, 213
Fred, 213
George A., 213
Joshua II, 213
Lela Virginia, 213
Springer
  Charles G., 91
  Kate Price, 91
Stanley
  Edith E., 159
  J. E., 165
  Melvin G., 159
Stansberry
  Emma C., 141
Stanton
  Bertha, 248
  Daniel, 248, 249
  Mary, 249
  Nancy, 248, 249
  Nancy Trent, 249
  Robert Olon, 159
  Schuyler, 249
  Sidney, 249
  Sidney Trent, 249
  "Sidney ""Trent "" Jr.", 249
  William, 249
Staples
  George B., 263
  J. J., 263
  James R., 263
  Maggie M., 263
  Margaret Anne, 264
  Mary A., 264
  Mathew S., 264
  Walter, 264
Staton
  Ellen, 108
Steele
  Baby, 58
  Old Man, 91
Steger
  Abe J., 224
  Alice Josephine, 224
  Elizabeth F., 224
  Ellen, 15
  Frances E., 15
  Frank Walker, 224
  Herbert D., 246
  Herbert D. Jr., 246
  Mary Spencer, 246
  Maryanne Baber, 224
  Nannie S., 224
  Sallie Hill, 225
  Susie M., 246
  Wm., 15
Steppe

Virginia Blackwell, 58
Stevens, 174
Stinson
  Ann R. Hubbard, 15
  Baby, 141
  Bettie Hudgins, 141, 142
  David R., 141
  Elijah M., 200, 201
  Elizabeth B., 201
  George W., 141, 142
  Ida, 142
  James Carlton, 142
  James Lewis, 201
  John J., 201
  John Thomas, 142
  John Willie, 141, 142
  Junius J., 201
  Junius S., 201
  Lelia B., 201
  Mary L., 201
  Mattie H., 141, 142
  Maureen Gordon, 142
  Nannie A., 200, 201
  P. Hubert, 142
  Thomas E., 201
  Virginia D., 142
  William D., 142
Stinson & Hubbard
  J. W., 15
Stout
  Novil E., 201
  Rosa A., 201

T

Talbott
  Barbara Jean, 92
  "Edwin Ellis ""Pete""", 92
  Gloria Faye, 92
  Raleigh A., 92
Talley
  Elsie Newton, 142
Tapscott
  Allen Walker, 225
  Annie Adkins, 225
  Clifford T., 225
  Joseph R., 225
  Lizzie Ayres, 225
  Mamie, 225
  Marjorie B., 226
  Mary Baber, 225
  Tucker, 225
  Vincent, 226
Tatum
  Thelma P., 142
  Willie E., 143
Taylor

Index

Acey W., 264
Annie T., 92
Arnie, 92
Beatrice C., 92
Elizabeth S., 264
Ellen T., 92
Fannie G., 175
George Cosby, 2
Herman M., 175
John E., 92
John L., 264
Mannie Sue, 175
Mary Davis, 264
Mary L., 92
Matt, 175
Robert, 92
Robert W., 92
S. Elizabeth, 264
Tiny Estelle, 92
W. H., 143
Willie Walker, 92
Zachary, 264
Taylor Burnley
  Eliza, 254
Thomas
  Albert B., 58
  Alice Farrar, 93
  Alma Gertrude, 143
  Andrew Jennings, 93
  Ann J., 59, 60
  Anna W., 58
  Annie B., 28
  Annie Martin, 250
  Annie S., 59, 62
  Baby, 143
  Ben L., 250
  Brian Keith, 28
  C., 250
  Carl Edwin, 175
  E. J. Mrs., 59, 60
  Elizabeth, 250, 251
  Elizabeth Pinnell, 175
  Elwood Campbell, 250
  Frances Worley, 61
  G. Gordon, 28
  George R., 59
  George V., 143
  George Wesley, 59, 61
  Gracie L., 59, 60
  Henry B., 175, 176
  Henry V., 175, 176
  Howell L., 175, 176
  Ida Poe, 59
  Irene Dawson, 59, 61
  J. Clarence, 143
  J. E., 250
  J. F., 28, 250
  J. H., 251
  J. L., 59, 60
  James A., 59, 60
  James E., 59, 60
  Janie H., 60
  John D., 59, 60
  Joseph B., 175
  Karen Elizabeth, 28
  Lottie A., 175, 176
  Mannie W., 143
  Margaret Elizabeth, 143
  Martha C., 59, 60
  Mary Emma, 60
  Mary H., 251
  Mary Lee H., 175, 176
  Minerva C., 28
  Morris L., 60
  Morris Lemuel, 59
  Nannie Dunsford Archer, 60
  Nannie S., 60, 61
  Nellie L., 175, 176
  Randolph King, 61
  Robert J., 28
  Robert V., 143
  Robert W., 250, 251
  Ruby Yancey, 143
  Sarah D., 28
  Sarah Josephine, 59, 61
  Stewart, 250
  Stuart E., 175, 176
  Terry Marie, 28
  Thelma G., 175, 176
  Thomas Edwin, 61
  Thomas H., 251
  Thomas J., 251
  Thomas R., 61
  Todd Baker, 176
  Walter E., 60, 61
  Willard Archer, 175
  William P., 59, 61
  William Russell, 61
  Willie E., 61
  Willie Elmore, 61, 62
  Willie W., 59, 62
Thompson
  Ann Scott, 264, 265
  Clemmie F., 264
  Emma Barker, 15
  George Paul, 93
  Georgia Y., 144
  Georgia Yancey, 143
  Gladys R., 144
  Gracie Geneva, 93
  H. Clinton, 144
  Horace Clinton, 143
  James Andrew, 144
  John W., 265
  Judith Jane, 144
  Oswald J., 15
  Wade H., 144
  William S., 265
  Wm. S., 264
Tillman
  John, 32
  Martha E., 32
Tinsley
  J. Walter, 144
Tolbert
  Andrew, 251
  infant son, 251
  Sallie, 252
  Susie, 251
  Thomas, 252
Toms
  Jonathan, 265
Toney
  Angus L., 252
  Anna F., 252
  Arthur Burnett, 252
  Bessie, 93
  Bessie A., 252
  Bessie Worsham, 93
  Carrie Etta, 270
  Ethel R., 144, 145
  Harold M., 252
  Harry James, 62
  Herman V., 252
  Howard W., 144, 145
  John Lee, 93
  John Leonard, 144, 145
  Kizzie Geneva, 144, 145
  Lemuel F., 252
  Leslie F., 252
  Lillian A., 62
  Lindsay G., 145
  Marion E., 144, 145
  Mary Lou, 93
  Mary N., 145
  Melvin Milton, 253
  Percy Arthur, 253
  Ressie Davis, 144, 145
  Rosa Pearl, 144, 145
  Russell L., 253
  Sidney A., 93
  Thelma L., 253
  Walter M., 93
  William Elmo, 144, 145
  Willie R., 145
  "Wrennie J. ""Teddy""", 253
Toyles
  Mary Helen, 201

Index

Trent
  Anna T., 62
  Catherine G., 62
  John G., 62
  Katie H., 202
  Robert L., 202
  Robert Lee, 202
  Stephen W., 62
  Susie R., 159
  Thomas T., 62
  Thomas W., 62
  William C., 159
  William Malcolm, 159
Trentham
  David H., 62
  Frances H., 62
  Lena W., 93
  N. Harman, 93
Treynor
  Nannie J., 265
Turpin
  Evelyn Hughes, 202
  Florence Louise, 202
  Johnson, 202
Twyman
  John J., 268
  Willie E., 268
Tyson
  Carroll Lee, 145
  Dorothy, 145
  Fred W., 145

U

Unknown
  children, 202
  Fannie I., 213
  Mattie, 213
  Thomas, 213
  Walter, 214

V

Van Keuren
  Marcella Childress, 28
Vanderwaal
  Frances Kidd, 246
  James D., 246
Vaughan
  Willie C., 159
Vaughters
  Eva Moss, 268
Viar
  Nannie, 94

W

Wade
  Alfred Byron, 176

  Sarah H., 176
Wakefield
  George E., 94
  Julia Call, 94
Wallace
  Joseph Denton, 63
  Sarah E. Bessie Dunkum, 63
Walters
  Louise Woodfin, 145
  Wilmer, 145
Walton
  John C., 202
  Ruby Davis, 202
Wash
  Alice Reese, 202
  Marvin Bruce, 202
Watkins
  Agnes, 214
  Milton E., 159
Watson
  Bettie, 165, 166
  Cleveland Walker, 165
  George Richard, 166
  John R., 166
  Nannie E., 166
  Tom, 165, 166
  William Robert, 166
Wayne
  Nora A., 268
  Samuel P., 268
Weaver
  Ada Ann, 246
  Betsey Ann, 246
  Charles Ray, 246
  Cora E., 246, 247
  Emma D., 246
  Floyd W., 247
  Oscar F., 246, 247
  Robert M., 247
  Saul, 247
Weber
  Anne Miller, 146
  Ophelia Deane, 146
  Richard Joseph, 146
Webster
  Field O., 226
  Mary S., 226
Weeks
  John Overton, 94
  Marvin O., 94
  William Clifton, 94
Weller
  Ida Kyle Davis, 146
  Thornton, 146
West
  Alice, 29

  Dudley Rogers, 29
  Eugene Francis, 29
  Jacob A., 29
  John Edmund, 29
  John Francis, 29
  John S., 29, 30
  Margaret Staehlin, 29
  Martha J., 29
  Sarah Elizabeth, 29
  Sue Roberson, 29
  Tyree, 29
Wheeler
  Charles Joseph, 146
  Ella Barger, 265
  John D., 265
  Judith A. S., 249
  Judith Ann Stanton, 249
  Mary Bransford, 146
  William, 249
White
  Arrianna M., 146
  Artie Hilston, 146, 147
  Bertha O., 146
  Chapman, 146
  Fountain E., 146
  H. Murray, 94
  John, 249
  Kate E., 94
  Mary F., 146
  Roberta Helen, 146, 147
  Sarah J., 147
  Sophronia Stanton, 249
  Wesley T., 147
Whiting
  Marguerite P., 147
Whitlow
  Minnie Dowdy, 247
  Minnie Dowdy, 247
  Rosa S., 94
  Wiley Hubbard, 247
Wilkerson
  Fletcher Smith, 202
  Joshua Holmes, 202
  William, 104
Wilkinson
  Ashby S., 226
  Carroll H., 147
  Essie B., 147
  Nannie S., 226
Williams
  Fred O., 30
  R. Garnett Agee, 30
Winfrey
  Annie E. T., 226
  Egbert B., 226
  Harvey E., 226

Index

Lottie S., 226
Wingo
  C. B., 203
  Mary S. Scruggs, 203
Wise
  Charles R., 247
  Charles Richard, 247
  Corbin Steger, 247
  Gracie Lillian Stables, 247
  Harry Edward, 247
  Harry G., 247
  Jennie B., 247
Womack
  Mr., 108
Wood
  Anna Hudgins, 30
  Christopher Shawn, 30
  Fred Glover, 94
  James Milton, 30
Woodfin
  Cora Banton, 226
  Donald Pierce, 147
  Edmund P., 147
  Geela Hanley, 94
  Iva Ford, 147
  Jennie Rebecca, 147
  Meade Painter, 147
  Ralph Pierce, 147
  Ray, 147
  Wiley Haskins, 226
  William Ray, 94
  Willie Taylor, 2
Woods
  Bertha Smith, 176
  Infant, 30
  Ira E., 30
  James W., 176
  Pearl A., 30
Woodson
  Anna May, 148
  Coleman, 107
  Drury Gilliam, 148
  E. Frank, 148
  Mary L., 148
  Olivia Rush, 179
  Polly W., 148
  W. Lafayette, 148
  William E., 148
  Willie Newton, 148
Wooldridge
  Josephine Oslin, 265
Wooten
  Inez P., 166
  Mr., 160
  Wiley L., 95
Wootten

Archie P., 148
Clifford, 270
D. Perkins, 148, 149
Garnette E., 148, 149
Hallie S., 270
Hallie Stanley, 270
James B., 149
L. Fleming, 148, 149
Virginia L., 148, 149
Wootton
  Bessie J., 149
  Inez Poe, 30
  Irving A., 149
  J. Cliff, 177
  Joseph W., 177
  Leland C., 149
  Lucy Boatwright, 149
  Mary E. LeSueur, 177
  Minnie R., 177
  Osten D., 30
  Samuel E., 177
  Wiley H., 149
Word
  Edith, 163
  Elsie Lila, 214
  Hester C., 163
  Howard, 163
  James N., 163
  Mamie, 214
  Mary, 214
  Richard Shelton, 214
Worley
  Ida Hicks, 177
  J. Cleve, 177
  Ruby E., 177
  S. William, 177
Worsham, 93
  Cora S., 95
  John D., 95
  "Mary Florence ""Jo""", 95
Wright
  Baby, 63
  Charlie, 271
  Elmo W., 63
  Elmo Walker, 63
  Emanuel F., 96
  Eva Mosbie Toney, 63
  Evelyn Joyce, 96
  Flora Estelle, 96
  Frances S., 63
  Joseph L., 63
  Maggie L., 101
  Mary Elizabeth, 96
  Phillip Archer, 63
  Thomas Jackson, 63
  William T., 63

Y

Yancey
  Bernard W., 149
  Edward Smith, 149, 150
  Elizabeth C., 150
  Elizabeth Christian, 149
  Ernie Pearcy, 150
  John G., 150
  Joseph W., 150
  Margaret A., 150
  Martha Payne, 149, 150
  Robert E., 150
  Rosa Payne, 150
  Sallie D., 150
  Waverly G., 150
  William Thomas, 149, 150
Young
  Garvis C., 247
  Lorraine A., 247

www.ingramcontent.com/pod-product-compliance
Lightning Source LLC
Chambersburg PA
CBHW071418150426
43191CB00008B/961